WILL TO POWER:
THE MISSIONARY CAREER OF FATHER MORICE

WILL TO POWER
THE MISSIONARY CAREER
OF FATHER MORICE

David Mulhall

UNIVERSITY OF BRITISH COLUMBIA PRESS
VANCOUVER
1986

Will to Power: The Missionary Career of Father Morice
© University of British Columbia Press 1986
all rights reserved

This book has been published with the help of a grant from the
British Columbia Heritage Trust.

Canadian Cataloguing in Publication Data

Mulhall, David
  Will to Power

  Bibliography: p.
  Includes index
  ISBN 0-7748-0254-5

  1. Morice, A.G. (Adrien Gabriel), 1859–1938.
  2. Oblates of Mary Immaculate — Biography.
  3. Missionaries — British Columbia — Biography.
  4. Indians of North America — British Columbia —
  Missions.   5. Carrier Indians — Missions.
  I. Title.
  BV2813.M67M84 1986   271'.76'024   C86-091343-0

International Standard Book Number 0-7748-0254-5
Printed in Canada

To My Mother and To The Memory of My Father

CONTENTS

ILLUSTRATIONS

Photo credits: British Columbia Provincial Museum, plates 23, 33; D. L. S. [A. G. Morice], *Fifty Years in Western Canada, Being the Abridged Memoirs of Rev. A. G. Morice, O.M.I.*, plates 1, 2, 13, 20, 21, 24, 25, 27, 28, 30; Provincial Archives of British Columbia, plates 3, 4, 5, 6, 7, 8, 9, 10, 11, 14, 15, 16, 17, 18, 19, 26, 31, 32.

PREFACE

A. G. Morice left France for Canada in 1880 in pursuit of a dream: to become a missionary priest-king. This book is about his attempt to realize that dream. Morice was, to quote Wilson Duff, "a man of forceful personality and powerful intellect" who between 1885 and 1903 "dominated" the northern interior of British Columbia.[1] During these years as the Oblate missionary to the Carrier Indians, Father Morice also became internationally known as an authority on their language and culture. This twin achievement caused Morice to become the best known of British Columbia's Catholic missionaries, but he has been misleadingly represented in an extremely laudatory biography written by a mysterious D. L. S—who turns out to be Morice himself.[2] Far from being meek and selfless, as D. L. S. suggests, Morice was an extraordinarily vain and egotistical man, obsessed with gaining power and recognition as a missionary, explorer, and Indian expert.

In his relations with the white world, he was a rebellious individualist whose quest for autonomy amounted to a kind of personal anarchy; among Indians he expected to become an authoritarian and undisputed ruler. The British Columbia frontier became a refuge where he could enjoy the kind of freedom to develop his individuality and to dominate others which was denied him in the more regulated and increasingly egalitarian societies of France and metropolitan Canada. Only the liberty of the colonial frontier seemed to make it possible for Morice to maintain his delicate psychic equilibrium. Before he became an independent missionary, he experienced periods of erratic behaviour, and after his missionary career was brought to a premature end, he reverted to his former troubled state—and stayed that way for much of his long life.

This said, I must emphasize that it was never my purpose to write a "psychobiography" or indeed a "psychohistory" of any kind. Psychobiography involves the "systematic use of organized psychological theory as an aid in narrating the story of a man's life," and the theory used is invariably Freud's or a variation on it. I have eschewed this approach with its inherent tendency to find "facts" to fit the theory, but I have nevertheless tried to go beyond stated intentions in order to gain a better understanding of Father Morice's actions. To have followed others in accepting uncritically Morice's account of his missionary service would have required me to ignore the evident validity of a statement made by a Canadian critic of psychobiography: "all men sometimes lie, equivocate, dissemble, and try to hide things, even from themselves."[3] In addition to shunning post-mortem psychoanalysis, I have tried to avoid both copious comparisons and detailed "context" descriptions. This book is neither a history of the British Columbia Oblates nor an attempt to describe the "typical" Oblate, which Morice definitely was not. It is influenced by G. R. Elton's definition of the biographer's proper task, to "tell the story, demonstrate the personality, and elucidate the importance of one individual; he should not be concerned with the history of that individual's times except in so far as it centres upon or emanates from him."[4]

The larger missionary enterprise of which Morice was a part does, of course, receive attention. In Canada and in other areas of European expansion, the missionary was the most conscious and by far the most effective agent of cultural change, and the natives' conversion to Christianity led to a profound reorientation of their lives. By 1900, the majority of British Columbia's Indians were Catholic, and thus the study of Catholic missionary methods and Indian reactions to them is essential for an understanding of the modern history of the province's native peoples. Although an attempt is made to examine Father Morice's motives for becoming a missionary, I concentrate on how he managed to build a veritable kingdom for himself among the Carrier. His multifarious talents and his boundless energy and determination provide a partial explanation for his success. But of equal importance was the existence of an environment which favoured his rise to a position of considerable spiritual and secular power. Since Morice's influence was established on a fur trade frontier, it is necessary to explore his relations with both the Indian trappers and the white fur traders. Also, since Morice was an Oblate and worked within the order's "Durieu System," it is important to consider the extent to which his use of Bishop Durieu's methods aided him. While the authoritarian nature of the system undoubtedly helped him, it could not have done so unless the Indians had felt that Catholicism would benefit them and that they must therefore tolerate the rule of its priest. This is a study, then, of the relationship between personality and circumstance: the personality of a fascinating and very ambitious missionary priest and the frontier circumstances which facilitated his ascendancy.

The most intriguing of these circumstances is surely the Indian interest in Christianity. It is also a subject which has not been satisfactorily treated by historians, no doubt because of the paucity of reliable evidence. All the available documents are written by whites, and, naturally enough, they contain misconceptions born either of ethnocentricity or of plain ignorance of what the natives were thinking. These limitations are even greater in Morice's case, for he kept no diary and his field notes have disappeared. Moreover, few of the private letters he wrote concerned Indian reactions to his work. This theme he usually dealt with in articles and books devoted more to descriptions of his missionary adventures and geographical explorations than to dispassionate analyses of Indian attitudes and actions. And even though there are fairly frequent references to Morice in Hudson's Bay Company and Indian Affairs Department documents, they too contain little about the vital matter of the Indians' perception of the missionary and his spiritual message.

Consequently, I left the archives for what anthropologists call "the field." At Fort St. James and in other villages around Stuart Lake, I found old people who still remembered the priest who had left them in 1903; others had heard of him from their parents. The number of informants was not great, but since many of the events and feelings they spoke about are not even hinted at in the written documents, their evidence proved invaluable. Generally, I did not use a tape recorder, since I found that it inhibited the elderly informants. In addition to drawing on this oral history, I used similar material recorded by Imbert Orchard for a radio series on the history of the British Columbia frontier.

The collection and use of this oral evidence posed methodological problems. The means employed to establish its validity are, however, the same as those used for written evidence: one person's oral testimony is compared with that of other informants and, where possible, with relevant documents. The crucial difference between oral and documentary evidence is that the historian or the sound archivist participates in the creation of the former. The interviewer influences both the quantity and the quality of the material collected. As J. L. Granatstein has noted, "careful preparation is required, and the interviewer . . . should already have done the digging through the usual archival sources." Thus prepared, an interviewer can take an active part in the gathering process, asking questions to stimulate recall and subtly challenging contradictory testimony. In their project on the Conservative Party, Granatstein, Stevens, and Oliver used what amounts to interrogation: "the questioning was deliberately planned to be rough and always probing. Contradictions were attacked [and] contrary evidence introduced."[5] While this approach is appropriate when interviewing veteran politicians who are accustomed to boisterous debates and question periods, it would so intimidate some oral history informants that they would try to avoid conflict either by pleading ignorance or by telling the interviewer what they thought he or she wanted to hear.

Granatstein's method may be too aggressive for general use, but the passivity of some interviewers is both more serious and apparently more common. In Canada, most of those collecting oral history are "neither archivists nor historians,"[6] and there seems to be a tendency for them to record and preserve whatever informants tell them. Unfortunately, this can lead to the incorporation into oral history archives of dubious material.[7] Ideally, the interviewer should combine the rigorous preparation and scepticism of Granatstein and his associates with a more empathic manner. I avoided abrasive questioning, yet I have discovered no major inaccuracies or contradictions in the oral testimony I collected from Carrier Indians.

To these patient and generous people I want to express my sincere thanks. Mrs. Lizette Hall and her husband Ralph put their house and Land Rover at my disposal and thereby greatly facilitated my work. At Fort St. James, Mrs. Hall and her brother, Mr. John Prince, provided me with particularly valuable information. My interview with Mr. Justa Hansen of Taché was also very useful. Tapes made by Imbert Orchard were put at my disposal by the staff of the Aural History Institute of British Columbia. The bulk of my documentary evidence came from the Oblate archives in Ottawa, and I wish to acknowledge the enthusiastic helpfulness of the archivist, Father Gaston Carrière, O.M.I. I would like to thank the ladies of the Hudson's Bay Company's London archives for the tea and chocolate biscuits and the governor and committee of the company for allowing me to use the archives. Mrs. Barbara Brown and Miss Milfred Soloman typed the manuscript carefully and quickly, and I gratefully acknowledge their services. My editor, Jane Fredeman, as well as John Herd Thompson, Robin Fisher, and Margaret Whitehead made useful and appreciated comments on the manuscript.

I am most indebted, however, to Frances, my wife, for her encouragement and forbearance.

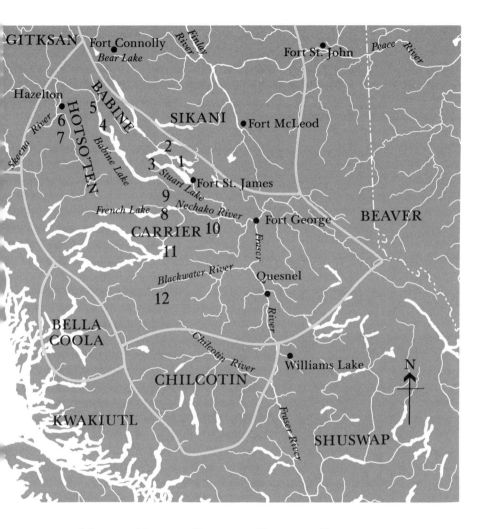

MAP OF NORTH CENTRAL BRITISH COLUMBIA

CARRIER VILLAGES

1 Pinché

2 Taché

3 Yekhuché (Portage)

4 Nit'ats (Old Fort Babine)

5 Hwotat (Fort Babine)

6 Rocher Déboulé (Agwilgate)

7 Moricetown (Keyor Hwotget)

8 Stella (Fond du Lac)

9 Natléh (Fort Fraser)

10 Stoney Creek

11 Cheslatla Lake (Lac Ste. Marie)

12 Alkatcho

1

THE MAKING OF AN OBLATE MISSIONARY

Adrien-Gabriel Morice, the future British Columbia missionary and Americanist, was born on 28 August 1859 at Saint-Mars-sur-Colmont in the province of Mayenne, France. On the following day he was baptized at the local Catholic church. His father, Jean Morice, was a wheelwright who had married his second wife, Virginie Seigneur, in July of the previous year. Two years after Adrien-Gabriel's birth, another child was born, and others seem to have followed, though Morice mentions neither them nor his parents in his disguised autobiography, *Fifty Years in Western Canada*. This omission suggests that his childhood memories were not happy ones, and the few pages devoted to his family life deal only with his ancestry and with the earliest manifestations of his unusually precocious intellect and memory.[1]

Yet in spite of this alleged intellectual ability, Morice readily admitted that he did not have a distinguished career at school. At the age of seven, he entered the local elementary school; there was, he later confessed, no "special brilliancy about his studies." He actually seems to have taken pride in his mediocre performance in the prescribed subjects. From his first exposure to institutional learning, Morice, always a non-conformist, resisted the routine and discipline imposed by the need to follow a curriculum. The youngster was only happy when he was busy with projects of his own, all intended for public consumption. He began with a hand-written newspaper, which he put out during the Franco-Prussian War of 1870–71. He read it to a group of old people he encountered on his way home.[2]

This established the pattern he followed for the rest of his life. Whether he was employed as a teacher, a missionary, or a church historian, he had his own pet projects. These literary sidelines consumed as much as of his time as his official duties, and they invariably brought him more public acclaim than did his job. Printing his own works gave Morice a large degree of independence. As a boy he ran a one-man show, and he was to insist on doing the same as an adult.

A desire for attention and influence seems to have been instrumental in directing Morice towards a career in the church. He could not have failed to notice the social prominence of the Catholic clergy in his native town, located in one of France's most Catholic and conservative areas. The wheelwright's son was tutored in Latin and Greek by a local priest, and in September 1873, at the age of fourteen, he entered the Lesser Seminary of Mayenne. Once again, his academic performance was mediocre, with the exception of Latin verse and music. Henceforth, music was to become another outlet for his creative individualism, while the epic tales of the classical heroes also seem to have inspired him.[3]

During the year he spent at the seminary, the young man discovered to his delight that he too could become a hero. The Oblate missionary, Bishop Vital-Justin Grandin, came to Mayenne seeking recruits for his Congregation's foreign missions. After Morice had heard his description of the Oblates' work among the Cree and Déné of the Canadian Northwest, he knew where his future lay: "That is what I want! To work and suffer for souls, to battle among, and conquer, the lowly of America, that is my vocation," he reports himself as thinking at the time.[4] The bishop's gripping accounts of the travels of his missionaries on the vast prairies and through the dense forests combined with the seminarian's romantic notions of America, gained from reading Chateaubriand's tales of the wild terrain and exotic peoples, to produce a feeling of ecstatic anticipation.[5] An outstanding figure in the Romantic movement, Chateaubriand was an eloquent and highly influential defender of monarchy and of Christianity. Much of his writing on America was a polemic against Rousseau's view of the "noble savage." Chateaubriand believed that the natives could greatly benefit from Christianity, and he presented the Jesuits of New France as heroes.[6]

Grandin had not neglected to stress the difficulties of the Oblate's life in the great Northwest—the climate, the isolation, and the many deprivations—yet it was the challenge that these difficulties represented which attracted Morice.[7] He had, after all, been brought up in a tradition which glorified the suffering and martyrdom of the saints. However, the influence of his Catholicism does not adequately account for the strength of the magnetic force which pulled Morice toward the barren North. Indeed, Morice's missionary career suggests that he was not particularly religious, and he showed little interest in the politico-religious aims of the missionary society which Bishop Grandin represented. Founded in 1816 by Eugène de Mazenod, the son of a nobleman ruined by the French Revolution, the Society of the Missionaries of Provence was renamed the Congregation of the Oblates of Mary Immaculate in 1826. De Mazenod was an ardent counter-revolutionary, and the members of his order were highly educated and disciplined, like the Jesuits. They were dedicated to "re-christianizing" the common folk of France, including the riff-raff of Marseilles and other cities. By 1841, word of the Oblates' work had spread, and Bishop de Mazenod was asked to send priests to Quebec. From there some went northwest into the territory of the Hudson's Bay Company, and in 1847 a contingent was sent directly from France to Oregon. Following the outbreak of hostilities between the natives and the invading American settlers, most of the Oblates moved north into British Columbia.[8]

Although Morice was the son of militantly monarchist and Catholic Mayenne, it was the Indian missions, not the Oblates' religious and political work among whites, which excited him. With the discovery of America's great wilderness, sensitive and unhappy European souls had a new alternative to their traditional escape into the past. Chateaubriand readily acknowledged the attraction of America for himself and kindred spirits. Morice probably saw the missions of Canada's rudimentary frontier society as an opportunity to escape the humdrum, civilized world of school curricula and rules. He might also have been seeking an escape from himself, hoping to find the "unalterable peace" and "spiritual childhood" found by the Jesuits in New France or the "repose" sought by Chateaubriand's troubled and highly individualistic hero, Réné, among the Natchez Indians.[9]

While Frenchmen of Morice's type often chose to escape to the American wilds, many of the nineteenth-century Britons—the famous explorer and missionary David Livingstone, for example—who sought more freedom than Europe allowed fled to Africa. For all these adventurers, European community life "implied not only impersonality and anonymity destructive of individuality, but civilization in general meant interdependence, the opposite of independence."[10] Morice seems to have been interested, above all, in his independence, and Bishop Grandin's Canadian missions apparently offered it. Excited, he asked the prelate how he could qualify as an Oblate. Grandin told him about the Juniorate at Notre-Dame-de-Sion in Lorraine where aspiring Oblates undertook several years of basic training. Full of joy and pride, Morice decided to be a missionary among the Indians. Inspired by this prospect, he seems to have worked harder than usual to prepare himself for admission to the Juniorate, which he entered in September 1874.[11]

His three years at Notre-Dame-de-Sion were relatively happy. But his irrepressible individualism and restlessness were such that once again he found it difficult to concentrate on the curriculum. This brought him into conflict with the director of the Juniorate, Father Alexandre Huart. For instead of giving his undivided attention to his studies, Morice followed his established pattern of devoting much of his time and energy to literary projects. Father Huart had obtained for him a rudimentary printing press, and with it he printed a book.[12] Morice had a remarkable ability to impress new superiors, who often agreed not only to permit him to engage in extracurricular activities but also actually provided him with the equipment he needed. They later regretted their actions, for his preoccupation with creative activities frequently became obsessive.

When he was not printing, Morice was likely to be "devouring" the *Missions de la Congrégation des Oblats de Marie Immaculée*. The *Missions* were mainly composed of letters and reports from Oblate missionaries in such far-flung fields as the frozen wastes of northern Canada and the scorching deserts of Basutoland. They are the Oblate equivalent of the more famous *Jesuit Relations*, and like the *Relations*, they are an important source of missionary and ethnographic information. Thanks to the Juniorate's director, Morice was allowed to read each day from the *Missions*. He read the whole collection, which came out in a stout volume annually from 1862, and then prepared lectures to give to the younger boys during their recreation period.[13]

There is reason to believe that Morice found a hero and model in the pages of the *Missions*. Nearly a decade later, his companion at the Fort St. James mission in British Columbia reported that Morice regarded Father Emile Petitot as the *"ne plus ultra"* of the perfect missionary.[14] The chubby and diminutive priest from Provence—the Indians called him "the priest shaped like an egg"—was by inclination an explorer who was only happy when heading over the horizon in search of new and untamed territory.[15] Petitot worked under Bishop Grandin in the Canadian Northwest, and at the time of Morice's Juniorate training, he was beginning to make quite a name for himself as an explorer, linguist, and anthropologist. Since Petitot wrote about Indians who belonged to the Déné or Athapascan language group, Morice became determined that he too would minister to Dénés. Consequently, he studied their language and culture well before he actually became a missionary.[16] Morice's later interests and achievements so closely parallel those of Petitot that it is difficult not to believe that Morice deliberately set out to emulate this "perfect missionary."

As well as stimulating Morice's scholarly pretensions, Petitot's writings must have greatly reinforced his romantic attachment to the exotic terrain and people of the Northwest, for Petitot made his missionary life sound like a wonderful adventure. He was even enthusiastic about the supposed beneficial effects of the Arctic cold, which included purification of the blood.[17] In addition to extolling its climate, Petitot meticulously studied and reported on the geography, geology, fauna, and flora of his mission territory, the present day Mackenzie District of the Northwest Territories.

Petitot also sought out the most remote and "primitive" native peoples. Despite his mortal fear of the Inuit, he made repeated requests to be sent amongst them and the most northerly Indians, the Loucheux.[18] Somewhat sickly himself, the young Frenchman admired and perhaps envied the strength and stamina of his taller and more powerfully built Indian companions. Morice must have read Petitot's admission in the 1867 edition of the *Missions* that he liked solitude, especially when it was occasionally punctuated by the visits of nomadic Indians. In the same letter, the missionary also confessed that he sometimes felt consumed by a profound and inexplicable melancholy. What the young Morice could not have learned from Petitot's letters and articles in the *Missions* was that his hero was not just depressed but seriously mentally ill during part of his missionary career.[19] Petitot's condition apparently rendered him incapable of living cordially with either his Oblate colleagues or other whites, hence the strength of his attachment to his life as an itinerant missionary among the tribes of the inhospitable Mackenzie. Like Chateaubriand's hero René, Petitot fled "civilized" places and people to seek peace among the "savage" peoples of America. He hated to leave this haven even to return to France to restore his shattered health and to have his maps and dictionaries published. Once in France, he begged his superiors to allow him to return to his "children of the forest" as soon as possible.[20]

Morice could not have failed to notice the recognition which Father Petitot received on his return to France in 1875. He was named a member of both the Anthropological and the Philological Societies of Paris; the Society of Geography, which had had his maps engraved, presented him with a silver medal for his map of the western Arctic; and at the International Congress of Americanists held at Nancy, he used linguistic, ethnographic, and archeological evidence to demonstrate the Asian origin of his Indians and thereby assert the unity of the human race. On top of all this, he received the title of "officier d'académie." When he was not receiving honours and giving papers, Petitot spent his sojourn in France supervising the printing of his Indian language dictionaries and translating books of piety in order that they might be printed in the syllabic script invented by James Evans, a Methodist missionary to the Cree.[21] For the young Morice, Petitot's career proved that an Oblate could combine the heroic, independent life of a missionary with that of an acclaimed savant.

Yet many hurdles still lay between Morice's ambitions and their realization. The first of these was the demanding year of novitiate he would have to undergo at Nancy in Lorraine before being formally accepted into the Oblate Congregation. After completing his classical studies in August of 1877, Morice started his difficult trial year. He later claimed that the discipline and control of emotions expected of a novice were not as trying as being forced to keep to the curriculum. But he stuck it out. On 15 August 1878, A. G. Morice took his vows and became Brother Morice, O.M.I. — Oblate of Mary Immaculate.[22]

A month later, he entered the Oblate Scholasticate, the school of theology and philosophy, at Autun in Burgundy. Fortunately for Morice, this new stage in his training was not so onerous. Once more he was allowed to indulge in "quite a few personal studies and free readings." The Roman ruins at Autun, for example, stimulated his interest in archeology, and during this year he used a new type of lithography to reproduce the lectures of one of his teachers. It is clear from his description of his printing activities that he was aware of a connection between his interest in literary production and his compulsion to work.[23] His multifarious hobbies were not just an assertion of his individuality; they were also a way to keep himself continually occupied. Morice seems to have been plagued by anxiety, and perhaps he coped with it by keeping busy. His great ambition doubtless also played a role. A few years later, when Morice was causing trouble for his superiors in British Columbia, the Oblate assistant general, Father Aimé Martinet, consulted the director of the Autun Scholasticate concerning his behaviour while he was a student there. The director replied that Brother Morice had been taken to task at Autun for the same faults which created problems for him in British Columbia: vanity, ambition, and insubordination.[24]

As well as being an academic preparation for the priesthood, the scholasticate was a period of additional probation. Yet despite his obvious unsuitability for the life of submission to superiors, modesty, and self-denial expected of an Oblate,[25] Brother Morice was permitted to take his perpetual vows on 9 October 1879. While the talented young brother was undoubtedly the beneficiary of the charity and optimism of his superiors, conditions in the mission field and in France must have played their part in the decision to keep him in the order. He was a man of great energy and intellectual ability, and he had a flair for languages. Such men were desperately needed as missionaries. Problems on the home front were equally favourable to him. All of Morice's seminary studies were undertaken during the first decade of the Third Republic, a time when anti-clericalism had become a major plank of republicanism in France; just as he was about to take his perpetual vows, the anti-Catholic sentiment was beginning to pass from rhetoric to action. In 1879, the French government was drafting laws that would seriously restrict religious orders. It was in this atmosphere of siege that Morice was accepted as an Oblate for life.[26]

The anti-clerical decrees of April 1880 were responsible for Morice's premature departure from France for the foreign mission field. Although the senior Oblate officers refused to abide by the constricting conditions laid down in the decrees, they did take the precaution of dispatching more than thirty scholastic brothers—men still studying for the priesthood—to the various missions outside France. One day these students were summoned to the father superior's office, and Morice watched apprehensively as his fellow students filed out one by one with their marching orders for Ceylon, South Africa, and other far-off, romantic places. When his turn eventually came, he emerged from the short interview with the great favour of an assignment to the missions of British Columbia. While he had dreamed of labouring in the Canadian Northwest with Bishop Grandin, British Columbia was quite acceptable. It was not as yet a white man's country, and Morice regarded the vast territory as a suitably formidable and challenging part of the Lord's vineyard.[27] The fact that Déné tribes inhabited its northern interior probably helped reconcile him to his orders.

The young Oblate was about to start a "new life."[28] On 26 June 1880, he and two other scholastics, Brothers Nicolas Coccola and Dominic Chiappini, both Corsicans, sailed from Le Havre. At the request of the bishop of Vancouver Island, the first Oblate had come to the British colony in 1849, but it was not until 1858 that the Oblate superior in Oregon, Louis d'Herbomez, brought most of his priests and brothers north to found a new and autonomous missionary vicariate. In Oregon, they had been bothered not only by the conflicts between Indians and the settlers but also by jurisdictional disputes with French-Canadian priests. The Oblates soon concentrated on the mainland, and because of Protestant competition, they tried to spread their influence rapidly. D'Herbomez, who was consecrated a bishop in 1864, made his headquarters in New Westminster, where he had built a church and begun a school. In 1865, he had asked a Quebec-based order of nuns, the Sisters of St. Ann, to provide the school with teachers. And by 1880, they had established six mission stations, from the Kootenays in the southeast to Fort St. James in the north.[29]

When Morice and his travelling companions arrived in New West-minster, they received a warm welcome from Bishop d'Herbomez, who, according to Morice, became especially attached to him.[30] But neither he nor the other brothers were allowed to dally in New Westminster. Instead, they were quickly packed off thirty miles up the Fraser River to the mission of St. Mary's (Mission City). During their years in Oregon, the Oblates had been influenced by Jesuit attempts at concentrating Catholic Indians in "reductions" — self-sufficient communities ruled by missionaries and cut-off from contact with traditionalist Indians and corrupting frontier whites — and it was the reduction model which was the inspiration behind the St. Mary's complex. It had a large wooden church, a farm, saw and grist mills, and a boarding school. The school's pupils worked on the farm as part of their preparation for settlement on the land in Catholic farming villages such as the one established at nearby Matsqui. The boys learned the "industrial arts," but neither they nor the girls were readied for assimilation into the white economy. Since the youngsters were worked hard and watched very carefully, it is not surprising that few enrolled and even fewer stayed to complete their studies. Morice and his Corsican confreres were assigned teaching and other duties, which they would perform while they were completing their training for the priest-hood under St. Mary's director, Father Alphonse Carion. Brother Morice was to teach catechism to the boys.[31]

But before he got down to his new job, he was delighted to be sent on his first mission into real "Indian country." Morice, Chiappini, and Coccola accompanied Father Casimir Chirouse Jr. to the village of the Squamish Indians to assist at a funeral. Various bands had been gathered by the Oblates at Squamish, located on the coast north of the future Vancouver, and it was becoming a showpiece for what has become known as the Durieu System. Bishop d'Herbomez's health had been failing for some time, and this meant that his assistant, Father Durieu, was able to reinforce and simultaneously subtly reorient the missionary practices developed by d'Herbomez and other Oblates in Oregon. As a young missionary, Durieu had become disillusioned with his colleagues' preoccupation with what he called "police matters," namely, the detection and punishment of "public faults" such as adultery, consuming liquor, and the holding of traditional feasts. While this "repression process" *(action de répression)* was, he later came to believe, a necessary step in the direction of conversion, missionaries must never forget that the spiritual remaking of the Indian was more important. Durieu called this second stage of conversion the "moulding process" *(action de formation)*. At Squamish and in all the native communities in which they were accepted as missionaries, the Oblates appointed Catholic chiefs, captains, and watchmen. The captain was the chief's deputy, and he usually administered the frequent whippings meted out as a form of public penance. The watchmen were spies and policemen who detected and apprehended suspected sinners. But as well as repressing "pagan" practices and the vices learned from whites, Durieu wanted these Indian aides to help the Oblates to uproot native spirituality and to sow in its place the seeds of Catholicism.[32]

Although Morice was probably not yet aware of the methods used by his fellow Oblates, he liked what he saw at Squamish. As the party approached from the sea, he was impressed by the large church, the whitewashed houses, and the three embossed flags flying from a big mast on the shore. Together the flags spelled out the Oblate slogan: religion, temperance, civilization. Brother Morice certainly believed that these objectives had been attained. In fact, some native customs persisted, and the Oblates' plans to create self-sufficient communities along the lines of the Jesuit reductions were never realized.[33] While the clandestine continuation of native practices suggests an incomplete success, it does not indicate a failure. Syncretism—mixing Christian and native beliefs—does not signify a rejection of Christianity. Indeed, it often precedes a more comprehensive conversion. Christians and other monotheists are so thoroughly imbued with exclusivist, "all or nothing" assumptions about religion that they cannot readily appreciate the incorporative, inclusive nature of Indian belief systems.[34] Thus, there is no reason to question the sincerity of the religious devotion observed by Morice at Squamish. The people were particularly attached to the sacrament of communion, and when they were not guilty of any public fault, Bishop Durieu allowed them to receive it once a month at New Westminster.

But what most excited the young reader of Chateaubriand and Petitot were the exotic situation and people at Squamish. At night, he and the other brothers slept "Indian fashion" under the blankets they had brought along. Father Chirouse, who regularly ministered to the Squamish people, got the only bed in the priest's house. During the day, Morice the aspiring ethnographer found time to observe with some sensitivity the native mourning customs. And when he wrote about his visit in the *Missions*, he followed Petitot in liberally seasoning his account with his observations. He also conveyed the same admiration and sense of being privileged that Petitot experienced in the presence of the strong and skilful "bons sauvages":[35]

to reach our canoes we had to accept the services of Squamish bearers, for whom our persons weighted no more than a feather. Soon we were gliding on the waves, leaving behind yesterday's weariness. The Squamish are able seamen. They use their paddles with remarkable

dexterity, and we were assured that last year they overtook the steamboat from Victoria.

What Morice termed a "mutual school" started as soon as the canoe
headed toward the mouth of the Fraser. Father Chirouse showed holy pictures and preached while the Indian oarsmen taught the eager new brothers
the Chinook jargon, a *lingua franca* first developed for the fur trade but
extensively used by the Oblates.[36]

Morice did not display as much enthusiasm for learning theology from
his tutor at St. Mary's. His habitual restlessness and tendency to rebel
against routine studies were probably increased by the excitement of the
trip to Squamish and the prospect of future missionary adventures. Nor
was his rejection of authority mitigated by his director of studies, Father
Carion, an irascible Belgian who had long been the tutor for budding
priests and the corrector of those going astray.[37] Impetuous and impatient,
Carion once confessed that he and Brother Morice had certain traits in
common. From the beginning, Morice refused to submit "with humility"
to Carion, and for two years the two were locked in combat. As well as
consistently being reluctant to dedicate himself to his assigned studies or
work, Morice generally refused to conform to the timetable of the Oblate
establishments in which he found himself. At St. Mary's, open hostility
was usually sparked by Morice's obsessional devotion to his two hobbies,
printing and music. In March 1881, Carion reported to Bishop d'Herbomez that he and Morice were on quite good terms before Morice decided
to print hymns. Carion gave him free rein until the young printer began to
stay by his press at night and catch up with his sleep in the morning.[38]

In the summer of 1881, Morice developed yet another sideline. He prepared and sent off to Bishop d'Herbomez a simplified alphabet for the
Stalo language spoken by many of the Indians of the Lower Mainland.
Morice hoped that Bishop Durieu would use his new alphabet, which was
probably syllabic in form, to print the Stalo catechism he was composing.
Not surprisingly, this first effort at creating a simplified script for writing
an Indian language came to nothing; Morice had had neither the time nor
the opportunity to master the Stalo language. The inspiration for this venture possibly came from the success of the Evans's Cree syllabics, for although Evans was a Methodist, his system had been adopted by Father
Petitot and other Oblates in the Northwest. Clearly, Morice was already
trying to lead the life of a great missionary pioneer rather than studying the
theology required by a humble priest.[39]

His increasing interest in music was partly responsible for this neglect
of theology. But at least teaching vocal and instrumental music was one of
his official duties. He found that the twenty-five or so lads, mostly métis,

who attended the school, had a real aptitude for music and were docile and easy to direct. Starting soon after he arrived, Morice rebuilt the defunct but once prominent band of St. Mary's School. Instruments were rescued from dusty corners, repaired, cleaned, and put to work. By June 1881, the band had eighteen instrumentalists and once again was able to join religious processions and civic parades. Morice's boys were also being taught to sing the Mass, and three of them were receiving organ lessons.[40] This was commendable, except that, as Father Carion observed, Brother Morice was sacrificing more important interests for the sake of music.[41]

Perfecting the sung Mass became particularly important to him, but to do so, he required an harmonium. Morice resolved to get one. His plan was to travel with the school band to the pioneer town of Yale and to the workers' camps strung out along the line of the Canadian Pacific tracks being blasted throughout the Cascade Mountains. The band would give concerts and, it was hoped, would collect enough money to buy the harmonium, though this was not the declared aim of the tour. Rather, donations were solicited to support the orphans at the school.[42] The little excursion lasted about twelve days and was a great success. The party, which had the local Oblate itinerant missionary, Father Jean-Marie Lejeune, as a guide, was given free passage on the Fraser steamer to Yale, where the local white Catholics printed tickets and programmes. After entertaining the gentlefolk of Yale, Morice and his troop visited the more humble abodes of the railway workers. They also played for Andrew Onderdonk, the general contractor, and his family.[43]

The adventurous little concert tour netted about $300, more than enough to pay for the harmonium, and Morice wanted to keep all the money. Carion and Lejeune thought it was unjust for the boys to see no return for their efforts. Carion accused Morice of organizing the trip entirely for his own ends, and Lejeune complained to Bishop d'Herbomez that Morice had been reluctant to play if money was not forthcoming, even when such playing was in return for free meals.[44] Throughout his career, Morice was to display a strong desire to acquire musical instruments, printing presses, and money which he could regard as his own. It seems to have been an important part of his drive to assert his independence, though it clashed with the vow of poverty which he had made when he became an Oblate. For this reason alone, Carion was justified in his insistence that Morice hand over most of the proceeds of the tour. Finally, Morice gave Carion the money above the $200 or so needed for his harmonium. This did not satisfy Carion, who thought the boys deserved a larger share of the funds, but Morice got his harmonium, since the bishop took his side.[45]

Conflicts over music did not end there. From the spring of 1881 to the summer of 1882, Morice and Carion were at loggerheads, and many of the confrontations between these two powerful personalities were, in Morice's opinion, caused by his tutor's failure to understand what was needed to have good music at the mission. Morice wanted the right to control all matters pertaining to music, and he threatened to abandon his musical duties if Father Carion did not promise to have a sung Mass every Sunday.[46]

But the debate on the role of music at St. Mary's was just a symptom of a deeper conflict between Carion and Morice, a conflict which reveals a great deal about Morice's character. As a student, he should have been learning theology and humbly submitting to the authority of his religious superior; he was doing neither. His anarchistic individualism had reasserted itself more forcefully than ever. When Father Carion reported on the progress of his three student priests in March 1881, nine months after their arrival, he noted that whereas Coccola and Chippini were devout, Morice had much pride and little piety. His attitude caused Carion to have serious fears for his student's future. A similar concern also prompted Father Lejeune to write to Bishop d'Herbomez. What especially grieved Lejeune, who operated out of St. Mary's, was Morice's almost total lack of a religious life. Indeed, Morice never appeared to bend his will in any matter. As for his studies and ordination, Lejeune added, he seemed to care not at all.[47] These observations strongly suggest that, for Morice, becoming an Oblate was a means to an end which had little to do with religion.

Lejeune went on to corroborate Carion's remarks concerning Morice's temperamental unsuitability for teaching. The brother much preferred giving orders to taking them, and his extreme measures had lost him the affection of the children. Just a few days before Lejeune penned these remarks, Carion had twice complained that Morice was unjustly punishing "les big boys." The lads had been forbidden to play their instruments, ostensibly because they failed to master the sung Mass. In reality, Carion felt, it was because he had given the boys some of the concert tour money. Father Carion was convinced that Morice was too sensitive and too easily offended to teach music.[48] But it was Morice's pride and rebelliousness which caused Carion the gravest concern. In July 1881, a year after the young man's arrival, his tutor told d'Herbomez that Morice was flattered, pampered, and given his own way too much. Instead, Carion counselled, he should be getting the rod while his character was still pliable. The bishop did not agree. Indeed, he was inclined to blame Carion's personality for Morice's failure to study and submit.[49] The initial period of friendliness and co-operation—a sort of honeymoon—which always characterized Morice's dealings with new superiors lasted much longer in his relationship with d'Herbomez than it had with Carion. This is not hard to explain. First of all, Morice had a facile pen, which helped him to persuade the bishop to accept his version of the duel with Carion, whom d'Herbomez already regarded as a troublemaker. Secondly, the bishop did not live at St. Mary's mission, and therefore he was not as conspicuous an authority figure as Carion. Consequently, Carion, not d'Herbomez, was the object of Morice's resentment. Morice always found it much easier to maintain friendly relations with superiors or peers with whom he did not have to live or work.

Armed with the bishop's tacit support, Morice's rebellion against Carion continued. Sometimes he used passive resistance, which his tutor found particularly irritating. He would refuse to attend recreation, to talk in Carion's presence, or to take part in class discussions. This mute avoidance was frustrating, but his refusal to confess his faults and his continued acceptance of communion was regarded as scandalous. His other forms of passive resistance included sleeping late and not going to meals. His periodic declaration of "strikes" represented a more active phase of resistance: he simply refused to study or to teach music. The denial of an unreasonable request was sufficient to throw him into a strange confusion and prevent his preparation for the priesthood. The erratic nature of Morice's behaviour perplexed Lejeune, who reported that he paid no heed to his superior and rang bells at odd times in order to create a disturbance.[50]

Occasionally, Morice became so desperate with his predicament at St. Mary's that he sought refuge elsewhere. In the summer of 1881, he longed to go and preach among the Sechelt Indians of the coast. Later on, he pleaded and threatened to be allowed to finish his studies at New Westminster. To remain at St. Mary's, he predicted, would cause a scandal, embarrassing Carion and exposing himself to damnation. In his more frantic moments, he found other reasons for "descending" to New Westminster: his watch was broken and needed the attention of a watchmaker; his toothache had returned and required a dentist; or his shoes must go to a cobbler for resoling. None of these arguments convinced Carion, who believed that what Morice really wanted was the freedom to do whatever he wished, since the imposition of discipline weighed too much on his heart.[51] Father Carion understood Morice well, and d'Herbomez seems finally to have accepted his and Lejeune's assessments of the young man's comportment, for Morice was ordered by the bishop to remain at Mission City.

Morice now knew that his only escape was to learn theology and become a priest. He wanted a rapid ordination, he told d'Herbomez in September 1881, in order to be rid of his tutor.[52] But despite his desire to escape from Carion, it was not until the spring of 1882 that he finally applied himself to the study of theology. Although Carion was aware of his student's motive, he responded magnanimously and reported that Brother Morice was now studying at full speed: in a few days he had learned more theology than he had in all of the previous year. This period of concentration and acquiescence was not without its relapses into restlessness and hostility, but Morice was finally able, Carion said, to surmount his character.[53] And he kept up this façade long enough to be ordained a priest on 2 July 1882.

Now, instead of being dispatched to realize his dreams of conquering "pagan" Indians, Father Morice was sent to New Westminster. Bishop d'Herbomez believed that his health was too delicate for missionary work. In his autobiography, Morice claimed that the terrible food at St. Mary's had considerably debilitated him, but his voluntary abstinence from meals and his agitated condition better explain his poor health. Throughout his life, Morice's periodic rebellions against the authority of his superiors were marked by physical deterioration, followed in some cases by hospital treatment.[54] In addition to the state of his health, Morice's ability to speak English well probably had something to do with his transfer to the Oblate *maison* at New Westminster. Its staff ministered to the city's elite as well as fulfilling the order's fundamental mission of serving society's unfortunates, Indian and white. Oblate priests visited jails, hospitals, and orphanages.[55] Yet this charitable work and the prospect of giving sermons to the "refined audience" at St. Peter's Cathedral could not provide Morice with the romantic excitement, the freedom, or the power which had attracted him to a career as an Oblate missionary. He was unhappy at New Westminster, and it was not long before a second, though equally unsatisfactory, transfer was ordered. The Oblate assistant general, Father Aimé Martinet, was making an official visit to British Columbia during the summer of 1882, and he posted Morice to the Oblate school at Williams Lake in the Cariboo district of the central interior. The reason for this transfer is obscure, but as the change was not to Morice's liking, it may have been to some extent a disciplinary measure. Unlike d'Herbomez, and in keeping with his name, Martinet was a strict disciplinarian who would not have been inclined to indulgence when dealing with a character like Morice. The assistant general reminded the British Columbia Oblates that they were members of a militant corps and that the success of the whole Catholic army depended on their discipline.[56]

Another of Martinet's policy recommendations may have influenced his decision to send Morice to Williams Lake. The increasing influx of white settlers meant that the Oblates' traditional missionary methods were now inappropriate. Martinet therefore instructed the missionaries to rely more on English language education and on imparting practical skills than on the rather arbitrary and authoritarian indirect rule system. The increased contact with whites which accompanied the settlement of the province, Martinet astutely noted, would make the native converts less willing to accept the Oblate regulations developed in Oregon. A change of the kind envisaged by Martinet would boost the importance of mission schools. Although at that time the school at Williams Lake was open only to whites and métis, Martinet's policy directives pointed towards racial integration in education. In any case, Martinet had chastized the Oblates for their failure to acquire greater fluency in English,[57] and there was a pressing need in the school for a man who spoke English well.

Founded in 1867, St. Joseph's Mission at Williams Lake was intended primarily to serve the northern Shuswap Indians, but its priests visited the Chilcotins and certain southern Carrier bands too. The Cariboo gold rush and the arrival of settlers had given the priests the extra burden of ministering to whites. The mission station had been built by Father James Mc-Guckin, an Irishman and a former commercial traveller. Dynamic and practical, McGuckin acquired an excellent farm, which, in addition to providing food for the mission, yielded a handsome profit from the sale of surplus produce. McGuckin also ran a ranch, and the farm and the ranch together contributed significantly to the cost of running Oblate missions elsewhere in British Columbia.[58]

Part of the profits were used to subsidize the operation of the mission school, which was established in an attempt to forestall the building of Protestant or state schools to serve the children of the district. Many of the youngsters were the progeny of irregular unions between native women and transient whites, and some of them had been abandoned. Father McGuckin supported these destitute children from the mission's revenue.

When the Williams Lake school opened in 1873, it had eight boarders and three day boys. By 1877, there were seventy-five pupils, forty-two boys and thirty-three girls. The girls were taught by the Sisters of Saint Ann. Although this school was not open to the Indians, formal education was regarded by many Oblates, and especially by McGuckin, as being potentially the best and perhaps the only way to make true Christians of them. This strategy certainly made sense, since the Indians of the Williams Lake mission district spoke four different languages and lived in such a dispersed and nomadic fashion that their missionaries sometimes had difficulty even finding them. Furthermore, the need to visit the mining communities of the Cariboo cut down on the amount of ambulatory evangelization that the few priests at the Williams Lake mission could do among the natives, and so the traditional Oblate system of itinerant missionaries relying on chiefs and watchmen was not a success. In 1878, eleven years after the mission was established, the local Indians had still not received much religious instruction, and only a handful were communicants. The priests could not learn the Indian languages and were not able to keep the chiefs orthodox and subordinate. Far better results could be expected from a school. The children from nomadic bands would stay at the mission and become thoroughly Christian and then return to implant Christianity among their people. McGuckin told Martinet in November 1878 that experience suggested that everything should be subordinated to the success of the school, and it is clear from the assistant-general's policy recommendation that he agreed.[59]

The job that Martinet gave to Morice was, in the light of this recommendation, an important one. He was put in charge of the Williams Lake school. He could have done an excellent job were it not for his self-confessed inability to "feel satisfied with a common, colourless career."[60] This must have been a disappointment for his superiors, for not only had he mastered English but, equally important, he had both the aptitude and the inclination to learn the native tongues too. McGuckin frequently regretted that his priests had neither quality, and he declared that ignorance of Indian languages was the greatest hindrance to native conversion. Even though his duties were important and the need for his talents obvious, Morice made no effort to reconcile himself to his new posting. Instead, his three years at Williams Lake were spent engaged in a revolt against his superiors. Rejecting the dull life of a teacher, he was determined to realize his long-held ambition of doing missionary work in the north.[61]

To Morice "the north" meant the Oblate missionary district which had its headquarters at Fort St. James and which extended over much of the northern interior of the province. It was the most vast and "uncivilized" of the Oblate districts in British Columbia—there were neither schools nor white settlers—and Morice could expect to lead the romantic life of a missionary explorer and savant if he were transferred there. The district's native inhabitants, the Carrier, were an added attraction, for they were members of the same Indian "race," the Déné, among whom Father Petitot laboured. Rather than studying Shuswap, the non-Déné language of the Williams Lake people, Father Morice set about learning the Carrier language from one of his métis pupils, a lad named Jimmy Alexander, who came from the Fort St. James area. The Déné languages became his new extra-curricular passion, and with Jimmy's help he was able to compile a short vocabulary.[62]

This enterprise indicates that Morice knew exactly what he wanted and where he expected to find it. He consistently alienated himself from his peers by his utter refusal to subordinate himself to collective endeavours. And this egocentricism was matched only by his desire to subordinate all those around him, something he could not realize in a European society.

His psychological marginality pushed him toward the geographical and social edges of his world. He was like Shakespeare's Prospero, whom Mannoni chose as a representative of the archetypal colonial in his provocative study of the psychology of colonization:[63]

> What the colonial in common with Prospero lacks, is awareness of the world of Others, a world in which Others have to be respected. This is the world from which the colonial has fled because he cannot accept men as they are. Rejection of that world is combined with an urge to dominate, an urge which is infantile in origin and which social adaption has failed to discipline.

Prospero, the Duke of Milan, was unable to deal with the world of people who argued with him, and he took refuge first in his library and then, after his overthrow, on a remote island. Alone with his young daughter and a "savage" slave, Caliban, and armed with magical powers, Prospero exercised an uncontested dominion over his human environment.[64] Morice sought the same kind of refuge, one peopled by a collective Caliban upon whom he could use the spiritual powers at his disposal.

2

TENDERFOOT MISSIONARY
AMONG THE CHILCOTIN

At Williams Lake, Father Morice made no attempt to reconcile himself to the role of schoolmaster, and his usual strategy of passive resistance soon caused d'Herbomez to give him yet another new job. The bishop probably thought that he had finally found a compromise that would pacify Morice. In January 1883, the maverick priest was given the task of evangelizing the Chilcotin Indians. Although he would continue to live at Williams Lake and help out at the school, Morice had won a minor victory. At last, he could satisfy his need for independence and conquest.[1]

The five semi-nomadic Chilcotin bands roamed the forests and prairies of that part of central British Columbia which lies between the 51° and 52°30″ latitudes and which is bounded on the east by the Fraser and on the west by the Coast Mountains. The origin of the name Chilcotin is obscure; the Indians called themselves *Noenai-Toeni*—"the men down here"—or simply *Toen*—"men." They are the most southerly branch of the Déné language group in Canada, and Morice liked to compare them with their American Déné brothers, the Apache.[2] By the 1880's, the once numerous Chilcotin had been reduced by disease to fewer than five hundred. There was a recognized division between the three bands from the plateau and the two from the mountains. The latter were called the Stone Chilcotin or the Snow Mountain People, and in their remote mountain fastnesses, they were better able to preserve their aboriginal culture than the Chilcotins of the lowlands, who had much greater contact with whites in search of furs, gold, and land.[3]

This contact was not always peaceful. The "Chilkodins" were first mentioned by Simon Fraser in 1807, and a trading post was established in their territory in 1830. It was later abandoned because of its isolation and what the fur traders regarded as the hostile attitude of the natives. Smallpox hit the tribe hard in 1862, and two years later a white man who suspected some Chilcotins of stealing food wrote down their names and warned them that they would be struck by another plague. The linking of the threatened action to the potent magic of writing was apparently the main cause of the "Chilcotin Uprising" of 1864 in which nineteen whites were killed. Most of the victims, who were either surprised in the night or ambushed, were workmen building the Waddington wagon road from Bute Inlet through the Chilcotin country to the Cariboo mines. A desire to loot the workmen's camps was a secondary motive for the outbreak of violence. The combatants' attempt to involve all the Chilcotin bands in a general uprising failed, and six of them were eventually hanged.[4] But this did not end the Chilcotin resistance to white encroachment. Although the Waddington road was abandoned after the 1864 troubles, prospective settlers arrived via the Fraser. During the 1870's, the Chilcotins chased off a number of these intruders, and while Morice was their missionary—from 1883 to 1885—there were only three white residents in the Chilcotin Valley.[5]

The Oblates fared somewhat better than the settlers. They were neither murdered nor scared off, but they did not obtain the meek submission and the mass conversion which they sought. In 1864, Father Leon Fouquet became the first Oblate to venture into their territory, and he left without even finding them. Soon after, however, contact was made by Fathers McGuckin and Grandidier. In the spring of 1866, the latter reported that one of the chiefs, Alexis, had not wanted to have the missionaries visit his band. Alexis, who had been appointed chief by Judge Cox after his co-operation during the troubles in 1864, was more receptive when Father McGuckin returned in 1873. McGuckin appointed the customary assistants for Alexis and reported that two other Chilcotin chiefs also wanted to have their complement of captain and watchmen. These chiefs were Ke-ogh and Anaham. Ke-ogh was weak and considered a poor chief; Anaham kept his band in thorough subjection and was, therefore, a "good" chief. The two Stone Chilcotin bands had no Catholic chiefs, but McGuckin assured Bishop d'Herbomez that one would shortly be chosen to take charge of both camps, whose combined population was only ninety-one. Once that was done, the job of converting them could begin. Father McGuckin wound up his 1873 visit to the lowland Chilcotin with a feeling of optimism: "a little patience and perseverance will succeed in making them pretty good Christians."[6]

By 1881 he was less sanguine. The priest assigned to the Chilcotins was not even a little persevering. Father Fréderic Guertin rather liked riding around visiting his charges, but he quickly gave up trying to learn their complex language. When he first met the Chilcotins in the spring of 1881, he found the experience intimidating. Guertin had none of Morice's passion for missionary work; he preferred his teaching duties. The bands he visited in 1881 had not seen a priest for three years, and there were a number of thorny problems for him to regulate, including the dubious status, in church law, of marriages which had been performed by a chief.[7]

The material progress of the Chilcotins was hardly more impressive. The deprivations suffered by the nomadic hunters upset Father Guertin, and he encouraged them to plant crops. They were not necessarily opposed to this kind of change — Guertin described Chief Anaham as "a man of progress" — but they had neither the seed nor the equipment. In any case, agriculture was impractical both climatically and topographically, though cattle ranching was later adopted with some success, but Guertin does not seem to have realized this. He had little or no understanding of the Indians' material culture or environment. According to him, large numbers of Indians were dying because they ate too much dried salmon and took too little exercise! Father Guertin did, however, take a useful census of the Chilcotin population in 1881. Out of a total population of 479, he noted that just 26 adults had been baptized, and those only because they were in danger of dying.[8]

Father Morice was not wrong, then, when he emphasized the difficulty of his first missionary assignment. The enthusiasm that he felt for his new duties was in stark contrast to Guertin's indifference, and Morice quickly threw himself into the task which Guertin found impossible: learning the Chilcotin language. With neither a written vocabulary nor a grammar, this was a formidable undertaking, but Morice knew that a knowledge of the language of his flock was essential for the success of any missionary.[9] Throughout the winter of 1883–84, he spent his afternoons visiting an intelligent old Chilcotin woman who, with her black husband, lived in a shack erected on land owned by the Williams Lake mission. Using the Chinook jargon as their common language, Morice coaxed out of this petulant lady enough of her mother tongue to compose a vocabulary of some six thousand words and to write a rudimentary grammar. He then translated the catechism, some prayers, and a few hymns. The young man who until now had found his studies boring was enchanted by the beauty and complexity of the language which his new missionary job required him to learn. It was a labour of love, and despite the extreme difficulty of the language, Morice seems to have suddenly acquired a great store of patience and perseverance.[10]

Armed with the rudiments of the Chilcotin language, he began his missionary excursions into the hunting grounds of the Chilcotin in April 1883. The purpose of the first visit was to introduce him to his new flock, and Father Guertin came along to do this. They crossed the Fraser via an ice bridge and headed for the camp of Chief Touzi, the Chilcotin camp closest to the Fraser. From there the two rode a considerable distance further west to Chief Anaham's village, where the inhabitants struck the tenderfoot missionary as not very Christian. The sod roofs of the cabins they had built in imitation of the whites were not conducive to cleanliness, Morice reported in the *Missions,* and they fried potatoes in caribou grease and served them up without forks. They eyed their new priest with cold curiosity, and Morice imagined that they were thinking that because he was young, he would not give them much trouble. Before long, it seems, they changed their minds and began to call him "the young priest with the strong words."[11]

Morice's second tour, again made in Guertin's company, was abortive. The chiefs came to fetch the Oblates on the appointed day, but they were more anxious to solicit political advice than spiritual succour. Two Chinese men had recently been murdered by Chilcotins, and the arrest of the suspected killers and their removal to prison had caused considerable panic. Chief Anaham reported that many of his band had fled into the forest for fear of imprisonment, and he asked Morice to calm the situation by writing to the Queen. The chief must have believed that the distant monarch could be influenced by the priest's appeal, an indication that the Chilcotin regarded the Oblate missionaries as potentially useful brokers in their relations with the white authorities. A decade earlier another Oblate, Father Jean-Marie Lejacq, had obtained a pardon for an escaped Indian wrongly convicted and sentenced to six months on a chain gang. In response to the latest request for aid, Morice promised to write to Dr. Israel Wood Powell, the superintendent of Indian affairs in British Columbia, if circumstances warranted it. The prospect of another major conflict with the whites had caused the Chilcotin to forget about the construction of the new church they had undertaken to build, and Morice felt that their preoccupation with political matters was such that no religious propagation was possible for the time being. After choosing a site for the church and pledging to bring along Father Georges Blanchet, the expert church builder, on his next visit, Morice and Guertin departed.[12]

The promise was kept. On 2 July 1883, Morice and Blanchet left Williams Lake on horseback to build a new church and priest's house at Anaham's camp. The ride was hard on sixty-five-year-old Father Blanchet, who had not ridden for many years. Upon their arrival at the village of Touzi's band, the most Europeanized Chilcotins, they found the crude log cabins deserted. The people had pitched their tents by a stream half a mile away. Morice preferred to see Indians living the more "primitive" camp life rather than being cooped up in smoke-filled cabins. As he approached their tents, the people began to cough and moan in order to prove their need for medicine. Missionaries were seen as doctors as well as useful intermediaries. Having dispensed the desired potions, Morice pushed on to Anaham's camp. When the party left the high plateau to enter the pine forests of the wide Chilcotin Valley, Morice spotted large forest fires and learned to his dismay that they had been set by the Indians. Without the smoke from these fires, the natives explained, the mosquitoes would so torment their horses that the precious beasts would run off. It was ingenious, as Morice observed at the time, but not very economical.[13]

On the evening of 7 July, five days after leaving Williams Lake, Morice arrived at Anaham's camp at the junction of the Chilcotin and Tlathenkoh or Anaham rivers. The camp was well situated on a prairie some forty feet above the river, and it was here that the Chilcotins had built their first church. Now a new church and a priest's house were planned; perhaps in the not too distant future, the "village" would become a permanent Oblate residence. Chief Anaham had considerable influence and could be a useful ally. He was also well-to-do by Chilcotin standards—he had a big log house with a plank floor—and he provided the visiting priests with flour, tea, sugar, and pepper.[14]

But Father Morice was not attracted by such civilized comforts, and he soon left for more primitive climes. Peken, chief of the Lake Louzkeuz people, had sought him out at Touzi's camp and told him that a group from the remote Alkatcho band of Carriers had arrived at Lake Louzkeuz and were hoping to see the priest. It was their fifth attempt to encounter a missionary, and despite a shortage of food, they had been waiting for two months. Leaving Blanchet to get on with the church, Morice headed for Lake Louzkeuz in the company of Peken and two of his young men. The journey was long and hard. For four days they rode a veritable steeplechase through thick pine forests. The pace was forced by the chief, who was so anxious to see the ailing son he had left at home that he seemed not to see mud-holes, rocks, or tree trunks. At one point, Morice's horse threw him into a tree trunk, and the resulting injury added to the discomfort caused by a chronic ailment which Morice attributed to the bad food and bog water he was forced to consume. But these discomforts were compensated for by the joy he felt at being in the company of his "poor children of the woods." He was especially moved, he claimed, by the sound of their hymns echoing in the forest as he read his daily office by the light of the camp fire. The boyhood dreams stimulated by Chateaubriand, Grandin, and Petitot were coming true. For the first time he was truly free.

The tenderfoot missionary noticed that the regularity with which these un-baptized and neglected natives performed their religious duties could scarcely be matched by those who enjoyed all the attention and graces of the church. Morice greatly admired, too, the Indians' ancient skills. He was particularly impressed by Peken's ability to interpret signs left in the forest by his band.[15]

Finally, after a grueling 150-mile ride, they reached Lake Louzkeuz. Peken's people rode out to shake the hand of the new *Yakastapayalthek* (the speaker for Him who is in the sky), and Morice immediately inquired after the distant people who had been waiting so long for him. He seems to have been as anxious to see them as they were to see him. Alas, they had departed just two days before he arrived. Fortunately, however, a mes-senger was able to catch up with two families and bring them back. Morice promised to visit them at home the following year.[16]

Then, with the aid of an interpreter, he began to preach his very first "mission." For the Oblates, a mission meant about a week of intensive religious activity, which comprised instruction, the celebration of the sacraments, and the judgment and public punishment of sinners. In the mornings and evenings, the sixty or so members of the Lake Louzkeuz band were assembled for moral and doctrinal lectures. Two or three hours in the afternoons were devoted to the catechism, which included rules of conduct in and out of church as well as sacred dogma. The Indians were summoned to each session by the blast from a horn, and upon entering their crude and humble church—the space between the logs was large enough in places to put an arm through—they bowed and made the sign of the cross. Given the fact that the people had exhausted their food stocks, attendance at these exercises was surprisingly good. Morice was pleased with the band's willingness to learn and to reform, which compared fa-vourably with what he called the semi-indifference of many Chilcotins. This greater zeal was a result, Morice believed, of their sense of isolation and their knowledge that the priest could not see them as often as they needed and wished.[17]

The Lake Louzkeuz people had a terrible fear of the devil and the "great fire," or so it seemed to Morice. He was besieged from all sides with questions about the gravity of this or that transgression: what kind of sin was it to eat before saying morning prayers, to enter the church without moccasins, or to collect wild berries on a Sunday when there was nothing else to eat? The Chilcotins were, like many aboriginal peoples in contact with Christianity, concerned above all to learn its taboos so that they could observe them and thereby reap the same material and eternal rewards as the white man and, presumably, avoid the physical torments of Hell's fire.[18] In New Zealand, for example, many Maoris began to observe the sabbath soon after contact with Europeans, and they often observed it in a more strict, even pharisaical manner than did most Europeans.[19] The Chilcotins had a frantic desire for baptism, and when Morice refused on the grounds that he did not know them well enough, there was a real uproar.[20] Baptism, it seems, was regarded as an important protective ritual. Morice's firmness was in conformity with Oblate practice elsewhere in British Columbia. He was beginning to put the Lake Louzkeuz people through the mill of the "repression process," the first half of the two-stage Oblate missionary method.

The use of public confessions and penances was a crucial part of that process, and both were more readily accepted than Morice's refusal of baptism. The two families from the Alkatcho band were admitted to the ranks of the catechists—those preparing for baptism—after each person had made the requisite *roenatsoewoelnoek* or public self-accusation of faults; any member of the band who had committed a "public fault" was punished by a public whipping. These penances were, according to Morice, accepted devoutly, and in some cases they were even requested. Perhaps the fact that the Indians traditionally linked physical discomfort and pain with spirit possession helped reconcile them to the penances. Certainly, neither the whippings nor Morice's doctrinal rigour prevented them from trying to keep him with them as long as possible. Owing to the Indians' penury, a five-day mission was all that Morice had planned, but at the end of this period, they prevailed on him to stay a few days more. He finally packed his bags after eight days and bade his "children" a sorrowful *adieu*.[21]

This mission at Lake Louzkeuz was the first missionary campaign of Morice's career, and he cherished his memories of the prayers the Indians offered before the miniature houses they built over the graves of the dead. These "humble children of the woods," as Morice liked to think of them, prayed to a Christian God they scarcely knew. Yet these touching scenes did not blind him to the fact that when he left the camp the *taeyen* or shaman would again assert his influence. Morice understood the Indians' culture too well to fall victim to the naive optimism displayed by some other Oblates. He did not despair, though; the people appeared to him to be co-operative, and he expected that their faults could be overcome.[22]

With this hope to console him, Morice began the long ride back to Anaham's camp. Thomie and Kwoelh, his unpaid Chilcotin guide and interpreter respectively, bagged hare and wild fowl to sustain the party, for the Lake Louzkeuz people had no food to send off with them, as was customary. They arrived at the junction of the Anaham and Chilcotin rivers only to find the camp deserted and work on the church hardly begun. A note left by Father Blanchet with Tom Hance, a settler who lived nearby, informed Morice that the Indians had headed for their fishing grounds on the Fraser two days before. Not being able to work on the church alone, Blanchet had returned to Williams Lake. Though disappointed, Morice understood the Indians' dependence on salmon, which they dried to eat during the long winter months. It was their daily bread: a good salmon run brought abundance and joy; a poor run meant famine and grief. So Morice kept riding until he reached the Fraser, where he expected to find the three Chilcotin Valley bands catching salmon. The gathering of the bands in one place would provide an excellent opportunity to give a mission. Once again he was disappointed. More than half of Anaham's band and the whole of another band were not at the fishing grounds. Some were hunting, and others were at Fort Alexandria, supposedly to fish for salmon but more likely, Morice suspected, to buy whiskey illegally from whites. Powerless to bring them back, he resigned himself to giving a mission to Touzi's band and what remained of Anaham's group.[23]

Father Morice hoped to visit the Stone Chilcotins when this riverside mission was over. These Indians hunted on the flanks of the coastal mountains whose snow-clad summits he had seen on his return from Lake Louzkeuz. Unlike the Chilcotin Valley bands, they still led a nomadic life untarnished by frequent contacts with whiskey traders and other representatives of European civilization. The prospect of meeting pristine Indians made Morice eager to begin the long journey to the mountains. But he was to be frustrated, for none of the valley people would volunteer to go with him as a guide or interpreter. All kinds of arguments were thought up to deter him from setting off: the trail was dreadful; the mountain Chilcotin were dispersed through the forest; and, besides, they were bad and primitive and Morice would be unhappy among them. When the eager young priest persisted, he was told by the valley Chilcotin that they did not know the way. And while he did not believe them, he was forced to abandon his project. As a consolation, he was told that the Stone Chilcotins came down into the valley in the fall, at which time he could minister to them. There being nothing else to do and nowhere exotic to go, Morice returned to Williams Lake. He had been away nearly six weeks and had travelled almost six hundred miles.[24]

Soon after his return, Father Morice wrote a long letter for publication in the *Missions*. The letter had a twofold objective: to describe the Chilcotins and to give an account of his work among them. He included a list of their violent deeds, but he was careful to explain that in murdering certain whites, the Indians were simply defending their land, the honour of their women, and their dignity. He felt no identity with the miners and workmen who had suffered the Chilcotins' wrath. Indeed, there was an implicit hostility towards men who by their very presence had corrupted his Indians.[25]

Part of the letter was devoted to the Chilcotin language. With the air of a savant and the thrill of a discoverer, Morice tried to give his readers an idea of the genius of that "blissful language." He explained, too, the affinity between the Chilcotins and the great family of Indians to whom Petitot had given the collective name "Déné-Dindjié." In making these comparisons, Morice was drawing on the linguistic writings of Petitot, and it is clear from the tone of the letter that he already regarded himself as an Americanist and, more specifically, as an ethnographer with a strong attraction towards linguistics. His enthusiasm for native languages was matched by the excitement he felt when travelling and living with true "savages," an excitement his published letter eloquently conveys.[26] Morice revelled in his escape from the mundane routine and discipline of European community life. Father Lacombe, the French-Canadian priest who became well known for helping to keep the Blackfoot "loyal" during the Riel troubles of 1885, was similarly delighted when he won the independence which his own mission in "untamed Indian territory" brought.[27]

But for Morice the release was not permanent. During the long intervals between his visits to the Chilcotins, Father Morice was expected to help out at the Williams Lake school and to abide by the rules of the Oblate order. So, despite his attachment to his new flock, he continued to demand a transfer to the Stuart Lake mission. Naturally, he backed up his demand with his well-tried and successful passive resistance tactics. When asked to instruct the children, he did so grudgingly and poorly. His superior, Father Julien Baudre, reported in October 1883 that Morice treated him with contempt and had been living cut off from the community for several months, studying and reading in his room. This inability to live amicably with his fellow Oblates and his concomitant desire to work with the most remote and least acculturated native peoples closely resembled aspects of Father Petitot's behaviour. Morice did, however, maintain good relations with Father Blanchet, the church-builder. Blanchet was a modest and easy-going old fellow who seems to have become Morice's confidant.[28]

Father Baudre's attitude was quite different. He found Morice intolerable and incorrigible, and he recommended that the bishop allow him to go to Stuart Lake, where he could be most useful. Above all, Morice would be both willing and able to learn the Carrier language, which was closely related to the Chilcotin tongue. But Baudre's motives were not entirely altruistic; he was desperately trying to rid himself of Morice. The bishop did not grant Baudre's wish. Instead, he consulted Father Martinet about Morice's continuing delinquency and was told that the young priest's record indicated that he must be watched carefully for his vanity and insubordination. Martinet believed that the best approach to adopt in such a case was to be firm but just. Care must be taken not to give Morice any reason to complain, for he would use this against them.[29]

In the meantime, Morice remained at Williams Lake and continued to visit the Chilcotins. In the winter of 1883–84, he spent two months among them. His first duty was to complete the church begun by Father Blanchet at Anaham's camp. Each morning he would have to do the rounds of the camp to stimulate the Indians' enthusiasm for the task, but once on the job both men and women worked well. Tree trunks were squared on two sides, and a church thirty by twenty feet slowly took shape before the admiring eyes of its creators. After a heated and humorous debate concerning the correct way to lay roof shingles—should one start at the top or the bottom?—the church was completed; the mission began.[30] As usual, one of the most important activities was the public confession. Among the "sins" which Morice and the other Oblates tried to outlaw was the traditional form of gambling. The most popular game involved passing a pair of small bone objects from hand to hand under the cover of a blanket and in time with the beating of a drum. When the drum stopped, one of the two players tried to guess which of his opponent's hands contained the winning bone. During his winter visit, Father Morice was a victim of the passion with which this game was played. A man named *Oezousi*, the Magpie, came with a horse from the camp of the Stone Chilcotins in order to take Morice and his paraphernalia to that camp. But when Oezousi reported for "duty," he had no horse. He had gambled it away during the night; his winter coat and head gear were also gone. But the young man was not perturbed and expressed his willingness to carry the baggage on his ample shoulders.[31]

Fortunately, the Stone Chilcotins had their winter camp not too far off in the Chilcotin Valley. Father Morice now had the privilege of ministering to the people he considered the most primitive in British Columbia. He found that they looked like most of the other Chilcotins: stocky with almond-shaped eyes, a prominent jawbone, and, along with other Dénés, straight black hair, small hands and feet, bronze skin, and sparse facial hair. Their dress was more distinctive because it had not yet been significantly influenced by contact with whites. The most important garment was a ground-hog skin cloak, worn with the fur inward and fastened under the chin. Around their heads they wore a band of beaver skin, and suspended from their necks were awls and tweezers made of copper. The awl was for making and repairing leather clothes and implements; the tweezers were used to pluck facial hair. Stone pipes, too, hung from the neck of the men and the women; the latter were inveterate smokers. Both sexes decorated their bodies with tattoos. In addition to putting lines on their faces, they adorned both faces and arms with crosses and designs of birds and fish.[32]

Father Morice found that these tattooed and fur-clad people responded well to his evangelical teaching. Indeed, he later remarked that of all the Chilcotins, it was they who were most encouraging. Their very simplicity was, he believed, an indication of innocence, and their minimal dealings with whites rendered them more docile in their attitude to missionaries. Oblate pioneers in Oregon had made the same observation: Indians who had little to do with the Americans were the simplest and most tractable; those with greater contact had their pockets full of money and were arrogant, insufferable, and entirely unconcerned with prayer. Like some of his predecessors, Morice was not dissuaded from his attachment to the notion of the "noble savage" by his exposure to real "savages." But the observations of Morice and other Oblates also suggests that there was, as in other mission fields, an initial enthusiasm for Christianity among the natives which was followed by disappointment with its failure to bring tangible benefits.[33] The longer the period of contact with Christianity and with whites in general, the greater the likelihood of disillusionment.

At the end of this first happy encounter with the Stone Chilcotins, Father Morice returned to the stifling routine of the Williams Lake Mission. His perpetual sulking and bad will continued and became, along with his renewed request for a transfer to Stuart Lake, a source of increasing anxiety and annoyance for his superiors. An exasperated Father Martinet was prepared to have the superior general send Morice a "first warning," a grave disciplinary measure. Three such warnings would bring a trial and possible expulsion from the order. However, Morice could not be expelled for refusing to talk to his superior, to attend recreation, or to play the organ. But, Martinet counselled, a close watch must be kept on this man "infatuated with himself." If things did not improve, Father Baudre should try to "faire explosion"—to force a showdown. He must take care, though, not to make unreasonable demands or to question Morice's motives, no matter how non-spiritual he suspected them of being. On the other hand, Martinet recommended that Bishop d'Herbomez refuse to transfer Morice because he would not change elsewhere and in any case they should not give in to him.[34]

Morice got an occasional respite from this struggle against his superiors by galloping off to visit his Chilcotins. On 18 March 1884, he left Williams Lake to visit the camp of Touzi's people at Tloesko on the Chilcotin River. Contrary to accepted practice, he did not even bother to tell Father Baudre where he was going, let alone ask permission.

Morice returned from Touzi's camp on 24 March, and on the 26th, he left for Fort Alexandria. The "fort" was an abandoned Hudson's Bay Company post about forty miles north of Williams Lake inhabited by Chilcotin and Carrier Indians. The village was formerly the northern terminus for the barges which brought the Hudson's Bay freight up the Fraser, but Quesnel, some forty miles further north, had now replaced it as the entrepôt of the area. Towards the end of 1883, the bishop had asked Morice to look after Fort Alexandria as well as the predominantly Carrier communities at Quesnel and Blackwater. He was now able to give catechism lessons in the Chilcotin language; the Carriers who lived along the Fraser called him the "Little Chilcotin."[35]

The mission at Fort Alexandria went well. The Indians had, according to Morice, improved considerably in the space of six months. Almost three years earlier, Father McGuckin had reported that they were "nearly all beyond the control of the priest and have been so for the past 2½ years."[36] With the exception of one man—"a villain, stealer of women and murderer"—they had now all confessed and were "well disposed." Morice also enjoyed some success in restoring broken marriages, a perennial challenge for the Oblate missionaries. An Indian woman was returned to the white husband she had left two years before, and a métis was persuaded to take back his wife, who had been living with another man.[37] Such were the fruits of a successful missionary excursion.

But these successes did not reconcile Morice to his situation. He remained obsessed with the idea of going to Stuart Lake, and his revolt, which had now lasted two years, was eroding Father Baudre's will to continue the fight. He no longer had the courage to face Morice's disdain and impertinence, and in the spring of 1884, he began to request his own transfer. In his opinion, Morice's condition was incurable; he was equally impervious to kind treatment and stern warnings. Consequently, Baudre recommended a remedy, perhaps expulsion, which Bishop d'Herbomez found too radical. Failing that, he implored the bishop to grant Morice his transfer.[38] Father Martinet, the Oblate assistant general, was still against any concessions to Morice. He felt that neither Morice nor Baudre should be transferred and that Morice, like any other subject, must submit to his superior. It was better for the foreign missions to perish for want of staff than lack of discipline. While Morice's individual acts were not serious enough to warrant the use of the most extreme measures against him, taken together and over a two-year period, they constituted grounds for sending him a first warning. This was duly sent to d'Herbomez in an open envelope on 28 July 1884, and the bishop was instructed to issue it if and when he saw fit. Martinet seems to have hoped that the official warning from the superior general would force the issue in a way that Baudre had failed to do. But the assistant general was not optimistic about Morice's reaction; his vanity, pride, and independence would probably cause him to revolt completely and leave the order.[39]

While he was the subject of such concern in high places in Paris, Morice used the summer months of 1884 to travel among the Indians from whom he expected humility, docility, and simplicity. His principal destination was the Carrier village of Alkatcho. He had just missed seeing most of its inhabitants the previous summer, and he had promised to visit them in 1884. Departing early in June, he gave a short and successful mission at Lake Louzkeuz and then, on 18 June, he pushed north towards Alkatcho with two guides.

At noon on the second day, the group paused at the abandoned Carrier village of Oelrak. While his companions prepared lunch, Morice's antiquarian appetite was whetted by the sight of two crudely carved columns. One had a square box on top and the other was partially carved out and sealed. Father Morice's guides were amused by his curiosity, and they laughed as they explained that the columns were repositories for the charred bones of Carrier Indians cremated according to their ancient custom. If the deceased was a married man, his widow was obliged to carry the remains of his bones in a satchel on her back—hence the name Carrier or *Porteur* given to the tribe by the whites. For the two or three years that she carried the bones, the widow had her hair cut off and her face daubed with resin, and she was the virtual slave of her late husband's relatives. The disappearance of this custom, Morice later wrote, proved what a precious gift Christianity had been for the native woman.[40]

His curiosity satisfied, Morice and his men began the last lap of their journey to Alkatcho. As they approached the lake the next day, Father Morice became excited at the thought of the happy throng of Indians welcoming their priest. He was to be disappointed, for the camp was deserted. But there was still hope: perhaps they were at their fishing place. The fishery was located twenty-five miles away on Long Lake, probably the modern Entiako Lake, which, according to Morice, had never been visited by a white man. Here they found a lone family: an old man, his wife, and their two young daughters. The rest of the band was by the sea, where they had gone to trade. At the insistence of their parents and despite his suspicion that one of the girls had reached the age of reason, after which baptism is only possible after a period of instruction, Morice baptized the two girls. There was not enough time to instruct and baptize the adults. Some years afterwards, Morice learned that the old man, Oestoes, had later died without either baptism or the consolation of a priest's presence at his death bed. But sensing the approach of death, Oestoes had attempted to perform what he considered to be the necessary ritual for the forgiveness of sins. He tied his wrists together like those of a criminal, and only after a considerable time lapse did he feel that he had paid off his sins. Shortly after releasing his bonds, he died.[41]

In the summer of 1885, Father Morice made the long trek to Alkatcho for the second time. This time the people were at home, and apparently Morice was regarded with extreme curiosity and anticipation. His first concern was to create the Oblate administrative apparatus, and a chief was appointed as well as a captain and the usual watchmen.[42] Anthropologist Irving Goldman, who studied the Alkatcho Carrier, believed that the Indians "approved of these appointments and apparently accepted the authority of these men." In the late 1930's, an Alkatcho man described for Goldman the important day when the Catholic priest they had heard about from their "neighbours" at Lake Louzkeuz finally arrived:[43]

> Father Morice came when I was a small boy. He came with an interpreter and three horses. He showed this Catholic business. He made camp some little way off. Some old men went over to see the White man. The old men came back and said, "It's a priest, he got big talk." We had heard from a long way about a priest. Now he came. An interpreter came and told us to go on the other side just a little way. Everyone came to the tent and sat outside. The White man sat inside. Then he came out and talked. "This people will all be Catholic by and by," he said. Then he talked a little bit and showed that Catholic business and he went back.

This willingness to accept the "Catholic business' should not be interpreted as true conversion, even though native religion did decline markedly following the arrival of the missionaries. Those whom Morice addressed were not rejecting tradition for a new life; rather they were engaged in a seemingly unemotional, "matter of fact" supplementing of one religion with another. In other contexts, this kind of religious behaviour has been called "adhesion," and the term could usefully be applied to the Alkatcho Carrier adoption of Christian rites and taboos.[44] Before encountering Morice, they had seen few whites, and for some time after his visit, their contact with whites was minimal. So it was obviously not the threatening presence of settlers and miners which had stimulated native interest in Christianity. Their fur-trading activities had, however, brought them the white man's weapons and implements as well as some knowledge of his ways. There was a strong desire to acquire these prestigious goods.[45] This covetousness and the receptive attitude toward new religious concepts and practices are related. Carrier religion was essentially pragmatic and this-worldly, as were the pre-Christian religions of Europe. It did not seek to transcend the material world but rather to manipulate it.

Both the intercession of the shamans with the spirits and the observation of the many taboos were expected to bring tangible benefits, above all, good health and material wealth.[46] Yet, since the Carrier had no traditional knowledge of the spiritual means by which they might gain greater access to the European technology, they seem to have sensed that they no longer fully controlled their situation. Robin Ridington has reported this kind of reaction to the fur trade among the Carriers' northern neighbours, the *Dunne-za* or Beaver, while Hilary Rumley believes that for British Columbia's native peoples in general, contact with Europeans upset assumptions about the power relations between the spiritual and material worlds and that adherence to Christianity promised a "moral equality" which would lead to the acquisition of equal wealth and power.[47] Apparently, the incorporation of Christian beliefs could be achieved either through native prophets, as among the Beaver, or via a missionary like Morice, as in the case of the Alkatcho. According to Goldman, when Father Morice sought out men to appoint as chief, captain, and watchmen, he "wisely selected the most prominent nobles and gave them positions within the church . . . which became analogous to the old honorific prerogatives." Perhaps, like Indian leaders elsewhere in British Columbia, the Alkatcho notables agreed to become missionary agents in order to bolster their rather weak traditional authority by participating in the new power structure introduced by the whites. In any event, by increasing the influence of both the priest and the chief, the appointments were "mutually beneficial."[48]

As it happened, however, Father Morice himself never returned to build on the foundation he had laid among the Alkatcho. Shortly after his return to Williams Lake at the end of his long summer tour, he received a transfer to Stuart Lake. But it was intended as just a temporary expedient, and under the circumstances, it seemed more like the end than a new beginning for his missionary career. His strategy of passive resistance and calculated aggravation had intensified since the first warning was served on him, and by May 1885 Father Martinet was preparing to send him a second. In the meantime, he asked d'Herbomez to encourage the errant priest to undertake a "retreat" with the bishop at New Westminster. This period of seclusion and religious contemplation away from the pressures of his duties would be Morice's last chance for salvation, Martinet vowed. For although Morice's behaviour was, on the surface, merely foolish and irrational, Martinet believed that deep down it was the result of an immense and overweening pride.[49]

Things came to a head in August 1885. By then Morice's revolt was more open, and in addition to refusing to perform some of his own priestly rituals, he tried to disrupt his fellow Oblates as they fulfilled their religious duties. One day while Fathers Guertin and Chiappini were saying their office, Morice walked up and down the corridor excitedly singing and clapping his hands. And though he found time to play the organ when he felt like it, he declared that he was incapable of getting up in time to celebrate the ten o'clock mass on Sunday. He also refused to give sermons. Father Guertin, who had replaced Baudre as the superior at Williams Lake, believed the case was hopeless. The young priest was now completely impervious; he could not be reached. As Guertin expressed it: "il ne donne aucun signe de vie: il est mort."[50] This extreme withdrawal may have been a deliberate tactic in Morice's campaign to get his transfer to Stuart Lake, but his unjustified feelings of persecution suggest some kind of mental illness. He had become convinced that his superiors were trying to get him to abandon his music, to which he was greatly attached.[51] However, if there was a breakdown, it was undoubtedly the result of the thwarting of his drive for independence, a product of his potent will to power.

Unable to cope with this unrelenting willfulness, the bishop sent Morice to Stuart Lake on 19 August 1885. He was to stay there until his fate was decided. This move was frowned upon by Martinet, who feared that Morice might be too free under the easy-going Father Pandosy, his superior at Stuart Lake. Pandosy had been among the five Oblates who had begun the Oregon mission in 1847, and he had remained at his post during the fierce fighting of the Oregon frontier wars. It was feared in Paris that Pandosy's eccentric behaviour, which was not specified, would provide Morice with evidence to embarrass the Oblates should he wish to do so. Yet, despite these fears, or perhaps partly because of them, Morice's superiors still desired his reconciliation—his conversion, as Martinet put it. If only he would submit, he could render great service wherever he was sent.[52] Talented missionaries were always in short supply, which helps to account for the many "second chances" which Morice received. But the battle of wills was coming to a climax; those in authority must now force the issue.

Morice was sent a second warning in late September 1885. He was charged with being in an "intolerable and habitual state of rebellion." A submission and a promise to mend his ways would allow his superiors to offer him the chance of joining a larger Oblate community, where he could have more spiritual support. But as long as he remained obdurate, he would be left at Stuart Lake. Martinet promised that if he warranted another warning, it would be the last.[53] While Martinet understood Morice quite well, he did not seem to realize that the last thing he needed was the support of a large Oblate establishment. Indeed, the absence of the normal constraints of religious community life at Stuart Lake was the best and perhaps the only cure for the rebel's malaise. At last Morice had his refuge. His superiors did not know it, but he had won.

3

WITH THE CARRIER:
THE MISSIONARY FOUNDATION, 1885–1895

Bishop d'Herbomez gave Morice his "marching orders" for the Stuart Lake Mission on 19 August 1885. The transfer was a temporary and desperate expedient, and the delinquent priest was not expected to remain there indefinitely. Either he would repent and be shipped off to a larger religious community, or he would continue his rebellion and face expulsion from the order. As it happened, he neither repented nor kept up his rebellion. Once he reached his refuge, he no longer had to rebel, and for the next eighteen years no attempt was made to integrate him into any other Oblate community. A man who could learn the Carrier language was needed in the district, and his superiors probably believed it was best to leave him on the margin of the British Columbia vicariate where he would cause them the least trouble. As late as 1904, when communications in the Northern Interior were better than in 1885, Oblate authorities admitted that the priests at Stuart Lake were virtual exiles.[1] It was a convenient place to keep a troublemaker, especially one who wanted to be there. But the situation was even more convenient for Morice. Having succeeded in getting himself exiled to a remote area where supervision was minimal, he could now begin to realize his dream of becoming a priest-king and savant. Between 1885 and 1896, when he left for a year in France, he established himself as an influential missionary and began to make a name for himself as an explorer and Americanist.

Morice sought out Stuart Lake precisely because he imagined that it would be ideal for his purposes. When he finally arrived there, he was jubilant. He regarded the Stuart Lake mission district as a perfect posting for both spiritual and physical reasons, though the two were related. The vastness and geographic isolation of the area meant that there were few whites to hinder the work of the missionary or to corrupt his flock. In particular, there were no Protestant ministers to compete with him. Another happy consequence of the minimal white presence, Morice believed, was the absence among the Indians of "arrogant fools who thought they were civilized because they drank shamelessly and could jabber a few words of English."[2] Morice's subjects would not be imitation Europeans but Christian *sauvages*—the elusive hybrid species that the Jesuits in Huronia had tried in vain to cultivate.[3] Since the Carrier were still living on the fur-trading frontier, they were not yet affected by the European ideas of religious and secular emancipation that Father Martinet had warned were coming with the settlers.

But Morice appreciated the remote and rugged terrain of the Northern Interior not only because it helped keep out such subversive notions. He loved the mountains, lakes, and forests for their own sake. Exploring them was both an escape and an heroic adventure; conquering them was an opportunity to appease his enormous lust for power and to put his name on the map literally. As an itinerant missionary, Morice would be responsible for ministering to remote and semi-nomadic bands scattered over the territory lying between the 53rd and 57th degree latitude and the 122nd and 128th of longitude, an area of approximately 64,000 square miles. Travel was not easy through the dense forests, over mountain ranges, and along the often treacherous rivers. The only trail fit for wagons was the nine-mile road across the portage from Stuart Lake to Babine Lake. Consequently, most travel was by the lakes and rivers. The natives, and Morice, used canoes and scows in the summer and toboggans in the winter. It was sometimes extremely cold—from 20 to 54 degrees below zero Fahrenheit—for months.[4] Like his predecessors, Morice was expected to make both regular and emergency visits to isolated Indian encampments throughout the year.

The increasingly sedentary Carrier made up most of this scattered flock, though Morice was also responsible for some bands of the nomadic Sikani. By 1885, the white man's diseases had reduced the total Carrier population to about 1,600 from an original population of perhaps ten times that number. They were divided among two principal linguistic and cultural subdivisions. Roughly a thousand people belonged to what might be called the central Carrier. For the most part, they lived around Stuart Lake and along the banks of the Fraser and its tributaries as far south as Quesnel. The second sub-group of about six hundred souls lived to the northwest on Babine Lake and in the Bulkley Valley.[5] The French-speaking employees of the North West Company had called them Babines—literally "pendulous lips"—because of the labrets they wore in their lower lips, and the name had stuck. The Bulkley Valley Babines, some of whom hunted as far south as François Lake, had a somewhat separate identity and they were known as the Hotsoten. Far to the northeast, on the western slope of the Rocky Mountains, roamed the Sikani, whose traditional way of life was quite different from that of the Carrier. The Oblate missionary from Fort St. James could only make intermittent contact with the 350 or so Sikani who came to trade at Fort McLeod, Bear Lake (Fort Connolly), and Fort Graham.[6]

At the time when the fur traders arrived in the early nineteenth century, the culture of the Carrier Indians was dependent on the availability of salmon and greatly influenced by their contact with coastal tribes. The Carrier moved with the seasons. In the summer they built elaborate weirs and basketry traps at fishing camps on the rivers. They dried their salmon catch for use during the winter, when they dispersed in the forest in order to increase their chances of finding firewood and game. The Carrier were divided into clans, each with its hereditary "nobles" who controlled the hunting and fishing territories and dominated the potlatch. But even the most influential of the nobles were not authoritarian chiefs.[7] Rather, they were "first among equals," and they had to depend upon persuasion and liberality to ensure compliance with their decisions, most of which concerned disputes among clansmen. Their matrilineal clan structure, the system of titled nobility, and the potlatch were all borrowed from the coastal tribes, and they were most firmly established among the Hotsoten.[8]

The Sikani had a quite different economy and culture. Not having access to salmon rivers, they ranged the forested uplands in pursuit of moose, bear, and other game. Constantly on the move in small patrilineal bands, they were only partially able to adopt ranking, potlatching, and other aspects of Pacific coast culture which they observed among Gitksan and Carrier Indians whom they met at the white man's trading posts.[9]

The presence of the fur traders led to major changes in the economic and social life of the Indians of the Northern Interior, especially among those Carrier who lived near the principal emporium at Fort St. James. The fort had been established by the North West Company's Simon Fraser in 1806, and both the North Westers and the Hudson's Bay men brought the technology and the culture of the white man. From the beginning, the Carrier manifested "a most pronounced admiration for the foreigners and their wares."[10] By the time Morice came to the area in 1885, their traditional culture had experienced considerable change; they were *not* the unspoilt noble savages that he liked to tell his readers about. Although the cultural transformation was for the most part voluntary and "non-directed"—not planned or directed by whites—it was nevertheless profound. Carrier men became trappers equipped with steel traps and guns, and control of the hunting territories passed from the titled nobles to heads of families. Many of the men and the women wore European clothes and built squared timber houses around the fur-trading forts. Their life became more sedentary, and they grew potatoes and other crops to supplement their traditional diet. As well as acquiring a taste for these foods and for utilitarian goods like guns and iron pots, the Indians wanted such "luxuries" as tobacco, tea, sugar, music boxes, sabres, and cowboy hats. Wage labour helped to pay for these consumer goods. Because of chronic staff shortages, the Hudson's Bay Company came to employ Carrier men as carpenters, farm hands, fur packers, and sailors; women were taken on as domestic servants.[11] The Carrier seem to have welcomed these opportunities to acquire the white man's skills.

The Carrier had also begun to assimilate the Christian religion long before Morice arrived. Something of a religious "reformation" had in fact taken place even prior to the establishment of an Oblate mission at Fort St. James on the shores of Stuart Lake. By 1850, the casual "preaching" of fur-trade personnel, including Christian Iroquois, together with syncretic beliefs spread by native prophets, "had so leavened the aboriginal doctrines as to occasion their drastic reinterpretation."[12] Originally, the Carriers solicited the aid of the many spirits of the animals and of the landscape. They believed that a pantheistic power animated the world and was "the cause efficient of rain and snow, winds and other firmamental phenomena," but this force was too inaccessible to be worshipped.[13] The "medicine" of the spirits which could be reached was obtained by the quest for a spirit visitation or through the intercession of the shaman. These same spirits were thought to demand the keeping of taboos; breaking them would bring physical punishment. The most elaborate and onerous set of taboos concerned the prolonged isolation of girls at the time of their first menstruation. The spirits of the animals were offended by any contact with menstrual blood, and they would not permit their bodily forms to be successfully hunted by a man who had such contact. Early exposure to Christianity's monotheism caused the Carrier to redefine this spiritual world, with the pantheistic force now being identified with the Christian God. Henceforth it was this God, called Utakke ("He who dwells on high"), and not so much the lesser spirits, who punished moral offences and taboo violations.[14]

The most dramatic intrusion of Christianity before the advent of European missions occurred in 1834, when the Prophet Dance spread with dramatic speed among the Carrier. Originating in Oregon, the cult involved a circular dance, belief in a supreme creator spirit, the confession of sins, and an expectation of world rebirth or resurrection. In the more southerly areas of the movement's activity, the native informants of anthropologists Boas and Spier related it to severe population loss caused by new diseases, especially smallpox, and Walker found that among Nez Percé cult members there was a "strong emphasis on acquisition of Euroamerican material culture."[15] In essence, the Prophet Dance combined hopes of resurrection and affluence, and in the absence of firm evidence linking Carrier prophets to the cult, it can only be assumed that it retained its original character after it reached them. One of the earliest of the Carrier prophets about whom anything is known is a woman named Bopa. She taught her followers that the dead "became white men on the far side of a great sea."[16] This preoccupation with death and rebirth certainly follows the Prophet Dance pattern.

So too did the religious teachings of a Cree-métis clerk in the employ of the Hudson's Bay Company. Later described by Father Morice as a "religious fakir," William McBean, who was in charge of a remote trading post, urged his Carrier clients to dance and promised them that if they followed him, they would turn into white men when they died. The teaching of McBean, an authoritarian and rather despotic individual, coincided roughly with the Prophet Dance agitation, which he was perhaps trying to exploit in order to establish a following. Dressed in white clothes and shoes, he warned the Carrier that if they listened to the "black coats" who would arrive shortly, they would turn black rather than white when they died.[17]

McBean's influence could not have been great, since the black-robed Catholic missionaries were certainly welcomed when they came in the 1840's. The teachings of the fur traders and of the native prophets had clearly created an interest in Christianity, and the priest could offer a more coherent formulation of it. And though the visits of Fathers Modeste Demers and Norbert Blanchet and the Jesuit John Nobili were "but skirmishes," the effects of what Fisher mockingly calls their "liberal sprinklings of baptismal water" were not as "minimal" and "superficial" as he suggests.[18] Soon after Nobili left the area in 1847, there emerged numerous native prophets, one in each of the major Carrier communities. They "counterfeited the work of the missionaries," to use Morice's description, and were the source of a "wonderful religious movement" which spread from the Carrier as far as the coastal Tsimshian people. The prophet most responsible for this movement was a Babine man known as Bini or Peni, who had changed his name from Kwes after he became convinced that his own mind *(pe-ni)* could penetrate those of his fellows. Bini also claimed to have died for three days, at which time he had visited the sky and had been told by the "Son of the Old Man" of an impending plague and great fire. To be saved from this cataclysm, the people were required to confess and repent their sins, to be baptized, and to marry "in the proper way"—all under Bini's direction. If they did reform, God had promised that the "poor should be made rich and the rich poor; that Indians would become white men and speak a new language; and that great dogs [horses] would descend from the sky." Noksan, a female prophet at Fraser Lake, foretold the same rebirth and plenty.[19] These prophecies are reminiscent of the cargo cults of Melanesia and of the early stages of conversion in the Pacific. In New Zealand, the Maoris at first conceived of Heaven as a place where they would be close to the Europeans and would enjoy an abundance of muskets and other European goods.[20] In both the Pacific islands and in central British Columbia, Christianity was viewed as the key which would open the doors of warehouses full of European "cargo." The Carrier apparently accepted European superiority, but they did not see it as racial in origin. Rather, the whites were a people whose superior technology presupposed a more effective religion.[21] Similarly, the Europeans appeared to the Samoan islanders to be "inferior, unhealthy and smelly," but their technology was admired, and, significantly, the Samoans "connected the possession of these goods not so much with the abilities and capabilities of Europeans themselves as with their forms of belief, their assumptions about power."[22] Like the Samoans, the Carrier wished to use Christianity to enrich themselves.

But the Carrier hoped for more than cargo. Bini, like the Prophet Dance prophets, promised resurrection, and the sick came to him to be healed. Although the Carrier had thus far been spared smallpox, other diseases introduced by the Europeans had taken a heavy toll. Father Nobili reported baptizing about five hundred children who then had the "happiness" to be "carried off by the measles," and the recurring prophetic theme of resurrection is undoubtedly and understandably linked to this disease mortality. American isolation from Old World pathogens meant that the Indians had no acquired immunity, and thus they were highly vulnerable.[23] Elsewhere on the Northwest Coast, the inability of the shamans to combat the new diseases is reported to have led to a loss of faith in their methods and to a feeling that the Europeans, who did not die in large numbers from smallpox or measles, knew "more and better" than the natives.[24] It can be assumed that the same sentiment was shared by the Carrier and that those who turned to Christianity as expounded by their own prophets did so in order to regain a sense of being able to control or influence the forces which determine human well-being. Their obvious inability to manipulate either the new wealth or the new sources of illness and death would have created the same decline in self-esteem as experienced by the adherents to the cargo cults in the Pacific.[25] The Carrier prophets offered a redemption from feelings of powerlessness as well as a restoration of prestige and integrity. A line from one of the hymns composed by Bini suggests a quest for a new status: "People entered the Great Father's House and became proud and wealthy."[26] Like the disciples of many prophets in the ancient world, Bini's followers hoped "to win personal knowledge of the secrets of the universe and a dignified status in it."[27] Among Amerindian peoples, attempts to use religion to rebuild cultures shattered by disease or military subjugation have been called "revitalization," and the word could appropriately be applied to the Carrier cults formed following the first missionary visits.[28] Unlike the reaction of the Alkatcho to Morice's mission in 1885, the prophet movement of the 1840's revealed a desire not merely to add Christian elements to Carrier culture but also to convert completely to a new life, as exemplified by the new baptismal names, the new language, and the new moral code.

In addition to serving his people, perhaps Bini was also, like other prophets, trying to legitimate a new and unprecedented authority. When he began preaching, he apparently was an ambitious chief and/or shaman involved in a struggle with a rival, and once he had established a following, he built a large house with a cross and a chimney and expected to be carried across streams by his disciples.[29] Bini's cult promised him a status equivalent to that of the missionary priest—a far more exalted position than any that the Catholic Church offered natives. Among the Déné of the Northwest, Petitot reported being visited by native prophets who were most anxious that he recognize them as his priestly equals, and one Cree prophet called himself a bishop. These "Christian shamans" seem to have been involved in a quest to recover the prestige lost with the arrival of fur traders and missionaries who, between them, controlled desired goods and, presumably, dreaded diseases.[30] In Bini's case, the new rank being sought was so much more elevated than that normally enjoyed by a chief or shaman that its popular acceptance required the simultaneous introduction of a different set of political values. And according to Max Weber, in societies where political legitimacy derived from age-old custom and tradition, "conscious departures from tradition in the establishment of a new order have . . . been due almost entirely to prophet oracles or at least to pronouncements which have been sanctioned as prophetic."[31] Thus, the cult offered prestige and power enhancement as well as a promise of group salvation.

By its radical and redemptive nature, the movement reveals itself as part of the long tradition of Jewish and Christian millenarianism, and Morice compared it to "messiah crazes."[32] The original Jewish millenium, to be ushered in by the Messiah, promised, as did Bini, both the resurrection of the "righteous dead" and a world of plenty. Later, among the Christians, it was Christ's second coming which was expected to bring about this material transformation. The great millenarian movements of the Middle Ages drew on this tradition, and they were stimulated by social and psychological changes similar to those experienced by the nineteenth-century Carrier. The growth of cities and of commerce drew peasants from the overcrowded countryside into the cities, where the traditions and security of manorial and family life could not endure. But the new wealth being produced in the towns brought little but frustration to these atomized urban masses. Then came devastating diseases, especially the Black Death, which was followed by the "greatest wave of millenarian excitement." The messiahs of the Middle Ages, like the Carrier prophets and those elsewhere in the colonial world, gained followers during "crises of mass disorientation." According to the leading authority on millenarian movements, "messiahs of this kind flourish not among the poor and oppressed as such, but among the poor and oppressed whose traditional way of life has broken down and who have lost faith in their traditional values."[33]

The sentiments behind the Carrier millenarian cult have been explored because by indicating the high expectations of Christianity, they help explain why the Carrier welcomed the Oblates. In 1867, the chief of the Fort St. James band met an Oblate priest at Quesnel and told him that his people had instructed him to bring home any priest he saw, "and if he be not willing to come, bring him by force." Upon his arrival at the fort, the priest was asked to appoint a chief and his assistants, and the people so desired baptism that they either pretended to be ill or greatly exaggerated their age. They were even eager to confess their sins and to submit to the penitential whipping that generally followed.[34] This co-operation impressed the Oblates, and in 1873 a permanent mission was established with Father Lejacq at its head. His assistant was Father Blanchet, the church builder. They acquired 320 acres of land adjacent to the Hudson's Bay Company post; under Blanchet's supervision the local Indians built the church of Our Lady of Good Hope. Its interior was finished free of charge by Simon and Billy, Carrier carpenters from Fort George. A mission house which contained a chapel, a "salle des sauvages," and the priests' living quarters—a kitchen and two bedrooms—was also constructed. Lejacq and Blanchet were happy together, and they seem to have been popular. Blanchet, already advanced in years, ministered to the people who lived near the fort as well as to those from the three other villages around Stuart Lake—Pinché, Taché, and Yekhuche—for whom the Mission at Fort St. James was a designated religious meeting place. He also laid out a new village near the church and encouraged its inhabitants in their vegetable gardening. However, neither of the two Oblates made a concerted effort to get the Indians to lead an entirely sedentary life. They apparently followed the fur traders in regarding the locally grown potatoes and other vegetables as a sensible supplement to the uncertain supply of salmon rather than as an alternative to the fishing and hunting economy. Of course, neither the climate nor the terrain were well suited to agriculture or to the concentration of population which it permits. Father Lejacq readily accepted the necessity of spending most of the year visiting the dispersed bands of Carrier, Babine, and Sikani trappers.[35]

This was the job that Morice was delighted to get in 1885. Later in his life, he acknowledged that Lejacq's work had "somewhat facilitated" his own task. He was less inhibited in his claims that the Carrier had welcomed him with "lively demonstrations of joy."[36] Their new *nahwoelnoek* (story-teller or preacher) was twenty-six and already quite bald. Although clean-shaven when he arrived at Fort St. James in 1885, Morice had a substantial black beard when he posed for a portrait photograph in 1894. In his autobiography, Father Morice described himself as "not bodily a giant, but of a quite middle stature, and rather inclined to obesity," and he hinted that he regarded his superior intelligence as a compensation for his unimposing physical presence.[37] One of the intellectual abilities of which he was most proud, and which was crucial for his work, was his gift for languages. Father McGuckin, the first Oblate to visit the Carrier, had insisted that their missionary must know their language, for Chinook was of no use at all among them. And when Father Lejacq left the area in 1880, he was equally emphatic about the need for a replacement who could learn the language, which was so difficult that some of the Hudson's Bay Company's métis servants who had been in the area for thirty years still could not speak it. Lejacq's assistant, Father Blanchet, declared that the language was "horribly difficult," and he had despaired of ever learning it.[38]

Morice, on the other hand, had long prepared himself for this challenge, and he threw himself into the learning of Carrier with relish. Despite his egoism, he was prepared to use a trial and error method of learning which put him at the mercy of his Indian tutors. A word or expression was explained to him, and he jotted it down. Later, he would proudly use it in conversation — only to find that sometimes his brave efforts were met with laughter. The natives found nothing more amusing than a mispronounced word, especially if it meant something quite different from that which the speaker had intended.[39] These humiliating incidents hastened Morice's acquisition of the language, whose great richness and complexity enchanted him. He found, for instance, that the verb "to break" had no single equivalent in Carrier. Instead, it possessed "no less than 110 particularizing substitutes, not one of which could be indifferently used for the other." The particular word used to describe breaking would depend on such things as what was being broken, the manner of the break, and the form of the object broken. Yet the Indian language was not without its deficiencies. When expressing abstract ideas and emotions rather than describing the material world, all the Déné languages were, in Morice's opinion, woefully inadequate. If a Carrier said, "my heart is sick," there was no way of knowing whether he felt "sorrow, melancholy, repentance, morosity, displeasure, etc."[40]

The language's other qualities and the benefits that Morice gained from knowing it more than compensated for this apparent flaw. Possibly his own troubled spirit appreciated the escape into a less introspective medium. His immersion in the alien language and culture of the Carrier was part of his flight from the European world. Because the language was so expressive, so wonderfully conducive to plays on words, Morice enjoyed countless hours of hilarity with his flock. Morice was the only white who spoke the Carrier language fluently, and his knowledge of it enabled him to gain what he considered to be his unique understanding of the people's culture and personality. With its tendency to exaggerate, the Carrier language revealed what Morice regarded as the Indian's childlike mind and his pride. Even when etiquette demanded modesty, as when fishermen deprecated their prowess, Morice believed that the Indians were really engaging in a subtle form of pride. Dismissing a good catch as trifling was a way of saying, "I am such a good fisherman that this is nothing to me."[41] These insights were useful to Morice the missionary and anthropologist, but the greatest reward that his command of the language brought was power. He was certain that it was this linguistic mastery which was, in his own immodest words, "to render him king of the country, especially if we join that linguistic achievement to his great impartiality and his astonishing penetration of the Indian character."[42]

But Morice did not become master of the language or of the people overnight. He had to work at it, and he did so with the kind of energy and singlemindedness which he had seldom found for his priestly studies. A former native prophet baptized under the name of Julien gave him countless language lessons, and for this Morice later expressed his deep gratitude. But when he was studying alone and could not resolve a problem, he would simply hurry out, confront the first Indian he ran into, and demand enlightenment. The entire native population thus became his human dictionary and grammar. Even with this assistance and dedication, however, Morice only learned a fraction of the language in his first year at Stuart Lake.[43]

He did not allow this to deter him from devising a means of writing Carrier within months of his arrival at Fort St. James. He learned that Father Lejacq had tried without success to introduce a version of Evans's Cree syllabics as modified by the Oblates for the Déné tribes of the North. There was certainly a demand for something of this sort. The Carriers' quest for knowledge was such that a missionary who taught them to read and write could expect to increase considerably his popularity and influence.[44] This, together with the fact that the Indians' ability to read prayer books and the catechism would facilitate his ministry, must have stimulated Morice's own ambitions to invent a simplified alphabet for an Indian language. And while he rejected Evans's Cree alphabet as inadequate to the task of rendering the many and complex sounds of the Déné dialects, Morice did borrow both the idea of signs representing syllables and the pointing of the signs in different directions to represent sound changes.

Morice regarded the latter feature as an "immense advantage which must be put entirely to the credit of Evans alone."[45] Evans had used eleven basic signs which could be placed in forty-four positions; Morice devised nine major and twenty-one minor signs with 180 possible positions. Despite the addition of signs and positions, Morice claimed that his system was easier to learn because it was more methodical and logical. In fact, according to its inventor, it made grammatical errors impossible.[46] But modern analyses of his scheme find many sounds not represented.[47]

This deficiency is not hard to explain. The syllabic alphabet was completed soon after Morice's arrival at Fort St. James, and it must therefore have been based on his theoretical knowledge of the Déné languages acquired from Petitot's linguistic works rather than on an intimate acquaintance with Carrier.[48] His approach was appropriate insofar as Morice wanted his syllables to be used by all Déné people, whether in British Columbia or the MacKenzie Delta. And a little later he presented the Cherokee with a new alphabet.[49] That Morice should have undertaken these formidable extracurricular enterprises at a time when he had just been given a new job certainly conforms to his consistent neglect of his routine duties in favour of ambitious literary projects of his own making.

As it happened, the "Déné Syllabary" did not give Morice the wide acclaim which he desired, but it was quickly adopted by the Carrier. In the course of his excursions, the new missionary gave instructions for five or six days in the district's four principal meeting places: Fort St. James, Fort George, Natléh, and Hwotat. Those instructed by Morice soon became teachers themselves; before long he was receiving letters from Indians he had never taught. They communicated with each other by writing with sticks in the sand or by chipping at a tree and writing with charcoal on the exposed wood. The syllabary gave them a useful means of communication, one that they could use in business letters.[50] But it had its limitations. For one thing, Morice was the only white man who could read it. It was to him alone that Indians would have to address their requests, religious or

secular. Naturally, he soon became the broker between them and other influential whites. Furthermore, by composing and printing prayer books
and even a newspaper in the syllabics, Morice established the kind of religious and press monopoly which would have been impossible if he had
taught English to the Indians. Control over this unique writing system
gave him great potential power. As Morice put it, "the fact that all his Indians knew in the shape of prayers, catechisms, etc., was due to him could
not fail to enhance his importance in their unsophisticated eyes."[51]

A more crucial means of acquiring power was the Durieu System,
which Morice was determined to implant in his district. The operation of
the system on the Lower Mainland greatly impressed him, and Bishop
Durieu seems to have become his model in the field of evangelization, as
Petitot was in matters pertaining to exploration and scholarship.[52] The indirect rule apparatus necessary for the first stage of the system, the repression process, had already been established in the Stuart Lake district, but
many pagan customs and attitudes had not been suppressed. Morice hoped
to complete the process and then to introduce the second and more important stage of Durieu's system, the "moulding process." Fear of the whip
and public humiliation would be superseded by fear of hell and an awesome respect for the sacraments. Above all, the success of the moulding
process required the breaking of the Indians' habit of regarding the sacraments as a pass for heaven—like a medicine which could sanctify them
without effort or sacrifice on their part.[53] Durieu insisted on complete spiritual acculturation.

The application of this policy in northern British Columbia was a formidable task for one man. There were fourteen "villages" or groups of Indians dispersed throughout the district, and Morice was able to visit most
bands just once or twice a year. Because it was impossible for the priest to
travel to the habitat of each band, certain well-situated locations, usually
Hudson's Bay Company posts, were designated as meeting places for a
given area. The local people were expected to congregate there at times
stipulated by the priest, and the chief of each band was given a small al-
manac showing the dates of future visits. The missions or revivals given at
the meeting places lasted about a week and were held about the same time
each year. Among the Carrier proper, the meeting places were at Fort St.
James, Natléh, Fort George, and Stoney Creek. The Babines of the lake
gathered at Hwotat, and those of the Bulkley Valley at Rocher Déboulé—
until Moricetown was founded. Morice usually met the Sikani at Mac-
Leod Lake. Apart from these regular visits, he would, when requested and
if the weather permitted, make special journeys to minister to the sick and
dying. On these trips as well as when he was "on tour," the Indians were
expected to fetch him and to provide transport, food, and shelter free.

Bishop Durieu insisted on this rule, intended to develop the Indians' generosity, to make them realize that the priest worked for them and to eradicate their mercenary attitude.[54] The rule also saved the Oblates considerable money and trouble, and men like Morice were sustained by the Indians for long periods. In 1887, for example, he left Fort St. James on 1 May and criss-crossed his vast mission district until September. Except for a two-day stopover at the Mission, the Indians transported and fed Morice all summer.[55]

Morice's mode of transport on these missionary perambulations varied with the terrain and season. He borrowed canoes, horses, toboggans, and sled dogs from the Indians, which sometimes created difficulties, especially in the winter. Morice would bundle up comfortably in furs and nestle down in the cradle-shaped birch toboggans used in the area, but each of the four dogs required to pull the toboggan would come from a different household in the village for which he was bound. As a result, they were more interested in fighting than in pulling as a team. Fortunately, the dogs' Indian masters more than compensated for their unruly behaviour. Morice always found them to be excellent guides and congenial travelling companions. Not being able to swim, he particularly appreciated their deft handling of canoes and their willingness either to carry him across rivers or, if the water was too deep, to pull him across on a hastily constructed raft.[56]

Father Morice made his first overland journey soon after settling in at Stuart Lake. An Indian arrived from Fraser Lake, presented him with a lynx skin, and asked him to come to administer the last rites to his dying brother. After a two-day ride they were at Isaac Qasyak's side. The villagers scrutinized Morice carefully as he dispensed his "medicine." They must have been impressed, for Isaac recovered, later becoming one of the area's best Christians. Indeed, Morice doubted that Isaac's piety could be matched by anyone in France. The behaviour of the Fraser Lake people conformed, on the whole, to Morice's stereotyped notion of the Carrier personality: tractability, naive simplicity, and a childish credulity, especially with regard to their confidence in the power of the priest and his prayers.[57] Together with the families from Lake Cheslatta and Lake François, they gathered at Natléh three times a year—at Christmas, in May, and in August—to be instructed by the priest. Located near Fort Fraser on the main water and land routes and the area's best salmon fishing spot, Natléh was an excellent meeting place.

The first regular visit Morice made to Natléh was at Christmas in 1885. That was the time of the annual "big meeting," and the Indians came to fetch him with two toboggans, one for his paraphernalia and the other for his ample person. A man walked in front of the convoy to break the trail and to encourage the dogs while another walked behind with a whip and exhalted them to hurry along. En route, they spent the nights lying on branches placed around the fire, one side of the body freezing and the other roasting. At least Morice had the use of a house once he reached Natléh; the Indians from surrounding villages had to make do with hastily constructed branch huts which provided little protection from the intense cold. During that first Christmas, the celebration of Midnight Mass and the other rituals was not marked by any particular glitter, for Morice did not yet know the language, and he had not yet begun to print the syllabic hymn books.[58]

In subsequent years, the Christmas festivities at Natléh were quite a spectacle. Morice introduced a "folk feast" in which the whole congregation participated in the recreation of the drama of Bethlehem. At last he had the freedom to indulge his musical fancy as he pleased. A choir of twelve girls sang the part of the angels and conducted a dialogue with the congregation, who played the shepherds. In their midst were a few young men who acted as narrators. When the cue came for the good people of Bethlehem to pray for the infant Jesus, the whole congregation sang the prayer in four parts. Morice was delighted with their performance and doubted that it could be reproduced in a French church. The climax to the whole celebration was the ritual of kissing the feet of a wax doll representing the baby Jesus while at the same time depositing a half dollar donation.[59] Christmas at Natléh became a big winter festival, and people travelled from as far afield as Fort George and the Skeena Forks. Those who gathered for the event in 1888 were disappointed when Morice did not arrive on schedule.[60]

The spring and summer meetings at Natléh were the occasion for another popular religious pageant. Stations of the Cross were erected by Morice in 1886, and though the less fervent needed prodding to assure their attendance at the other mission exercises, their zealous attachment to the re-enactment of Christ's suffering never faltered. Obviously, the Carrier appreciated the introduction of these Catholic dramas. For a long time they had been influenced by the coastal peoples with whom they traded, and they had borrowed many customs, notably the potlatch. However, Carrier ceremonialism had remained underdeveloped compared to the rich theatricalism of the coast ceremonies, and the introduction of Morice's religious pageantry perhaps allowed the Carrier to feel that they could now put on a good show too.[61]

The Indians displayed similar enthusiasm for another feature of the spring and summer meetings with Morice—learning the syllabics. In 1886, about twenty children were given three days instruction. A year later, and without further tutoring from Morice, twice that number could read and several could write. It appears that, in his absence, the children and young adults had gathered almost every day to study what the most advanced among them had written. More than seventy wanted to take the eight-day "course" Morice offered in 1887, but he could only handle forty-five. That summer the salmon run had failed, and the people were on the verge of starvation. Yet they stayed at Natléh until the mission was over, living on berries from the nearby woods. A month or so later, one of the younger graduates of the summer course sent Morice a letter asking for medicine for his sick brother.[62] The Carrier were finally learning the white man's "magic" of literacy and had one more reason for regarding the priest as useful.

Not surprisingly, the missions at Natléh were an important part of the Indians' lives. They harmonized their winter and spring hunting with the priest's visits, though in August they were traditionally at Natléh for the salmon fishery. At the spring and summer meetings, Father Morice settled disputes ranging from the delineation of a hunting territory to the status of conjugal bonds. Such arbitration was usually accepted, though there was an occasional conflict.[63] But what really provoked resentment and hostility was Morice's opposition to the potlatches that usually accompanied the gathering of the different bands. Among the Carrier, the main function of the potlatch was to validate the inheritance of a title by the person who gave the feast. People from a group other than the celebrant's bore witness to the succession and were rewarded with food and gifts. Without a potlatch, there could be no legitimate claim to the titled status that was such an integral part of the traditional economic and social system.[64] While they condemned it in principle, Morice's predecessors had realized the importance of the potlatch to the Indians and had permitted small and regulated feasts. They had a quite understandable fear of antagonizing the people by being too severe. And despite the legal proscription of the potlatch in 1884, the local Indian agent took the same position. He believed that the custom would gradually die out and that any attempt to enforce the ban would be costly and might provoke trouble.[65]

Morice was neither so flexible nor so cautious. If the Indian was to become a new man and not just a baptized pagan, he must abandon all his beliefs, bad and indifferent. For Morice, the potlatch was definitely to be counted among the bad. It was an occasion marked by envy, gluttony and, above all, by the display of "simply phenomenal pride."[66] Morice shared Bishop Durieu's determination to destroy the Indians' pride. It was the sin that most horrified Jesus Christ, Durieu believed, and one of the principal objectives of the second stage of his missionary method was to "eradicate" this pride from the hearts of the Indians. In its place his missionaries would plant and cultivate humility.[67] But this was not the only reason for

Morice's opposition to the potlatch. Such large gatherings of people were not conducive to morality or civil order.[68] Perhaps, too, Morice had a personal motive for wanting to destroy the potlatch: an aspiring priest-king could not comfortably contemplate the continuation of an ancient and important social ritual which he did not control. Moreover, the demise of the potlatch would weaken the traditional social structure and the leadership of the titled men, thereby strengthening his position.

In any event, during his first spring visit to Natléh in 1886, Father Morice declared, in the name of Bishop Durieu, that these feasts must be renounced. This reversal of Oblate policy provoked an outcry against him. The potlatching did not stop, and the following year Morice backed up his edict with a threat to refuse to allow participants in potlatches to confess their sins. This seemed to have the desired effect, and Morice reported to Bishop d'Herbomez that he was making progress.[69] In reality, clandestine potlatching continued for many years, with the feasts often being held immediately before or after the meetings at Natléh. The potlatch remained an important part of the syncretic ritualism developed before Morice arrived. While he demanded total rejection of tradition, the Indians of the Natléh area still achieved a creative integration of the old and the new. The European priest preached total subordination and a wholesale religious transformation; the Indian parishioner practised pluralism despite proclaiming submission and Christian orthodoxy. This development is revealed by the nature of the All Saints' Day celebrations in 1888, as recorded by the Hudson's Bay clerk at Fort Fraser. The people gathered at Natléh to honour and pray for their dead kinsmen, and since Morice was not present, the chief gave a little sermon at the church door. Then everyone went to the cemetery, and after fixing up the graves and saying prayers over them, they had a potlatch. The making of house-like tombs and fences for the graves of the dead was apparently an important part of the new potlatch ritual.[70]

The same enthusiasm was not forthcoming when Morice asked them to do some building for him. In 1886, he pointed out the need for a catechism house in which to hold classes and told the Indians to get on with erecting it. At the same gathering, he permitted some of the most spiritually advanced among them to begin preparations for their First Communion. The other Indians were appointed to watch over them. The following year, after learning that the catechism house had not been built, Morice refused to admit any of the men to communion, including those who had been preparing themselves under his immediate predecessor, Father Charles Marchal. The men did not budge; neither did Morice. He believed that the Indian character was such that a leader could never go back on his word without losing his authority. Consequently, the women received their first communion, and he left—after hearing at least two hundred public confessions, baptizing seven children, and marrying five couples.[71]

Morice's refusal to avoid confrontation was hard for the Indians to understand or cope with. Morice himself spoke of the Western Déné as having a "general gentleness of disposition"; another anthropologist wrote of the Déné "ethic of noninterference with another's behavior."[72] Even the most influential Carrier noblemen were not authority figures.[73] Obviously, these traditional attitudes and practices did not prepare the native people to handle the authoritarian and assertive personality of a man like Morice. The advantage which the aggressive colonizing European had over certain native peoples was noted by Warren Hastings, the controversial governor of Bengal:[74]

> There is a fierceness in the European manners . . . which is incompatible with the gentle temper of the Bengalee and gives the former such an ascendant as is scarce supportable, even without the additional weight of authority.

Despite their stubbornness over the catechism house, the Natléh people usually avoided conflict by publicly bending the knee before Morice's demand for a total subordination and religious acculturation.

He faced similar problems elsewhere. When he visited the Fort George band during his first spring tour in 1886, he found that the people shared the inability of the other Carrier to persevere. They were unable to resist temptation, and being just one and a half days' journey from Quesnel, their greatest temptation was liquor. In the course of the mission, many of the Fort George people were fined for having tasted the forbidden "whiteman's water." Imposing fines for drinking was a general Oblate policy. Usually the penalty for the first offence was one dollar, but it became more severe in proportion to the number of transgressions. Morice probably used whatever he collected to provide for the maintenance of the church and for the relief of widows and orphans.[75]

There is no doubt that the Carriers' new missionary shared the determination of other Oblates to outlaw alcohol. Every chief appointed by the Oblates received as a symbol of office a flag with three words embossed on it: "Temperance, Religion, Civilization." The order of the words is significant. "Civilization" could only come after "Religion," which, in turn, could not be successfully introduced before "Temperance." The first stage of the Durieu System was designed to achieve this "Temperance," which meant stamping out all pagan customs and ending drinking. The two objectives had a great deal in common, however, for drinking had become part of the traditional ceremonial life among some tribes. Even the clandestine drinking parties that were organized after the beginning of Oblate presence have been described as "an arena for the reaffirmation of old cultural forms and values."[76] As a result, the Oblates placed great emphasis on the detection and punishment of drinkers. On the Lower Mainland, zealous watchmen even arrested and handed over to the police non-Indians who brought liquor onto the reserves. Gambling, both traditional and modern, was also a target of the "Temperance" campaign, and during his Fort George visit, Father Morice condemned and punished offenders.[77] It seems that native leaders welcomed this attempt to curb the abuse of alcohol.

Morice undertook the first of his rare visits to the Sikani (Father Blanchet took charge of them while he was Morice's companion at Stuart Lake from 1887 to 1897) in the spring of 1886, after his return from Fort George. Morice regarded the Sikani as more simple, more honest and more moral than the Carrier, their superiority being attributed to their habit of wandering in small bands of related individuals and to the absence of potlatching. Because the Sikani had no horses with which to fetch him, Morice rode to rendezvous with them at Long Lake in the company of some natives from Fort St. James. Once at Long Lake, he and his Carrier companions discovered that the Sikani had waited so long that their food stocks were exhausted and one band had been forced to leave.[78] The lack of provisions meant that Morice's mission would have to be brief because the remaining Sikani band members could not feed themselves or him. Two important tasks were nevertheless undertaken: some work was done on their future church, and a bonfire of gambling paraphernalia was made. The church had already been started by Indians from Fort St. James since the Sikani had not yet acquired European skills. Now Morice set the Sikani to work for the first time with saw and plane, presumably under the supervision of his Carrier companions. The other achievement, the making of what Morice called "a fire of joy" of the gambling sticks and drums, was regarded as an indication of the mission's spiritual success, for the Sikani were great gamblers. As well, they were still very much under the sway of the shamans, though Morice claimed no success on that score.

Nevertheless, Morice set off on the return journey to Fort St. James in good spirits. One of his companions was Joseph Prince, an influential Fort St. James Indian who worked closely with both the Oblate missionaries and the Hudson's Bay Company. Joseph was carrying an old, large-calibre revolver, and when a partridge suddenly crossed their path, Morice grabbed Joseph's gun and shot at the bird. The bullet found its mark, but in his impetuous haste Morice held the gun too close to his face, and the recoil caused the hammer to pierce his cheek just below the eye.[79] It was their second minor shooting accident of his spring tour, and it is probably as indicative of his enthusiasm to throw himself into the outdoor life of his mission district as it is of his general ineptitude in such activities.

Fortunately, his facial injury was not serious enough to disrupt his spring and summer tours, and after a short stopover at the fort, Morice left in late June to make his first summer call on the Babines. They were not his favourites, for he felt that they were neither as simple and moral as the Sikani nor as tractable and amenable as the other Carrier groups. About three hundred natives had their home bases in two villages on the shores of Lake Babine; the village of Hwotat at the northern end of the lake by the Hudson's Bay post was their meeting place. In the summer it was a five-day journey from Fort St. James, though Morice always visited the Stuart Lake villages of Pinché and Taché en route. The summer travel by canoe would be much more pleasant than Morice's first visit to the Babines the previous winter. Father Marchal had usually made his winter trip to Babine in late January, but the fact that there was a new priest was relayed along the "Indian telegraph," and the Babines arrived to fetch Morice early. He suspected that they were anxious to see how accommodating he would be. It was a seven-day toboggan ride over the lake ice, and during the latter part of the journey, the priest's party was joined by people from Old Fort Babine who were also headed for Hwotat to attend the meeting.[80]

Once at Hwotat, Morice was eager to begin his mission, but he was frustrated by his inability to communicate effectively. Convinced that the interpreter was giving a ridiculous meaning to his French, he tried Chinook—but to no avail. English was no good either, because the interpreter did not know it well enough. Reluctantly, but in desperation, Morice resorted to the "French of the mountains," a pidgin French introduced as the *lingua franca* of the area by the métis in the employ of the fur companies. Its vocabulary was more or less French, but its syntax came from the Indian languages. When, for example, Morice wanted to explain that the devil was master of almost the whole world when the son of God became man, he had to express himself as follows: "L'bon Dieu son garçon quand çá i devient la même chose comme nous autres, le Yâble c'lui-là quasiment tout le monde son bourgeois."[81] Finally able to make himself understood, he thundered against the Babines' rampant "paganism." It was not that they did not follow the Catholic taboos and rituals; they often did. But they also thought that Catholicism was compatible with their ancient beliefs and customs, which they could not conceive of abandoning. If the Christian God was slow to cure a sick relative, it was only natural to turn to the shaman. They were not bad, Morice believed, just weak. Their great fear of death and what he considered an excessive love of near relatives drove them to the shamans. The pattern of syncretism was well established, and Morice had a hard struggle ahead of him. Yet he returned from his first winter visit to the Babines convinced that his strong words had had some effect.[82]

He was less sanguine when he returned in the summer. In his absence the Babines had taken up all their ancient customs. Now was an opportune time to confront them with the prohibition first announced at Natléh: the potlatch feasts which had been allowed to continue as a temporary concession must be abandoned forthwith. As at Natléh, there was a great outcry. One of Morice's Indian assistants was knocked over, spat at, and threatened with sticks because he wished to uphold the word of the "Great Speaker"—the bishop. Morice found the Babines to be a shrill, vociferous group at the best of times, but when the congregation of about two hundred souls was joined in its protest by four or five hundred howling dogs, the din was devastating. Fortunately, someone detected the comical nature of the scene and burst out laughing. The young people joined in, and the tension was relieved. But this hilarity did not mean that the Babines had accepted Morice and his new laws. Some of them even continued to play their games of chance with visiting Gitksan while he was still giving his mission, and the following winter Morice waited in vain for them to collect him at the fort. Although he accounted for this failure by saying that the Babines were too stingy and lazy to send sled dogs for him, obviously they did not care to fetch a priest who refused to compromise with or accommodate tradition.[83]

Things came to a head the following summer. The Babines fetched him, but they refused to feed him while he waited at Hwotat for everyone to arrive for the mission. They were saving all their food, including enough sacks of flour to practically fill two houses, for a potlatch to be held when Morice left. Not wishing to starve and having nothing useful to do, he decided to spend a few days with the Hotsoten—the Babines of the Bulkley River. But before leaving, he publicly swore that anyone who took part in any feast would not be allowed to confess when he returned to give the mission.

Even before he arrived back at Hwotat, Morice learned from his "secret agents" that a big potlatch with the distribution of blankets had indeed taken place with the participation of all but a few young girls and the infirm old people. It was Bishop Durieu who suggested to his missionaries that they should appoint, in addition to a chief and watchman, two "commissaires" to be their eyes and ears. One of their most important tasks, Durieu recommended, was to report on the deficiency or delinquency of chiefs.[84] Naturally, these spies were detested, and when Morice returned to Hwotat and announced that he would confess the children only and then return to Fort St. James, the people "broke out into a torrent of vituperation and abuse'' against his unknown agents. Although they were still attached to their potlatches and shamans, the Babines valued the rites of the Catholic Church, especially baptism and confession. They did not want to be abandoned, and they tried hard to prevent Morice from leaving. Nobody would lend a canoe or act as oarsman. Finally, and only by flattery and cajoling, he managed to convince three Carrier visiting from the fort to return there with him. Even then the Babines did not give up. The shamans allegedly tried to conjure up a wind to oppose Morice and to unleash the forces of nature against him. But the priest's incantations were more powerful; he got a good tail wind and reached Fort St. James safely.[85]

The abandonment of the oft-warned Babines seems to have been undertaken with the consent of Bishop Durieu, with whom Morice corresponded. The next move on the priest's part certainly conformed to Oblate missionary practice. Morice attempted to separate the ''quiet'' Babines from the ''bad'' and to get the former to establish a new meeting place for themselves. The incorrigibles would be left to wallow in their paganism. Old Fort Babine, also known as Nit'ats, was considered the best location for the new meeting place, and under their influential chief, the people of the village began to build a church.[86] Hwotat was too near the haunts of the worst Babines, and it was also along the route frequented by the notorious ''Atnas.'' This Carrier word for ''stranger'' was applied mainly to the Gitksan of the Skeena River, with whom the Babines had a longstanding trade and social relationship.[87] Morice blamed the Babines' tenacious attachment to the old customs, particularly the potlatch, on this contact, and he tried to limit it. Like many men of his time, Morice was prone to racial and ethnic stereotyping. The Gitksan were the inland branch of the Tsimshian, whom the Oblates had abandoned entirely because they were hopelessly and stubbornly ''pagan.'' Since the Gitksan were thus, in Morice's words, of ''Tsimpsian parentage,'' they were regarded as corruptors of his more amenable Carrier. By persuading the ''quiet'' Babines to congregate at the Old Fort, he hoped to cut down on their contact with the Gitksan at Hwotat.[88] On the Lower Mainland, Bishop Durieu and his assistants frequently dealt with troublesome groups by inducing the amenable ones to move away from the others.[89] However, Morice could not implement his plan successfully, and he temporarily abandoned all the Lake Babines.

This did not discourage him from planning the same kind of strategy for the Hotsoten. The converts among the Bulkley Valley people were to be removed from the influences of their traditional fishing villages at Rocher Déboulé and Keyor Hwotget. Under Morice's supervision, they were to begin to build a model community. Rocher Déboulé had been designated by Father Lejacq as the Hotsoten meeting place, but Morice considered it a bad choice because it was too near the Gitksan and the ''wolf''—the

Protestant minister at Hazelton.[90] Father Marchal had also disapproved of the Rocher Déboulé location; after trying without success to persuade all the Hotsoten to move back up the Bulkley to their ancient village of Keyor Hwotget, he gave up on them. Morice first made their acquaintance in the summer of 1887 when, instead of waiting without food at Hwotat, he decided to see if the Hotsoten were as bad as everyone made out. Having met with some of them at Keyor Hwotget, he decided that they were for the most part full of goodwill but "very ignorant." He offered them a last chance to mend their ways, provided they agreed to quit both Rocher Déboulé and Keyor Hwotget, which was on the route used by the Rocher Déboulé people, and to renounce shamans, gambling, all potlatches, Indian dances, and "bad songs." Those who chose to forsake their culture could move to the new village and meeting place site already selected by Morice. Located on a flat river bank just three miles from Keyor Hwotget, the future village would nevertheless be away from the corrupting traffic of the telegraph trail, the area's principal thoroughfare.[91]

The new settlement was Morice's creation. Using a plan which he regarded as superior to that drawn up by Father Blanchet for Fort St. James, he marked out future house sites and planted a cross where the church would be built. A nearby trader even agreed to establish a store there, thus eliminating the need to travel to Rocher Déboulé to trade. Eight heads of families, including the chief of Keyor Hwotget, made the required renunciation, and Morice appointed Denis Chenulyat as head watchman to keep an eye on them. Henceforth they were called the "people of Moricetown," though it took a few years for the new "town" to rise.[92]

On his return to Fort St. James in the late summer of 1887, Father Morice could not wait to spread the news of his new enterprise. Excitedly, he told his new colleague at the mission, Father Blanchet, about Moricetown. But Blanchet was not impressed by this "big news," for it added to his conviction that Morice cared only for his own glory and getting himself talked about.[93] He communicated his concern to Bishop d'Herbomez, who expressed astonishment that Morice was giving his own name to the new village. Impertinently, Morice retorted that he was quite prepared to call the place "d'Herbomeztown," except that he doubted that the natives would be able to pronounce it. The bishop declined this offer because it was not compatible with the modesty expected of an Oblate missionary. Such modesty was foreign to Morice's character, as was truthfulness, it seems. At the time of the conflict with Blanchet and d'Herbomez, he claimed that the Indians had insisted on the name "Moricetown." But in his memoirs published in 1897, he claimed ignorance of the reason for the town's name.[94] The hamlet of Moricetown still exists alongside the Bulkley River, between Hazelton and Smithers.

The Moricetown controversy was just the first of many issues which brought Morice and Blanchet into conflict. Blanchet, who had served at Fort St. James with Father Jean Marie Lejacq, returned there in September 1887 to replace Father Pandosy as the resident priest and director of the mission. While en route from Williams Lake, Blanchet learned from whites and Indians at Fort George that they disliked Morice because of his abrupt manner, his inability to tolerate any opposition, and his unwillingness to combine gentleness with force. Once at the fort, the old man found Morice in good health but regretting the departure of Father Pandosy, with whom he apparently got on quite well. The likely reason was that, as Martinet had anticipated, Pandosy had given the rebel the freedom of action he so desired. Morice was used to being severe with his Indian flock, and now he was worried that the new director would be too sympathetic to the Indians and would undermine his authority. His fear was well-founded, for Blanchet believed in the adage that "one caught more flies with honey than with vinegar." He hoped that age and experience would mellow Morice, enabling him to make better use of the personal qualities, especially his linguistic skill, so well suited to his vocation. Blanchet was impressed that after just two years in the area Morice could preach in Carrier without an interpreter.[95]

The wise old man had neither the aptitude nor the determination needed to master that language, but Blanchet was endowed with the priestly virtues that Morice so conspicuously lacked. If either one of them had possessed the positive qualities of both, he would have been an ideal missionary. An Oblate historian has described Blanchet as "a model of candor, simplicity, humility, and charity" — another St. Francis. While he had originally prepared for the priesthood, Blanchet had spent most of his career as a lay brother, since he believed that the loss of a finger in a shooting accident had rendered him unworthy to celebrate mass. Only in 1872, at the age of fifty-four, did he agree to be ordained in order to be able to go with Father Lejacq to establish the Stuart Lake Mission.[96] Two priests were needed in such a vast district, and Blanchet undoubtedly wanted to work with Lejacq, to whom he was devoted. But his humility and late ordination made it difficult for him to accept the responsibilities of the priesthood, and during the eight happy years he spent with Lejacq, he apparently still acted more like a lay brother than a priest. His relations with the Indians were relaxed. When Marchal replaced Lejacq in 1880, he was horrified to find them coming in to smoke a pipe on Blanchet's bed or to borrow his tools. Known affectionately among the Indians as their "dear old grandfather," Father Blanchet was much loved by the people of Fort St. James, Indian and white.[97] The informality and kindliness that endeared Blanchet to the Indians was in marked contrast to Morice's austere authoritarianism, though such a demeanor was not rare among Oblate missionaries on the Pacific coast. The regal aloofness cultivated by the Oblate pioneers in Oregon had prompted a visiting inspector to remind them that they may be masters, but above all they were fathers. Bishop Durieu, Morice's model, considered it more dignified to speak to Indians through an interpreter because they were used to Queen Victoria's prestigious officers addressing them in that manner.[98]

With Morice aspiring to that kind of dignity and authority, clashes with Blanchet were inevitable. But it was more than a question of manner: Blanchet objected to Morice's willingness to abuse his priestly prerogatives to ensure obedience. He vehemently opposed Morice's refusal to accept confession from those who did not promptly obey his commands. In addition to depriving the Babines of confession because they had persisted with their potlatch and the men of Natléh for their failure to build a catechism house, Morice threatened to deny confession to those who did not attend every sermon he gave during the last two days of the All Saints' mission at Fort St. James. Blanchet was astounded. As far as he was concerned, a priest could only refuse confession to somebody who had been formally excommunicated. The limit of his power was to withhold absolution when the penitent disobeyed him without a valid reason. Catholic theologians taught that access to confession should be easy, not difficult. Besides, Blanchet reasoned, how could any priest, without a grave lack of charity, force people to rest in a state of sin for months or even years just because they had missed a few sermons?[99] These humane and doctrinally well-founded arguments were rejected by Morice, who challenged Blanchet to suggest a better way to maintain discipline. He resented the soft old man's interference, and he told Blanchet that he managed well without unsolicited advice. Morice became really reproachful when he learned that Blanchet had unknowingly confessed someone who had not attended all the mandatory All Saints' sermons.[100]

But Blanchet did not relent. At first content to counsel Morice not to adopt extreme measures impulsively, he later reported Morice's denial of confession and his severe demands on those wishing to become communicants to the bishop. On the question of confession, Bishop d'Herbomez endorsed Blanchet's position: a simple priest could not use the denial of confession as a disciplinary measure.[101] The issue of admission to communion was submitted to Bishop Durieu when d'Herbomez became ill. Blanchet told him that Morice required aspiring communicants to publicly declare their desire and then to begin a probationary year. Those guilty of any grave public fault during that year were disqualified. Father Blanchet believed that these severe requirements, together with the rule of public confession before communion, encouraged people to hide their sins and so abuse the sacraments. Another important and theologically sound objection he raised was that Morice treated communion as a reward rather than as a potent aid for avoiding sin and helping sinners back to righteousness.[102]

Morice dismissed these arguments as naive and impractical. Blanchet wanted Indians to be treated like white Catholics and believed that they should all have made their first communion long ago; Morice insisted that the Indians were big children, who could not be treated like whites without serious consequences for the work of the mission. In a direct appeal to Bishop Durieu, Morice argued that the removal of the rigid requirements for communicants would deprive him of one of the principal means he had to stimulate them to behave well. Consequently, he ignored the citations Blanchet produced from the theology books and continued with the communion regulations he claimed to have inherited from Father Marchal. Morice was sure that Marchal had been instructed by Durieu, and he therefore felt obliged to conform to his practice without reference to theology.[103]

In fact, Morice was following Durieu's instructions to the letter; in criticizing Morice's practice, Blanchet was unwittingly launching an attack on the Durieu System. The cult of the Eucharist that Durieu had created was central to the moulding process, which hoped to replace pride with humility and to develop a fearful respect for the sacraments. In 1884, when he instructed Father Lejacq about the implementation of his system, Durieu emphasized the need for a discriminating rigour in dealing with Indian converts.[104]

Morice was vindicated. Indians, said Durieu, were not to be treated like whites, at least not until everyone in the community was a communicant and had respect for the sacrament instilled in him by the severity of the training period. Communion was not to be used as an encouragement or spiritual tonic for ailing neophytes who returned to the "vomit" of their sinful ways as soon as the priest disappeared. Oblate missionaries were not to cast pearls before swine.[105]

Durieu issued precise instructions for the preparation of communicants. Essentially, he described the method he employed with the Squamish and Sechelt people, and he expected his missionaries to follow suit. If their applications survived the requisite public scrutiny, prospective communicants became members of a probationary group, the *Iah'anshout* society, and underwent a sort of group therapy which included individual and group confessions as well as denunciation by the whole congregation. During the priest's long absences, the *Iah'anshouts* were surveyed, reprimanded, and guided by an official whose special title was the "J.C. [Jesus Christ] watchman." His authority was considerable; even the chief, watchmen, and the captain were obliged to go to him if they wished to become probationers. When the priest arrived to give his mission, the J.C. watchman gave him a progress report on his charges. They were then required to kneel before the priest during the catechism class, and all those present were invited to describe their faults. Bishop Durieu believed that constant exposure to public scrutiny and denunciation would keep the probationers on their toes and help the priest detect hypocrites. This probation usually lasted for several years before and after the first communion, and it ensured that communicants were a minority destined to be models and examples for the community at large.[106]

The ritual surrounding the sacrament was embellished and painstakingly executed to impress the Indians with the sanctity of the sacrament. On the eve of the communion day, the communicants scrubbed themselves and their houses and were encouraged to be meditative and quiet, taking special care to refrain from business talk and story telling. In the morning they quietly donned their special communion clothes; no talking was permitted until after the ceremony. The church was prepared with equal care. Bishop Durieu considered some of the more humble Indian churches unworthy to receive the Sacred Host. In decorating the chosen church, the Indians vied with each other to provide the most beautiful flowers and cloth for the altar. Once the church was ready, the Host was introduced with all the pomp and ceremony possible. Just before the changing of the bread and wine, ten stalwart young men would slip out of the church and shoulder their double-barrelled shotguns. As the tabernacle door opened, they fired a thunderous salute. Durieu wanted all his missionary priests to adopt these rituals and to repeat them faithfully whenever communion was given.[107]

This cult of the Eucharist was obviously incompatible with Blanchet's conception of the sacrament. His stand against Morice's somewhat milder and more orthodox practice was futile, though it does show that Durieu's ideas were not accepted by all the British Columbia Oblates. Indeed, Blanchet's strong reaction to Morice's methods suggests that such severity was something new to him, and he was one of the five Oblates who had founded the order's missions on the Northwest Coast. In fact, a major change in the Oblate missionary system had taken place since Blanchet and Lejacq worked together in the 1870's. Bishop Durieu had become deputy to the ailing d'Herbomez in 1875, and from then until the latter's death in 1888, Durieu gradually took command. Henceforth, greater emphasis was placed on spiritual or psychic acculturation, which was to be achieved through the "moulding process," with its cult of the Eucharist and religious dramas like the Passion Play. Bishop Durieu wanted his Indian converts to "disregard the tinsels of the world and set their hearts on things imperishable." His refinement of the Oblate missionary method was formulated in detail by 1883, and in that year the bishop began to send Father Lejacq a series of letters explaining how it could be applied.[108]

The trend had been observed and criticized earlier by Father Martinet on a tour of inspection in 1881. He reminded the British Columbia Oblates that it was not their job to make church laws, and he suggested instead that they seek guidance in the instructions for foreign missions written by Mgr. de Mazenod, the founder of the order. He also felt there should be a relaxation of the puritanism evident at the Oblate missions. If the Indians were denied honest recreation, especially games, they would reject Catholicism as too severe and turn to the dubious recreations of the whites, presumably drinking and frequenting brothels. But what most disturbed Martinet was that the segregationist preoccupation of Oblate missionary methods was out of step with the changing nature of British Columbia society. The influx of more white settlers and Protestant ministers meant that the Oblates were no longer all powerful; consequently they could not continue to employ in their dealings with the Indians methods that would not be used with whites. To survive in the new, competitive conditions, they must be more circumspect.[109] Though logical and realistic, these arguments failed to convince Durieu to steer a radically new course.

This suited Morice perfectly. Durieu's authoritarian severity and love for religious ceremonies coincided with Morice's personal preferences and with his romantic ambition to become the priest-king of Christian Indians. In 1888, the bishop acceded to his request to replace Blanchet as curé of the Fort St. James area while he continued to be the itinerant missionary for the whole district. But Blanchet still impeded his monopolization of influence and power, for he stubbornly claimed certain prerogatives as a father confessor, particularly the right to decide whether or not his penitents were ready to receive first communion. This became yet another source of conflict. Naturally, Morice believed that he alone, as director of the mission, should decide such things. In letters to Bishop Durieu, he complained that Blanchet was too lax and timid. He allowed people who gambled, sang, and absented themselves from sermons in defiance of Morice's orders to make their first communion; he also saw nothing wrong with Indian feasts, and, in Morice's absence, he lent out plates and forks for feasting.[110]

Morice could not stand for these actions, and he kept up pressure on Blanchet until he wrote in desperation to Durieu begging for a transfer before Morice drove him mad. It was the first time in his long missionary career that he had made such a request, but he claimed that Morice was impossible to work with. Blanchet agreed that the young man was perhaps too gifted for his own good. Certainly he was talented, but he had an extraordinary opinion of his own ability, and he would not tolerate any advice or interference. He had to be in total command, and he could be callous and cruel in his relations with the Indians. He delighted in catching people out, especially those whom Blanchet had allowed to receive communion. With his command of the Carrier language, Morice had the upper hand. He refused to hear the confession of a woman who had failed to attend some prayer meetings, even though this prevented her from making her Easter duties, the mandatory participation in the sacraments of penance and communion at Easter time. Knowing no other language than her own, the woman was unable to confess to Blanchet. Blanchet noted that Morice much resembled the similarly talented Father Petitot, his idea of a perfect missionary, but he hoped that Morice would not end up like Petitot, who had been forcibly removed from his mission district and confined to the St. Jean de Dieu mental hospital in Montreal in 1882.[111]

Fearing the same fate for himself, Blanchet eventually conceded defeat and offered to remain with Morice in the capacity of a lay brother. He would look after the priests' house and the garden and have little to do with the spiritual work of the mission.[112] All theological and jurisdictional disputes would thus be avoided. Except for his annual summer visit to the Sikani, Father Blanchet remained at Fort St. James under these conditions until his retirement to Williams Lake in 1897. Now that Blanchet was subordinate and subdued, Morice was happy with the arrangement; Blanchet could do all the time-consuming and demeaning chores. Once again, Morice had not only survived a conflict but had won. In the ruthless crushing of his opponent, he was indirectly aided by the ascendency of Bishop Durieu and the spread of his methods.

As well as helping Morice defeat Blanchet, the methods used by Bishop Durieu on the Lower Mainland encouraged him to persevere in his battle to subjugate the rebellious Babines and to intensify the spiritual acculturation of the central Carrier. Visits he made to the villages of Squamish and Sechelt in 1888 and 1890 provided him with a living model and enhanced his already strong commitment to the Durieu System. Although he undoubtedly exaggerated them in publications clearly intended to praise Bishop Durieu, the piety and discipline of the coastal converts contrasted sharply with what he regarded as the wild and pagan ways of some of his own flock. Particularly impressive were the militaristic organization and splendid ceremonies he saw.[113] The people of Squamish and Sechelt had long been accorded Durieu's personal attention, and it was with them that he developed his moulding process to its highest level. An elite corps called the Guard of Honour of the Sacred Heart was established to act as a model of Catholic fervour and enthusiasm, and such elaborate pageants as the Indian Passion Play were introduced.[114] Inspired by the transformation that he claimed Durieu had wrought and aided enormously by epidemics that terrified the Babines, Morice demanded unconditional surrender from them within a few years of his visits to Durieu's model villages.

The principal aim of Morice's 1888 trip was to attend a "retreat" at New Westminster. He also wanted to consult the bishop, probably concerning his theological disputes with Blanchet. But what Morice most looked forward to were visits to Sechelt and Squamish. His keen interest in far off Indians was apparently shared by his Carrier congregation, for he had often told them of the great progress made by the coastal Indians under Durieu's care. As a result, many Carrier wanted to be allowed to accompany their priest to "the land of the horizon."[115] Louis and James from Fort George were the lucky ones chosen, and they left home with Morice on 1 June. James's luck soon ran out. At the rapids twelve miles below Fort George, he and Louis portaged Morice and his personal baggage and then returned to shoot the white water. But their canoe capsized in the fast spring flood, and James was swept away. Louis managed to swim to safety, and though he was injured, he walked back to Fort George for aid, leaving Morice to spend the night alone on the river bank. Anxiety kept the priest awake. Under traditional law, Morice would be held responsible for James's death because the young man had died in his service. James was the son of the chief of the Fort George Carrier and the father of two young children. All this weighed on Morice's mind. The next day he was relieved to find that the griefstricken relatives did not reproach him but instead reassured him as he departed with a new canoe and crew.[116]

Ten days later he arrived in New Westminster. There, along with sixteen other Oblate priests, he undertook a retreat. Afterwards, the priests exchanged their tranquillity and meditation for the calculated clamour and sensuality of a big "Christian Potlatch" at Squamish. Morice travelled with Father Lejacq in a flotilla of seventy-six canoes carrying more than seven hundred Fraser and Douglas Indians and their Oblate spiritual guides. On approaching Squamish, the canoes of the Lower Fraser Indians were adorned with Venetian lanterns; statues of Mary and Joseph were mounted in two of the biggest canoes. After an exchange of cannon salutes between the hosts and the seaborne guests, the Squamish band played a welcoming piece as the people went through the usual welcome ceremony.[117]

It was eight years since Morice had first been at Squamish. He noticed quite a change. The houses were bigger and cleaner, and the small church of white-washed planks had been replaced by a more imposing structure, paid for by the congregation. But what most impressed Morice was the demeanour of Bishop Durieu's subjects. They were dressed in dark uniforms, had an impressive military bearing, and obeyed the chiefs like veteran soldiers. Even the children sported uniforms, each village having its own distinctive outfit.[118]

The religious dramas were presented and performed with skill and flair. Stagemanaged by Bishop Durieu and his assistant Father Casimir Chirouse, they were essentially didactic and revivalist in intent, designed to impress the fundamental dogmas of Christianity upon what Durieu and his lieutenants regarded as the vulgar and materialistic mentality of their Indians.[119] Father Marchal, an enthusiastic supporter of Bishop Durieu, believed that since the Indian's senses were more responsive than his intellect, words and arguments were less effective than actions.[120]

This resort to drama might not have been necessary if more Oblates had mastered the native languages.[121] But the processions and the Passion Play were more than educational devices. Although not planned as such, they provided a social and psychological compensation for the loss of traditional ceremonies and the potlatch. Both the "pagan" and the Catholic meetings provided for inter-group competition where large and conspicuous expenditures were prominent. The time and money spent on regalia and fireworks during the Catholic feasts resembled in function the traditional potlatch distributions and probably accounts for their great popularity. The periodic festive gatherings also helped, the Oblates believed, to revive the waning enthusiasm of the Indians and to keep them out of mischief. At the end of the 1888 meeting at Squamish, Father Morice witnessed a spectacular night-time procession and firework display. That particular spectacle became an annual event. As a tribute to the Blessed Sacrament, it was part of Bishop Durieu's cult of the Eucharist. The total cost of the altars, candles, and fireworks used during the procession held in 1894 amounted to $2,000—quite a potlatch![122]

But the most spectacular and successful of Durieu's productions was the Passion Play. Morice saw it for the first time when he returned to the coast in 1890. Reminiscent of the Mystery Cycles of the Middle Ages, this "American Oberammergau" became the central feature of the yearly big meeting of the Lower Mainland Indians. It was prepared and executed with the utmost care. Apart from making the costumes and learning their parts, the actors bathed, fasted, and meditated before the play, in preparations resembling the purification procedures used before entry into a traditional secret society.[123] The Passion Play itself began with a penitential procession on its way to Calvary. It passed the Stations of the Cross being performed by Indian actors. The congregation filed past and saw Christ's judgment before Pontius Pilate, His scourging, and His crowning with thorns. The procession stopped at a raised stage built around a huge cross bearing a life-sized statue of the crucified Christ. A weeping and dishevelled Mary Magdalen embraced the feet of the statue. Once the crowd was settled and hushed, an ingenious device was activated and blood began to flow from the statue's forehead, side, hands, and feet. As it fell on the hair and clothing of Mary Magdalen, the crowd was seized by great emotion, and everyone knelt to pray. They were then called upon to repent and to avoid renewing Christ's agonies by repeating their sins. The ceremony had a great impact on those who watched it, Indian or white, Catholic or Protestant.[124] A production at Kamloops, for example, so affected a white man that he became mentally unbalanced and tried to crucify himself. An excommunicated Shuswap chief experienced a sudden reconversion after he watched it, and he returned to chastise his people and literally to whip them into line with Oblate expectations.[125]

Morice too came away from the big meetings of the coastal tribes inspired with an ideal and determined to spread it. While a degenerate and free-thinking Europe was undermining the traditional influence and power of the Catholic Church, Bishop Durieu had, in Morice's opinion, succeeded in building Christian civilization among Indians who only forty years before had lived by rapine and murder.[126] Now it was they and not the Europeans who were the truly civilized of Christendom. And Morice the Oblate publicist did not hesitate to attribute this dramatic change to Bishop Durieu's wisdom and to a missionary method allegedly based on a thorough understanding of the Indian character.[127] The dramas which stressed punishment and pain were probably a response to what missionaries would have regarded as a lack of appropriate guilt feelings, especially concerning sexual behaviour, and to their awareness that the breaking of traditional taboos was expected to have unpleasant physical consequences.

Morice needed inspiration and a methodological guide as he returned home to tackle the thorny problem of the Babines. Abandoned for "insubordination" in 1887, they had since given themselves up, reported Morice, to such "pagan" practices as gambling, potlatching, and adultery. Yet certain Christian rituals and taboos continued to be observed. They did not eat meat on Fridays, and morning and evening prayers were recited in the church.[128] Like the people of Natléh, they were developing their own syncretic religion. Unfamiliar with the uncompromising monotheism of Christianity, religious pluralism seemed perfectly natural and reasonable to them. They would probably have agreed with the Roman senator who had tried to justify the retention of pre-Christian altars in the Senate House: "There cannot be only one path to such a great secret."[129] While the Babines rejected the priest because he refused to tolerate their pluralism, they still considered themselves Catholic and evidently believed that they could continue to gain the benefits of prayer and abstinence. But the events of the next two years provoked some doubts about the wisdom of the partial nature of their commitment to Christianity. In the winter of 1887–88, a measles epidemic carried off more than thirty Babines, mostly children. Then in the summer a number of fatal accidents occurred. Finally, in February 1889, Alexandre, an hereditary noble and shaman at Old Fort Babine, was struck down. From his deathbed he declared that God was punishing them. He sent for Morice and counselled the people to reconcile themselves with him.[130] Fear of the priest and his God was becoming stronger than their faith in traditional remedies that proved so ineffectual against European diseases. Among the Carrier, it was supposed that the Catholic priests, who did not marry and have children like other people, were beings apart who had a distinct genealogy and were endowed with great knowledge and power. The Babines were thus incredulous whenever Morice was unable to answer theological questions, usually concerning the exact degree of sinfulness attached to a trivial transgression of Catholic rules. These reactions convinced Morice that the Babines considered the priest as something akin to a powerful shaman, with power over life and death. For his part, the moribund shaman Alexandre, feared that he might die before Morice arrived. So he confessed before an image and then expired. Morice was not too disappointed with this turn of events, since he could exploit the idea that Alexandre was destined to die without a priest because of his shamanistic activities. It was an opportune moment too, he thought, to achieve a durable reconciliation with all the Babines of the lake.[132]

The people at the Old Fort were asked to travel with him up to the new fort at Hwotat for a mission. But his request met with a cool reception. For the past year a feud between families in the two villages had been simmering, and the Old Fort people feared that a combined gathering might bring it to the boiling point. A boy from the Hwotat family had drowned when a canoe capsized; his companion from the Old Fort had managed to swim to safety. Since the survivor was held responsible under Carrier law, the dead boy's uncle vowed to seek revenge. Morice nevertheless persuaded the Old Fort people to set off for Hwotat, but once they arrived he realized that their fears were well founded. The atmosphere was so tense that he could achieve nothing without a resolution of the feud, which was compounded by a dispute over hunting grounds. Fortunately for Morice, an Indian agent had recently been appointed for the Northern Interior, and he happened to be at Hwotat en route to Fort St. James. Mr. R. E. Loring ordered the feuding families to appear before him; when one group refused, Loring went pistol in hand to fetch them. After long negotiations and the payment of compensation, Morice and Loring managed to settle the affair.[133]

Loring then returned to his base at Hazelton, and Morice began the delicate job of religious reconciliation. At first, attendance at the mission was poor, and some Indians made attempts to disrupt it. The "Devil's clan," as Morice called his adversaries, beat their drums "and invited their fellow men to gamble and dance, as a protest against the priest's intentions." Much of this animosity was apparently directed against Morice's severity rather than against Christianity *per se*. Morice considered few Babines pious enough for baptism, and he had insisted there could be no salvation without it. Consequently, one man told those attending the services that they were wasting their time going to church and observing church rules. Despite this harassment, Morice concluded the first part of the meeting with a sense of satisfaction.[134]

The second stage proved more problematic. The sermons and prayers of the retreat stage were followed by the usual routine of settling social difficulties and eradicating "public disorders." The separation and punishment of "unduly united" couples was, as usual, the most troublesome of the disorders. The chief had been unable, and probably unwilling, to persuade a baptized married man called François to leave his mistress and return to his wife, Marianne. But Morice accomplished this end by reminding François of the possibility of premature death without the opportunity to confess. Then the trouble started. During the night, François's abandoned and humiliated paramour fled to the forest vowing to hang herself. Now, according to Indian law, Morice was responsible for her act; her brother, a shaman, grabbed his gun and resolved to kill Morice before the night was out. Unaware of this threat, Morice was sleeping in the priest's house along with a lad called Patrick,[135] who served him as a sort of "houseboy."[136] At any rate, Patrick and Morice were suddenly awakened by the boy's frantic mother, who exhorted her son to flee before he too was shot. But Patrick stuck by Morice and was in fact joined by another loyal young man bent on protecting the priest. The would-be assassin was eventually calmed down and disarmed, and the following morning his sister was found, alive and well, cowering in the corner of someone else's house. This incident and a similar one which had occurred at Natléh in the spring of 1886 show that Morice took quite a risk when he donned the magistrate's robe. Yet he claimed that although it was generally the Indians' instinct to resent correction, especially when passions were involved, their common sense and faith usually prevailed.[137]

There is another explanation for their restraint: the people were afraid of Morice and his God. They were repeatedly told that epidemics and accidents were God's way of punishing them for their failure to submit. Ultimately, it was fear that persuaded the Babines to accept Morice. He was aware of this and referred to the influenza outbreak which finally undermined resistance to him as "an eloquent and persuasive missionary."[138]

In the winter of 1893–94, the Babines of the lake learned that the Bulkley Valley natives were succumbing to the scourge. They were terrified. A party was hastily dispatched to fetch Morice three weeks before the time fixed for his winter visit, and even the least fervent prayed hard. The Carrier Indians, including the Babines, attributed some illnesses to minute physical substances, but they believed that the pathogens were made and spread by malevolent persons. In this particular case, it was Morice's rival, the Protestant minister at Hazelton, presumably the Church Missionary Society's John Field, who was suspected. Consequently, they called upon Morice to save them and promised to submit en masse if he succeeded. At the same time, they were wise enough to impose a rigorous quarantine. All contacts with the infected Hotsoten were curtailed. Even when the clerk at Fort Babine offered three the times the usual rate for a letter to be delivered to Hazelton, there were no takers.[139]

Their caution and faith were rewarded. Not one case of flu was reported. They kept their promise to Morice, and henceforth he was able to praise their "good dispositions." By the way of thanksgiving, and in order not to be outdone by the Gitksan on the Skeena who had a bell donated by English Protestants, a subscription campaign was begun to buy a large church bell.[140] The substantial contributions were often collected by the Hudson's Bay Company. A certain "Bear Lake Tommy" gave ten beaver skins and $10 in gold dust. In the spring of 1895, the Company brought the 450-pound bell up from Quesnel. A large number of Indians, including most of the Hotsoten from Rocher Déboulé and Moricetown and even a few protestant Gitksan, gathered at Hwotat during Morice's winter visit in 1896 for the "baptism" of the bell.[141] There can be little doubt that their adherence to Catholicism had a certain integrative effect on the Carrier. Projects like the bell purchase and the periodic missions and pageants brought various bands together.

Father Morice seems to have enjoyed rituals and he was therefore most disappointed in 1892 when Bishop Durieu cancelled a scheduled visit and ruined his plans to stage a reception and *fêtes* like those which he had witnessed on the coast. He believed that these religious festivities helped explain the success of the Oblates' Lower Fraser mission district, and Durieu's visit would have been an opportunity for Morice to demonstrate how well he was applying the bishop's missionary system. When the visit was called off, Durieu gave Morice permission to confirm in his name. The confirmation ceremony was performed at Fort George, Natléh, and Fort St. James.[142]

Apparently, the Babines and the Hotsoten were not yet advanced enough for this sacrament. Because of their remoteness, they had in fact been somewhat neglected by Morice, which he regretted. So in 1892, he undertook a prolonged visit to the Bulkley Valley. His main objective, however, was to counter the encroachments of Methodists. The embryonic Moricetown was threatened by the development of the Methodist model community at the junction of the Skeena and the Bulkley. On 16 July 1892, Morice left Hwotat with its chief and two of his young men. That the Hotsoten failed to fetch him indicates that they were not yet an integral part of his missionary circuit, as were the Carrier proper and the Babines of the lake. To reach Moricetown from Hwotat it was necessary to go via Hazelton, and for the first time Morice made the journey on horseback. The Babines had just acquired their first horses, and though the chief was proud of his mount, he was also apprehensive about riding it. A third horse carried Morice's provisions; the two young men walked.[143]

Morice loved these journeys through the luxuriant forest and over the rugged mountains of his mission district. The space and grandeur of the wilderness seem to have tranquilized his agitated soul. The austere beauty of the mountain passes particularly enchanted him, and he was in high spirits as the little party wended its way along the Bear or Suska River. The mountain flanks of boulders and stunted shrubs was the habitat of ground hogs and mountain sheep, both of which were easy to shoot and good to eat. But after two chilly nights under the stars, the relaxed missionary was glad to spend a quiet day in the comfort of the Loring home at Hazelton. The village's only other permanent white residents were the family of Mr. Field, the Church Missionary Society's man on the Skeena, and the Hudson's Bay staff. Although Morice refused an invitation to visit "at home" with the Field family, he was happy to accept the hospitality of the Lorings, who treated him very well.[144]

The next day Mr. Loring ferried him across the junction of the Skeena and Bulkley Rivers to the site of the nascent Methodist village. It comprised a house for the minister, what Morice called his church-cum-school, and two other houses. One of these was inhabited by a Gitksan family and the other by the minister's few Hotsoten converts. He did not meet the minister, but an encounter with one of the converts convinced Morice that, rather than producing Christians or even anti-Catholics, the Methodists were simply creating arrogant upstarts. The convert proudly sported a watch and asked Morice the time in order to check its precision. Nothing antagonized Morice more than a pretentious Indian, and he consoled himself with the thought that his Indians needed only the sun to regulate their daily activities.[145]

He was glad to get on his way to Moricetown. There was as yet no autonomous community there, though both Morice and Loring came to use the name when referring to the fishing village of Keyor Hwotget. Those Hotsoten who had pledged to reform still lived at Keyor, but they were known as the Moricetown people. Morice was proud of the town site he had selected in 1887, and in 1889 Simon from Fort George had come with him to erect the walls for the future church. But since then spring flooding had turned the area into a temporary lake, and another site had to be selected. In the meantime, one of the large aboriginal houses at Keyor was chosen to be a church, and an eight-day mission began. The Hotsoten were still firmly attached to their traditional beliefs, and in his efforts to pry them loose verbally Father Morice had to compete with the thundering of the nearby waterfall, where the salmon were caught in baskets. Any temptation he had to shout was stifled by the pain of a chronic lung complaint — the result of the convulsive vomiting provoked by an overdose of medicine. Despite these distractions, the people were attentive, though through fear, Morice admitted, rather than through love.[146]

The Catholic doctrine of the indissolubility of marriage proved, once again, to be a main stumbling block, and from it other problems developed. Morice confronted them all with his usual uncompromising severity. His stern application of dogmas and rules repeatedly produced hostility. On this particular occasion, he refused to give an illegitimate child the customary baptismal medal. The child's father, who presumably regarded the medal as an important talisman, protested vigorously and glared menacingly at Morice.[147]

But a violent confrontation was avoided, and the missionary left "Moricetown" to retrace his steps back to Hazelton and thence to Hwotat. Since the Hotsoten had just finished their trapping, a party of twenty or so decided to travel up to Hazelton with Morice to trade their catch. Loaded down with fur packs and suffering in the intense mid-summer heat, they and their dogs could not keep up with Morice's "tame moose," as they called his horse. Thus, after reaching Hazelton and spending half a day resting with the Lorings, Father Morice ended his twelve-day visit to the Bulkley Valley. But he almost did not make it to Hwotat; harsh treatment of his horse put him in mortal danger. While making a steep climb on the pass, the animal came to a fallen tree blocking the trail. Morice spurred him on without pity — only to be tossed off when the horse jumped. One of his feet became entangled in the stirrup, and he found himself upside down, in an undignified and dangerous position. Fortunately, his Indian guides managed to release him without causing the horse to bolt.[148]

These occupational hazards neither discouraged nor intimidated Morice. Indeed, by making his life seem all the more dangerous and romantic, they probably spurred him on. Henceforth, he went to Moricetown via Hazelton every summer. The third of these annual trips, in 1894, was particularly rewarding. Since his last visit, the ranks of the Hotsoten had been decimated by the flu that had so disconcerted and reformed the Babines. The epidemic was the revengeful hand of God, Morice insisted, and he pointed to the fate of one of his principal rivals, a famous shaman, as proof. Not only had he been powerless against the flu, but he had also suffered the horrible punishment of having his body eaten by the dogs. A measure of Morice's ascendancy was his ability to persuade the people to move the log church from the first, ill-fated Moricetown site to a new one. The whole job only took four days—three days to float the logs three miles down the river and just one day to reassemble them. It took twenty to thirty men and women to haul the logs to and from the riverbank, and Morice later reported, condescendingly, that they enjoyed the exertion as long as it did not last too long.[149] By his standards, the Hotsoten were finally making progress. They were more deferential and attentive, and they had shown willingness to work on their church. The fact that they still lived in the traditional houses of cedar planks, grew few vegetables, and kept horses rather than the more productive cows does not seem to have perturbed Morice. It was Loring's job to worry about the absence of agriculture and the building of squared timber houses. The willingness of the Protestants to provide schools, medical attention, and material assistance was regarded by Father Morice as a kind of bribery.[150]

What he wanted was spiritual or psychological acculturation and subjugation rather than material "progress." Protestant missionaries, and most of his Oblate colleagues, usually made no distinction between spiritual and material civilization. Morice did, and he regarded the latter as a truly "bad gift." Unlike the Indian agent and the Protestant ministers, he wanted to cultivate a Christian Indian, not a replica of the diligent working man of Victorian England.[151] His charges should have no need for watches, schools, or the English language—even if they thought otherwise.[152] Neither should it be necessary to substitute agriculture, ranching, or any industrial enterprise for their viable trapping, fishing, and hunting economy. In terms of native personality and behaviour, the Indian would be allowed, indeed encouraged, to retain traits which were judged to be compatible with Christianity. Morice liked to think of the Carrier as being "like big children," and he had no desire to change that. Likewise, he cherished what he described as their naive confidence in the power of the priest and his prayer.[153] No shaman or priest would ridicule a belief in either the supernatural or in the ability of some men to manipulate it. Anthropologist Diamond Jenness studied the spiritual life of the Bulkley Carrier in the 1940's, and he found that they "have always lived in an age of miracles, and even today they look upon the interference of the supernatural world as an everyday affair, and see supernatural forces at work in the most trivial events." Fear of the spiritual forces inhabiting the mountains remained strong enough to induce "periodic hysteria."[154] These beliefs must have been at least as strong in Morice's time, and he set himself the Herculean task of harnessing and redirecting them. Fear of the mountain spirits and recourse to the shamans would be replaced by the prospect of Hell fire and the saving grace of the sacraments.

The rewards that the conversion of Indians brought to the missionary were substantial. The Catholic Indian was more fervent than his white counterpart. On his death bed, for example, the Indian often displayed a serene faith rare among whites. Those whom Morice attended frequently experienced a "sort of extasis," and some even claimed to have seen angels. In contrast, whites too often approached imminent death with terror. Morice and other Oblates also favourably compared the Indians' generosity with that of whites. Even when it came to financing institutions intended for the use of whites, the missionaries could count on the Indian convert to be more generous than the average white Catholic.[155] Much of this Indian generosity was stimulated by a skillful exploitation of the prestige and high social status that accompanied generosity in traditional Indian cultures. Indians who failed to provide free transport and food or to pay for the building of their church could be shamed by comparing them to more generous bands.[156]

Of course, not all aspects of aboriginal behaviour could be softened and pushed into Morice's "Catholic Indian" mould. Although he did not care to see his Indians adopt the materialistic culture and ethos of Europeans, he nevertheless attempted to radically change native thought and habits. Potlatching, shamanism, traditional laws concerning marriage and divorce, and Indian notions of righteous revenge were all rejected. A more respectful and charitable attitude toward the elderly and such unfortunates as orphans was encouraged. In 1890, an entry in the journal kept at Fort Fraser lamented the heartless rejection of two Skeena River Indians by the Fort Fraser Carrier. However, the writer hinted that the last person qualified to teach them charity was their priest—"a Levite over again."[157] The fur trader might have taken the same attitude toward Morice's efforts to bring the role and status of Carrier women more into line with European practice. This was a major social reform, since it inevitably implied a new division of labour and a change in the status of men. The Carrier woman was not, according to Morice, "the queen of the home as with us, but a servant, a drudge and almost a slave.[158]

In his attempt to liberate them, Morice occasionally told women to stop overloading themselves, but they were reluctant to obey for fear that their husbands might beat them. The men aggressively defended the traditional division of labour. They did not understand the European roles of king and queen and charged Morice with acting in contradiction with his own preaching, according to which the father was master of the family. Surely, they asked, the master should not work, for then he would be a workman and not the boss? This logical argument was reinforced by the observation that God made women broad across the hips in order to carry loads.[159] With this kind of opposition, it is fortunate that these social reforms were far from being a priority for Father Morice.

His major concern was with gaining influence. Consequently, he concentrated his considerable energy, determination, and courage on the task of undermining native individuals and institutions whose hold on the people represented a rival authority. By 1896 he could claim some success. The resistance of the Babines had been broken, and Moricetown was beginning to take shape. True, the ban on potlatching was a sham, but the pretence itself indicates that the Indians wanted to stay on good terms with the audacious little Frenchman. Like Blanchet, they ultimately opted for public subordination rather than confrontation. Deference was evidently perceived as the most appropriate attitude to adopt when dealing with such a powerful and useful figure. Dunning has described how, among northern tribes, the leadership of the shaman or the great hunter "waned in the face of the growing prestige and power" of the white contact persons.[160] A student of missions in New Zealand has insisted on the importance of the "relative prestige, or *mana*," of the groups involved in an inter-group contact: "The greater the prestige of a group, the better its prospect of influencing behaviour."[161] Together, Morice's association with the prestigious white group and his Catholic magic, which was believed to have saved individuals and whole communities from death, enabled him to become the spiritual patron of the Carrier. He also became an important broker for them in their relations with the fur traders and the government.[162] The Indians therefore tolerated him, though they liked neither his personality nor his efforts to stigmatize beliefs and rituals to which they were still attached.

Throughout his vast district, Morice was transported, fed, and housed free of charge. Indians financed many of his purchases and activities and helped to build his churches.[163] And the simplified Carrier alphabet he devised provided him with a unique means of instructing and communicating with his flock. In establishing this kind of relationship with the Indians, Morice was laying the basis for his independent little kingdom. His influence among the Indians was to be a crucial weapon in his fight to replace the Hudson's Bay Company's Chief Factor as the paramount white authority figure in the area.

4

THE ACQUISITION OF PARAMOUNT POWER, 1885–1896

When Father Morice arrived at Fort St. James in 1885, the Hudson's Bay Company's chief factor was still the paramount white authority. Gradually, however, the priest became a feared spiritual patron. His religious dominion was translated into secular power as he assumed the role of broker in relations between the Indians and the "Honourable Company." His ability to command obedience from the Indians and to gain favours for them from the company enabled him to undermine the position of both the chief factor and the Indian chiefs who had previously acted as go-betweens. A similar pattern marked the relationship between Morice and the Indian agent at Hazelton, the only white man apart from Hudson's Bay Company officials who could compete with him. Morice resented the occasional and peripheral encroachments of Protestant missionaries and of his fellow Oblates from other mission districts, but they did not really pose a serious threat. Neither did the miners and settlers, who did not come in sufficient numbers to disrupt the fur trade or to challenge his dominant position.

Before Morice's arrival, the relations between the Oblates and the fur traders at the fort had developed into a mutually beneficial *modus vivendi*. Despite religious differences, the members of the two groups seem to have had no sense that their respective roles were incompatible. Contributions from fur trade officers and clerks financed the first visit of Catholic missionaries to New Caledonia, and they and the Oblates who came later always received free transportation and other aid.[1] When Father Lejacq established a permanent mission at Fort St. James in 1873, the chief factor, Gavin Hamilton, received instructions from the company office in Victoria to "work together with the Priests . . . [whose] influence with the Indians will avail us much."[2] The Oblates would encourage diligence and the prompt repayment of debt and would work to abolish gambling and the potlatch, both of which the company regarded as wasteful. While the whites did not understand that traditional games of chance were not a pastime but an economic activity whose objective was to acquire goods for potlatching, they knew they competed with trapping. In 1888, for example, Chief Factor MacFarlane condemned "this pernicious, I might say very wicked system which so adversely affects the morals of the Indians, and the interests of the Company." Potlatching was similarly condemned. Although the need for potlatch goods might encourage Indians to trap, the institution was seen as "foolish," especially since the Indians sometimes potlatched with supplies provided on credit for furs they would eventually bring in.[3] Co-operation with Oblate missionaries who would attack these institutions made sound business sense.

Oblate dignitaries felt the same way about the company. Peaceful co-existence was essential, and the Oblate pioneers in the Pacific Northwest were given instructions to this effect by a visiting inspector from the Red River Mission. They were to do nothing to hinder the commerce of the trader and should only interfere in trader-Indian relations if there was a grave threat to religion. To irritate the traders might cause them to use their influence against the missionaries.[4]

In the Northern Interior, Father Lejacq and company officers developed a relationship of friendship and mutual aid that went well beyond these guidelines. Lejacq told the Stuart Lake people that he could not baptize anyone who had an unpaid debt. This provoked great consternation among the trappers, but it obviously pleased the company.[5]

Some friction between priests and fur traders was, however, to be expected, for they sought influence among the same clientele and used the same chiefs as agents. Indeed, an "unresolved power conflict" is inherent when there is more than one high-status white in a frontier community. There can be no consensus about who is the paramount authority, and the conflict becomes more pronounced when one of the competing parties has previously enjoyed a monopoly of high status,[6] as was the case with the chief factor at Fort St. James before the Oblates arrived.

The early traders at the fort had conferred the title of "Chief" upon a respected Carrier nobleman named Kwah. He was expected to be the company's spokesman, to keep the trappers busy, and to help resolve conflicts between white and Indian.[7] It was in the interests of the company to boost Kwah's authority. To ensure co-operation and, presumably, to help finance the generosity expected of native leaders, the company paid chiefs substantial annual gratuities. Its officers also treated them with respect. When Kwah died in 1840, his son, called ''The Prince'' by traders, was designated as his successor by the company.[8] The Oblates too chose The Prince as their chief in the indirect rule system. But upon his death in 1882, it was the missionary, not the chief factor, who chose his successor. Taya, the new chief, was The Prince's brother and had been his captain in the Oblate system.[9] Since the chief was an important broker for the two white patrons, a sort of rivalry for his loyalty seems to have developed from time to time. In 1885, a company report on the Fort St. James district blamed the missionaries rather than white miners for the fact that the Carrier were becoming less tractable and ''very troublesome.'' The priests allegedly had ''no scruple in using every means in their power to curry favour with the Indians and undermine any influence we traders may have among them.''[10]

This accusation could not have been fairly levelled at the founders of the Stuart Lake mission, but Morice was certainly guilty of the charge. In 1887 he invited a free trader named Frank Guy to establish himself at Fort St. James in direct competition with the company. Guy, a Frenchman and apparently a devout Catholic, set up shop near the Catholic mission and had his Sunday dinner with Morice and Blanchet. Guy's presence naturally put the Oblates in a delicate position vis-à-vis the company, and Blanchet admitted to Bishop d'Herbomez that he had to be careful not to offend. The bishop recommended that good relations be maintained with the company, which had rendered them service in the past and could do so in the future.[11] There was nothing that more obsessed and frightened the Hudson's Bay officers than free trade ''opposition,''[12] and Morice's involvement with Frank Guy was therefore seen as a serious threat to the fruitful co-operation between the Oblates and the fur traders. It was the equivalent of the chief factor inviting a Methodist minister to build a church for Indians beside the fort.

Morice's machinations were certainly neither inspired or supported by his fellow Oblates, nor were they provoked by the company. The other priests who had worked in the area praised Hudson's Bay officials for their generosity and friendliness, and the chief factor in 1887, Roderick MacFarlane, was in sympathy with the aims of the order.[13] Nor was there any trace of conflict related to the changes in the Indians' culture resulting from their conversion to Catholicism. Company officials did not seem to resent the time taken by the Indians to travel to and attend the missions at the various meeting places. Instead, they readily adjusted to the Oblates' calendar of meetings and holy days. MacFarlane, for example, instructed his man at Stoney Creek to travel up to Natléh for the Christmas mission in order to be available to trade with the assembled trappers. He appears to have regarded the religious festivities as opportunities to attract trade.[14] The Catholic ceremonial gatherings probably reduced traditional trade and potlatch contact with their now Protestant western neighbours, which would have pleased the Hudson's Bay Company. At Fort St. James, relations between priests and fur traders were certainly cordial. Just when Morice was inviting Guy to challenge the company's cherished monopoly, its officers' mess ran out of tea, sugar, and rice and had to borrow three weeks supply from the Oblate mission.[15]

Yet despite this fraternization and mutual aid, there was no doubt that the Hudson's Bay Company was still the paramount white agency in the region. It was the chief factor, not the mission director, who wrote to the provincial premier about such things as the need for government welfare and conservation laws. MacFarlane was also in a better position than Morice to command loyalty from the chiefs and leading Indians. In return for their aid in encouraging their people to refrain from idling, to pay their debts, and to stay away from free traders, the chief factor could offer them wage labour, favours like ploughing their land, and privileges such as going behind the counter at the stores. Above all, annual gratuities worth hundreds of dollars were judiciously dispensed.[16] MacFarlane's influence obviously stood in the way of Morice's monarchical ambitions, and the priest probably invited Guy to Fort St. James to weaken MacFarlane's position.

Guy's presence did seriously disconcert MacFarlane. The Frenchman was a well-liked and able rival, who not only took trade from the company but forced it to pay extravagant prices in order to compete. Free traders operating out of Fraser Lake and other outposts, together with the storekeepers at Quesnel, formed a "powerful and well equipped opposition" which had already robbed the company of its traditional monopoly. Now Guy was setting up shop on the doorstep of its regional headquarters.[17] That was a declaration of war, and MacFarlane tried to eliminate his new enemy by outbidding him. When that did not work, Guy was offered a handsome sum to retreat to warmer climes. He accepted, much to MacFarlane's relief, for in spite of the substantial credit he gave, Guy had been making a good profit.[18]

Surprisingly, Guy's association with the Oblates did not jeopardize their good relations with the company. MacFarlane does not seem to have known that it was Morice who had invited Guy, and the chief factor became quite friendly with "his Reverence" — as he called Morice.[19] Both men had scholarly pretensions, and after MacFarlane left the area in 1889, they corresponded regularly. MacFarlane sent Morice his papers on birds, and Morice described his linguistic and anthropological research. They flattered each other, and in 1892 MacFarlane seems to have suggested that his friend might one day be made a bishop. Morice passed on the latest gossip about the fort's white and Indian inhabitants—births, marriages, deaths, transfers, and promotions—as well as messages of goodwill from MacFarlane's former clients.[20] Their unlikely friendship really blossomed after MacFarlane left the area. In this respect, Morice was following the pattern that had marked his relationship with Father Carion, his tutor at Ste. Marie: resentment and hostility toward those in personal and competitive contact with him, followed by a desire for a friendship once the superior or equal was geographically distant and no longer a rival. He valued MacFarlane's letters and friendship, but he was incapable of establishing this kind of intimate peer relationship with those among whom he lived and worked.

That included W. E. Traill, who replaced MacFarlane as chief factor. During Traill's tenure from 1889 to 1893, his dealings with Morice were marked by both conflict and co-operation, and Morice was decidedly the dominant partner. Traill did not like Morice, but he was forced to use him as a broker in his relations with the Indians. For various reasons, he could no longer depend on the chief to bring in the trade. While earlier chiefs like Kwah and The Prince were relatively loyal and efficient agents for the traders, by 1889 Taya was neither. One reason was that Taya's authority as chief was far from secure, owing to resentment over the way he acquired the rank. The Prince's oldest son, Joseph, had expected to become chief when his father died, but Father Marchal chose Taya, Joseph's uncle and father-in-law. Taya was already an old man, and Marchal probably expected that Joseph would soon assume the high rank for which he had been groomed. He was the protégé of the Oblate pioneers Fathers Mc-Guckin and Lejacq, who had taken him down to Williams Lake when he was twelve to be taught farming and "mechanics" as well as Catholicism.[21] Father Lejacq learned the Carrier language from him, and Joseph became fluent in English and French. His knowledge of the white man's languages and skills, together with his "half-breed" status—his mother was a métisse—seem to have given him a feeling of superiority and to have increased his resentment against Taya. Presumably as a result of his prolonged and intimate contact with whites as a youngster, Joseph had an authoritarian personality more akin to the European than the Carrier norm. He and Taya were regarded as rival chiefs, and Joseph was supported by his four burly brothers. The five were known as the "Prince Boys."[22] Taya was, of course, supported by his family. Eventually, the feuding Fort St. James band split into two warring factions.

Economic changes and rivalries aggravated this political factionalism and served to reduce Taya's authority further. While the Prince Boys took on jobs like wood-cutting, freighting, and sailing the company's schooner, Taya and men of his more conservative type stuck mainly to trapping.[23] Because of their greater reliance on wage labour, the Princes were becoming less dependent on the intercession of the chief with the company—to obtain credit, for example. Nor were they as impressed by the largesse he could dispense from his gratuities, as full-time trappers were. The brothers were the most prominent members of an expanding group no longer relying solely, or even predominantly, on trapping and hunting. The bigger this class became, the weaker was Taya's political leverage.

But it was the influx of free traders which was most responsible for destroying the status and power of the company's chief. With the "opposition" traders nearby, the trappers' need for the chief's favours was reduced. Indeed, Taya himself was as anxious as the other trappers to sell his furs to the highest bidder and to accumulate as much credit as possible. Guy had given Taya considerable credit, and when he left, Taya took his furs to another free trader at Giscome Portage. For this act of "disloyalty," he lost most of the $200 worth of gratuities which the company gave him each year. His rival, Joseph Prince, continued to sell his skins at the fort and was rewarded with such jobs as sawing lumber.[24] Taya, an independent trapper chieftain, was not interested in this new kind of perquisite; he still wanted the old rewards like "Jawbone"—credit. In his study of the impact of the fur trade on the Indians west of Hudson's Bay, Arthur J. Ray has shown how competition between fur traders "had the effect of increasing factionalism and tensions within bands, creating a more unstable political and social climate."[25] The same thing happened in the Northern Interior of British Columbia: the loss of the Hudson's Bay Company's near monopoly reinforced factional antagonism and led Taya to commit political suicide. Since he could not resist the free traders' forbidden fruit, he was of little use to the company in its fight against them.

So Morice became, in effect, the company's chief. By now he had learned the Carrier language, and the company needed a new agent with influence within the native community to persuade the Fort St. James Carrier to trade "at home." It was especially important to keep them from going to Quesnel. The town had been created as an entrepôt for the Cariboo mines, and though it declined with them, it still boasted two hotels and seven stores, which were the company's major competitors.[26] A constant battle was fought to keep the Fort St. James Indians from trading there, and Traill was losing.[27] In 1890, many trappers were antagonized by his strict credit policy; they retaliated by taking their fall hunt to Quesnel, where they expected to get higher prices, a better variety of trade goods, and illicit liquor. One of Traill's assistants believed that whiskey was the town's principal attraction. In any event, the Indians' behaviour at

Quesnel was considered so bad that Morice severely chastized them on their return and effectively put Quesnel off limits. He also stopped buying the mission's provisions from Quesnel, provisions which had almost certainly been fetched without charge by fort trappers trading there.[28]

The Indians resented Morice's interference, but Traill was delighted. Henceforth he agreed, in the interests of sobriety and morality, to let the priest hire the men to carry the company's mail to and from Quesnel.[29] This was a much sought-after job, and Morice's right to allocate it naturally increased his power in the Indian community. By the same token, it reduced the chief factor's patronage and influence. But a more serious consequence of this new development was Traill's tacit recognition that Morice alone had the power to stop the trading at Quesnel. His reliance on Morice spelled the end of the paramountcy of the Hudson's Bay Company's chief factor in the Northern Interior. From now on, his freedom of action and even of speech would be restrained by his need to placate Morice.

These constraints were hard for Traill to accept. As an Anglican lay preacher and former justice of the peace, he found the Oblate system of public confessions and penitential whipping distasteful; as a fur trader and storekeeper with an enlightened self-interest in the material prosperity of his clients, he objected to the priest siphoning off their money. Morice's ability to extract donations and subscriptions for organs, bells, printing equipment, and general running expenses was so great that in 1892 Traill had to stop paying cash for furs, "which cash instead of circulating falls into his hands."[30] In turn, Morice began to suspect that Traill was attempting to undermine him.

There were more serious suspicions. The priest believed that the chief factor was actively discouraging Indians from donating to the Church and stirring up opposition to the use of corporal punishment, allowing himself to be regarded as the "protector" of those fleeing the "chastisements" of the watchmen.[31] The Oblates' use of the whip had become controversial throughout British Columbia in the summer of 1892, when Bishop Durieu's former assistant, Father Chirouse, was sentenced to jail for one year for sanctioning the severe whipping given to a young Indian woman at Lillooet. News of the affair soon reached Fort St. James, and a concerned crowd of Indians was told by Mr. Peter O'Reilly, the reserve commissioner and a former stipendary magistrate in the area, that public penance by whipping was illegal.[32] Traill was present at the gathering, and those Indians who resented the punishments meted out by Morice and his chief may have sought Traill's advice and protection. Apparently, those Indians already associated with the Hudson's Bay Company as wage earners were also the most likely to rebel against whipping. This was particularly true of the Prince brothers, who, because they regarded themselves as métis, seem to have considered that they should be exempt from "Indian" punishment.[33] They saw Traill as their natural ally, for they could recognize the simmering animosity between their employer and their priest.

What brought the conflict to the boiling point was Morice's conviction that Traill was spreading malicious rumours about him. The hostility was now out in the open, and a scalding and wide-ranging debate ensued. The fort was only five minutes' walk from the mission house, but Morice preferred to vent his anger by writing to his rival. Not being "quick at repartee," he resorted to doing battle on paper, where, in his own words, his "inflexible logic or mordant sarcasm" could be used more effectively.[34] But Traill proved quite capable of parrying the lethal thrusts of Morice's pen. On the question of whipping, he told the priest that it was not only illegal but also did not have the "desired effect, but quite the contrary—If you can't teach your people by moral suasion, you can't make them better by corporal punishment."[35] Morice had already stated that those who opposed whipping only wanted "more liberty to use and abuse" native women, and he now dismissed Traill's arguments as naive and illogical. How could it be illegal to whip people for immorality when Canadian courts did it every day? And as Indians could not be expected to behave better than whites, then "moral suasion" had to be reinforced by physical punishment. The Oblate system had been devised by bishops and priests and practised for "some 40 years"; surely a fur trader could not pretend to challenge it?[36] Morice was not concerned that the Oblates were not civil magistrates passing sentence according to law. The government had permitted them to act as policemen and judges for so long that their repressive activities were regarded as normal. Many of the province's newspapers certainly took that position and denounced Father Chirouse's conviction as unjust.

These editorials echoed Morice's arguments and greatly strengthened his case. Essentially, the editors contended that although Chirouse might be guilty of violating the letter of the law, he should not have been convicted, because whipping delinquents was an old tribal custom which the government had wisely permitted to continue. The Indians were still a "semi-civilized race," and the government had "winked at" the whippings ordered by the priests and chiefs because of the "good results" obtained.[37] Indians were treated like children throughout the province, *The Daily Colonist* observed, and it would therefore be "just as wise for the magistrate to punish a father for administering reasonable chastisement to his children" as to convict a missionary or an Indian chief for ordering a punishment "according to the tribal usage."[38] In fact, there is no evidence to indicate that penitential whipping was an aboriginal custom in British Columbia, but the Oblates managed to convince many people—perhaps even themselves—that it was, and these editorials and other protests succeeded in obtaining a pardon for Father Chirouse. The series of dissenting editorials was printed in the Oblates' British Columbia magazine, *The Month*, a copy of which Morice gleefully sent off to Traill with the instructions: "Read and be convinced!"[39]

Traill was not swayed. But he was not going to allow his Anglican and liberal indignation to disrupt relations with the Mission and threaten trade. On the day before receiving the editorials, he assured Morice that he would not complain as long as the watchmen did not seize company employees at the fort; if delinquents were caught and whipped at the Indian village, he would not protest.[40] Even this did not satisfy Morice. He wanted an unconditional surrender; he menacingly suggested to Traill that it "would be a great mistake to suppose that I am unaware of the many breaks [*sic*] of the laws both *divine* and *human* which could be charged against even others than employees."[41]

The chief factor was unmoved by these personal threats, but he could not ignore Morice's economic offensive. Early on in their debate, Morice informed him that henceforth he would revert to his earlier habit of getting all his supplies, except coal oil, from Quesnel and would have them brought up free of charge.[42] Obviously, Morice's loyal Catholic Indians would fetch the supplies and at the same time take their furs to Quesnel and stimulate others to do so. Traill was both annoyed and puzzled. He assured the priest that the company charged little more than cost price for the provisions and reminded Morice that his bulky mail, which included many books and journals, was transported without charge. If Morice insisted on going to Quesnel, then the company would have no choice but to charge him the "usual rate to outsiders" for his coal oil. Still, Traill clearly wanted to placate the priest and to end the conflict. He implored Morice to let him know "wherein I have given offense." The veteran fur trader wrote to the missionary, assuring him that he had had thirty years of excellent business relations with "gentlemen of your persuasion" and regretted that "it has of late been otherwise."[43]

This letter had the desired effect. Morice revealed his gravest suspicions. According to reliable informants, he claimed, Traill had spread "miserable calumnies" concerning his "private conduct" via a letter to Mr. Charles Ogden at Fort George. It was also alleged that he owned a copy of an "infamous" anti-Catholic book and that he taught his children stories about the immorality of priests. Traill was openly accused of exploiting Morice's self-confessed hypersensitivity regarding morality by

...her Morice (right, at 27)
...ned as an Oblate at the Ju-
...ate at Notre-Dame-de-Sion,
...orraine, France (below).

Morice's predecessors in British Columbia included (from left to right): Bishop Louis D'Herbomez, Father (John Pandosy, Father Georges Blanchet, Father Jean-Marie Lejacq, and Bishop Paul Durieu.

Morice's dreams were fulfilled when he was assigned to Fort St. James (below); the Indians came from their (above left) to Our Lady of Good Hope Church (above right), which had been built for Fathers Lejacq and Bl

Morice (above right, at 35) worked extensively am
the Indians, forming Moricetown (bottom), hol
masses with Sikani Indians (below right) and In
women (above left), and publishing a Carrier n
paper (left).

...ce had close, if not always pleasant, relations
...Alexander Murray, a chief factor (above left, with
...ife and daughter) and with Indian Agent Richard
...st Loring (above right).

...ce was often in contact with the Hudson's Bay Company post at Fort St. James (above) and often travelled to
...company forts, such as Fort McLeod (below right). Roderick McFarlane (below left) was one of many company
...als in the area at that time.

Father Morice photographed the Stuart Lake M[...] (above left), and he visited the Carrier Indians [...] Mary's Lake (bottom). Chief Taya (above right [...] chosen by the missionaries to succeed Carrier l[...] "The Prince" as chief. Louis Billie Prince (left) [...] became chief of the Carrier tribe at Fort St. Jam[...]

(above) Morice often encountered shamans, or medicine men, in his travels. Landing freight at Fort St. James (below left) was a costly and difficult process. Morice often travelled around the province, relying on his Indian guides, such as Isaac Qasyak, Thomas Natil, and John Stene (bottom right) to pole the boats up rivers (above right) and portage between rivers and lakes (right).

Morice (above left, at 70) left behind an Oblate l[...] when he left British Columbia. While Indians su[...] the Tsimshian (left) retained many traditional cus[...] others followed the Oblate teachings, seen at a [...] at Fort St. James in 1913 (bottom). Our Lady of [...] Hope Church (above right) remained a symb[...] Christianity long after Morice's departure.

circulating such stories to punish Morice for his firmness.[44] Exasperated by these vague accusations, Traill had the offending letter sent to Morice and promised to make a public apology if Morice came up with any proof of his guilt.[45]

Morice read the letter and was forced to admit that he had been deceived. But no apology was proffered. On the contrary, he tried to justify his suspicions by claiming that "nobody would have a right to be considered *human,* not to say *manly* who would not resent active and constant opposition to his conduct as long as this does not encroach on others' rights or duties."[46] This remark, together with his belief that Traill's alleged slanders were the principal weapon in his supposed campaign against the priest, reveals that Morice was primarily concerned with maintaining his authority and freedom of action. The passion and panic that the slightest challenge to his rule evoked is entirely consistent with his lifelong drive for unbridled power.

Fortunately, he calmed down once his worst suspicions about Traill were proven to be unfounded. His plans to buy supplies at Quesnel were cancelled.[47] Traill was happy to accept a new *modus vivendi.* He recommended that they agree to differ on the question of corporal punishment and assured Morice that he had no intention of causing him any trouble or weakening his influence. In particular, he would not turn his fort into a "sort of City of refuge" for those fleeing from the watchmen. With these commitments, Traill expected the correspondence to end and the matter not to arise in conversation. Morice agreed—provided that Traill promised that his opinions about whipping would not be voiced in front of the Indians.[48] The priest's ability to exploit his influence among the company's Indian clientele was so considerable that its chief factor had to forsake both his freedom of action and his freedom of speech.

Ultimately, harmony was restored. Soon Morice was busy hiring men for the company's mail trip as before. These appointments were frequently conditional on the men paying off part of their company debt from the fee of about $40 paid for the two-hundred mile round trip. But the priest and the trader began to develop more than just a mutually convenient business relationship. Once Traill had acquiesced, Morice set out to cultivate his personal friendship. He sent him an academic paper to have its English checked for mistakes, borrowed his books, and asked his opinion regarding the classification of certain plants. Perhaps Morice was trying to sweeten the bitter pill of subordination or to show how magnanimous he could be in victory. When, in March 1893, it was rumoured that Traill was to leave the district, Morice claimed to "sincerely hope" that it was not true.[49] But it was. The business affairs of the district were not going well, primarily because of the scarcity of furs and the competition of free traders. Despite his careful management, Traill was apparently held responsible.[50]

He was replaced by A. C. Murray, who was already serving in a senior capacity in the district. Murray was obviously under pressure to improve the financial state of the local operation. One austerity measure he decided to take was to tell Father Morice that henceforth he would have to pay to have his mail brought from Quesnel; by the time he left the priest's house, however, Murray had not only agreed to continue the free mail service but had also offered Morice a "donation" of $50. He gave this money on the explicit condition that Indians stopped taking their furs to Quesnel for approximately one year. Morice had once again threatened to send Indians for his mail and provisions if the company did not oblige him. Murray knew that the Indians would make these long trips without remuneration, and he was equally certain that they would take their own furs and thereby stimulate a general move to Quesnel. Another "rush" to the town would be "ruinous" to Murray.[51]

But his $50 donation was nevertheless a gamble. The priest's ban on Quesnel had not stopped Fort St. James trappers from travelling there a number of times in the previous year.[52] Morice's conflict with Traill, which would have made him less willing to put pressure on his Indian parishioners to comply with company wishes, is a partial explanation. But the reconciliation between priest and chief factor did not stop the traffic. Morice's authority was not absolute. Indeed, the worst offender was Chief Taya, supposedly the priest's deputy. Taya liked to show his independence. As a traditional trapper with little interest in wage labour, he did not have to ingratiate himself with the whites, including Morice, who dispensed this patronage. Probably Taya also resented Morice's close ties with his rival, Joseph Prince—who was on very good terms with the Hudson's Bay Company—and was therefore reluctant to comply with the priest's ban.[53]

Murray was, however, hopeful that Morice was as influential as he seemed.[54] To get the priest to try a little harder, he agreed to pay favourable prices for furs handed in to Morice as subscriptions to his Carrier newspaper. No money changed hands; the value of the furs was simply deducted from the Mission's account. But at the various trading posts, company officials collected furs, cash, and gold dust for Morice. On one occasion in 1895, the clerk at Fort Babine handed him $128.00, apparently part of the collection for the new church bell.[55] But these favours and the "donation" seem to have paid off. In the spring of 1894, the chief traded at the fort. Most of the other trappers must have done so too, for Murray was delighted to record in his journal that he had done $800 worth of business in one day—the most successful day in many years.[56]

He was not so pleased with his dependence on Morice. It made it difficult for him to resist the priest's intrusion into his personal life. His wife, Mary, was an Indian, and Morice was her confessor. A nervous woman subject to seizures, Mrs. Murray was terrified of Morice, who apparently used her as a source of personal and business information.[57] Murray probably did not mind Morice sending the altar linen for his wife to wash, but the priest's interference in his domestic affairs caused him "much annoyance" and on one occasion brought him into conflict with one of his subordinates.[58] Although the details of the incident are unclear, it involved Mrs. Murray, Morice, and others. In the course of his attempt to clear up the matter, Murray accused Charles French, the clerk at Fort Babine, of being too frightened of Father Morice to reveal what he knew. Something about Morice's personality and demeanour certainly inspired a fearful respect among whites and Indians alike. But French vehemently denied that he was "afraid of that son-of-bitch," whom he vowed he would never forgive for the mischief he had made between himself and his boss.[59] Murray might have shared French's opinion of the priest's pedigree, but he dared not say so. According to Murray, Morice was not liked by the Indians either, though he did have "much influence" with them. Consequently, Murray hoped for the company's sake that conflict could be avoided. In this he was backed up by the company's manager in Victoria, Mr. R. H. Hall, who counselled patience and reconciliation.[60]

The company officials' reliance on Morice allowed him to encroach on their business prerogatives. Some of his letters to Murray read like those that would be exchanged by executives in the same company. As well as choosing men whom he thought deserved the mail job—even if Murray thought otherwise—Morice also got involved in the discussion of what should be paid to them for the trip. In February 1895, he suggested that Murray change the date of the spring pick-up at Quesnel because the pre-arranged date did not suit him.[61] On other occasions, however, Morice assumed a regal, authoritative tone when addressing Murray on company matters. Just before Christmas in 1894, he offered the chief factor some "friendly advice on a subject which might lead you into trouble." It had come to his notice that Murray was either selling or giving away bottles of liquor to his employees. He was reminded that his predecessors, MacFarlane and Traill, had "promised" never to do so. He also notified Murray that some of the local men hired by the company, especially the Princes, were not "half-breeds" as they liked to claim; rather, they were "Indian quarteroons," having just one European grandparent, and giving them liquor was illegal. Morice was in any case against even genuine "half-breeds" having liquor. Joseph Prince, who seems to have been a more useful and reliable aide than Chief Taya, was quoted as an authority on this matter. According to him, the promise of a "half-breed" not to share liquor with Indians was "absolutely worthless as once he has tasted the drug he forgets all about it [the promise]."[62]

Morice's objections to liquor distribution were motivated by more than the usual religious and moral considerations. Drinking at Fort St. James was apt to provoke violent confrontations between Indian factions, and Morice believed that he must prevent them. Although he denied he was threatening Murray or assuming the role of a policeman, he nevertheless reminded the chief factor that he had, in a letter to the superintendent of Indian affairs in Victoria, "constituted" himself as being responsible for the "peace of this place."[63] Essentially, he was serving Murray with formal notice that the chief factor was no longer the paramount civil authority in the area.

Legally that mantle should have fallen on the ample shoulders of Mr. Loring, the Indian agent, but Morice usurped his authority as assiduously as he had that of the various chief factors. Loring lived in far off Hazelton and rarely journeyed to Fort St. James. By discouraging Loring's visits and by assuming responsibility for what the agent should have been doing in the Stuart Lake area, Morice minimized government interference and the possibility of a challenge to himself.[64] This arrangement suited Loring, who, according to Morice, recognized the "priest's transcendent position in the same sphere, and, instead of trying to thwart him in his operations, shrewdly made him serve his own ends, or, rather, do his work."[65] It would be closer to the truth to say that each made the other "serve his own ends." Loring's agency was vast, covering the territory of the Gitksan as well as the Carrier, and he was glad to have Morice to help settle disputes in what he called "the interior." Allegedly a former German aristocrat — Baron Loring von Wilke — Loring had spent many years prospecting in the United States before becoming a police constable and then a prison officer in British Columbia.[66] Just before his appointment as the first Indian agent at Hazelton, he had married the widow of Phillip J. Hankin, a former colonial secretary in pre-Confederation British Columbia, and it was rumoured in the Hazelton area that he owed his job to his wife.[67]

At Fort St. James the Hudson's Bay Company hoped that the Indian agent would be a useful mediator. In March 1890, Traill wrote to Loring expressing his regret that Morice had "deterred" the agent from making his first visit to the fort; the chief factor urged him to come that summer. But it was not until 1892 that Loring finally arrived, and a two-year interval elapsed before complaints and a reprimand from Victoria resulted in a second visit.[68] What needed his attention most was the violent factionalism among the fort Indians. Though the conflicts were precipitated by the consumption of liquor from Quesnel and often concerned control over economic resources like hay meadows, many involved the perennial rivalry between Taya and Joseph Prince.[69]

In all likelihood, both of them used the repressive apparatus of the white man's religious and political systems in their feud. Since Taya was the chief and Joseph the government's Indian constable, each had legitimate power at his disposal. The old chief was cantankerous, eager to assert his authority, and violent; Joseph was ambitious and equally prone to violence.[70] Unlike traditional Carrier leaders, these men were eager to acquire and exercise personal power. They were familiar with the coercive authoritarianism of the early fur traders and of the missionaries, and they were not slow to use similar methods. This acquisition of authoritarian political power was an important part of the acculturation process. The duel for paramountcy among the Carrier of Fort St. James was repeated in other Oblate-influenced villages, and it sometimes led to bands splitting into separate communities, one led by the chief and the other by his rival, usually a captain or watchman.[71] This kind of fission may have been inadvertently stimulated by the Oblates' deliberate policy of not trusting chiefs and secretly appointing commissaires to spy on them and report their deficiencies. Morice may have played Joseph off against Taya to be sure that his own position remained secure. What is certain is that Morice's absence from the Fort during the spring and summer and his absorption in his research, writing, and printing in the winter months gave both contestants ample opportunity to use the authority vested in them.[72] Morice was interested in power rather than mere administration, much of which he left to Indians like Taya and Joseph.

The rivalry between the two was common knowledge throughout the area, and early in September 1890 news reached Fraser Lake that Taya had killed Joseph. Nobody seemed surprised. As it turned out, however, Taya had actually shot his other son-in-law, Jean-Baptiste Thayoelli. Immediately after the incident, he claimed not to have known which of his two sons-in-law had received the fatal blast from both barrels of his shotgun. According to the story he told Morice, he was drifting down the Stuart River at night when he shot at what he thought was a bear feasting on fish. Following the blast, a horrified human voice cried out: "My father-in-law, what are you doing? Oh! My God! Holy Water."[73] The figure then fell, dead. Taya panicked, and without stopping to find out which of his sons-in-law he had killed, he went to Morice for advice and protection. He feared the blood revenge that could follow even an accidental killing in traditional Carrier society. Taya must have been equally conscious of the suspicions that would be aroused if Joseph turned out to be his victim.

Morice nevertheless persuaded him to remain in the village rather than fleeing into the forest; the body was sent for and its identity established. Jean-Baptiste's family was distraught with sorrow, but when Morice went to comfort them and to appeal for a more moderate display of grief, he too was so distressed to see the "gaping hole" in Jean-Baptiste's body that he began to weep and had to rush out and return home with a sense of failure. Father Morice obviously had a strong emotional commitment to his Indian "children," and as long as his power and reputation were not involved, he was capable of showing sympathy and affection toward them. His diplomatic talents were also considerable, for at the funeral Jean-Baptiste's family and Taya received communion together.[74]

But this dramatic tragedy did little to mitigate the factional rivalry. The Hudson's Bay Company people wanted Loring to put an end to it. They probably hoped, too, that Loring would moderate Morice's influence among the Indians. Such was not to be the case, for Loring increased rather than diminished Morice's authority. The agent understood neither the Carrier language nor culture, and when he came to Fort St. James, Morice interpreted and mediated for him.[75] Once again the missionary proved an indispensible broker for a potentially competitive white patron. As a result, consciously or not, the government was bolstering Morice. Even before Loring assumed his duties in 1889, Captain N. Fitzstubbs, the stipendary magistrate who handled Indian matters, congratulated Morice and his Oblate colleagues on being "foremost in support of Law, Order and Discipline" and asked him to persuade the Oblate-appointed chiefs to be invested as special constables.[76] Elsewhere in British Columbia the Oblate system was similarly strengthened by the appointment of the Catholic chiefs and watchmen as policemen.[77]

Other denominations were not always looked upon so favourably. In 1889, Fitzstubbs reported to the provincial attorney-general that the Methodists on the Skeena River were preaching "disloyalty and discontent," and six years later the Hudson's Bay clerk at Fort Babine told Murray that the whites of the area were far more impressed with Morice than with the "crazy Methodist parsons such as roam around Hazelton."[78] Throughout the British Empire, Protestant missionaries, including British Columbia's William Duncan and Thomas Crosby, were often men of humble artisan origins without the classical education given to Jesuits and Oblates.[79] Morice's learning clearly impressed whites and Indians alike and added to his prestige.

Morice had an angry encounter with a Protestant "minister of error" and his followers in 1892. The Methodist cleric confronted the priest near Hazelton. He wanted to know if it was true that Morice was preaching that Methodism was an off-shoot of the schism of the amorous Henry VIII and that its minister was leading the Indians to Hell.[80] Not only did Morice admit this, but he also accused the Methodists of trying to buy souls with material aid. The Methodist natives took umbrage at these remarks and vowed not to allow the Catholics to cross the Skeena to visit Mr. Loring. A violent confrontation was narrowly averted, and Morice eventually reached Loring's dwelling. The agent promptly summoned the impertinent Methodists. Morice was relaxing at the piano when they arrived. Loring gave them a severe reprimand, and one of the group, who was alleged to have insulted Morice, was told that he would have received a two-month jail sentence if the priest himself had heard the remark. The agent emphasized that the Catholic priests were important personages and had to be treated accordingly.[81]

Morice's importance as a mediator in times of crisis justified this support. When, for example, he arrived at Babine for his winter visit in February 1896, he found an official letter from Loring waiting for him. It contained the surprising news that the Babine's chief, Alec Typee, was suspected of pilfering $1,200 worth of merchandise from the Hudson's Bay warehouse by skillfully removing and then replacing the roof shingles. The goods were stored in the woods for later distribution at a potlatch. The letter went on to relate how five special constables sent by Loring in January had been fired upon and forced to flee. As an alternative to calling a military expedition, Loring asked Morice to read a letter to the Indians assembled for the mission and to prevail upon the suspected chief to give himself up.[82] The letter promised that rough and indiscriminate justice would be meted out to those who harboured fugitives: "the whole of the respective village would suffer; the government would not stop at the very extremes such as burning the village, destroying the contents of their salmon-caches and hunting them down to the last man."[83] When he read the letter, Father Morice further accentuated the futility of resisting "people who were [as] numerous as mosquitoes on a sultry day" and who would certainly carry out their threats. It would be best, he insisted, for the chief to give himself up and rely on the impartial justice of Mr. Loring. If he was innocent, as Morice claimed to believe, then he had nothing to fear.[84]

Their conviction was no doubt sincere. Loring himself was somewhat perplexed by the crime and assured the deputy attorney-general that the Indians of the Northern Interior were for the most part more law-abiding than whites. One thing was certain, storing goods in an isolated and unguarded warehouse like the one allegedly robbed by Alec would never even have been contemplated in a "community of whites." At Fort St. James, Loring continued, theft was so unusual that Mr. Murray and his family slept with their doors unlocked. Loring therefore felt justified in promising Alec a light sentence if he were found guilty after surrendering.[85]

Chief Typee weighed the combination of threats and inducements. Then, according to Morice, he declared that no man could make him give himself up, but the priest was the representative of God, not a man. Although Morice's intervention must have made it easier for Alec to surrender without losing too much face, the threat of violence was probably what tipped the scales. A military expedition had been sent up the Skeena in 1888 when rebellion threatened after police shot a fleeing murder suspect. After that show of force, Magistrate Fitzstubbs had reported that the Indians were now aware that whites in isolated areas were not forgotten or unprotected. Exaggerated accounts of the number and power of the soldiers had reached even the deepest regions of the interior.[86]

During his trial before Loring, the Babine chief admitted his guilt and revealed the whereabouts of his booty. True to his word, Loring gave Alec a mild three-month jail sentence—to be served in Hazelton.[87] In his memoirs, Morice claimed that he alone was responsible for averting a violent confrontation, but Loring emphasized in his own report that his letter had "had a salutory and overawing effect."[88] The agent had been criticized for neglecting the Carrier, and he was obviously not going to admit his dependence on Morice. Morice tended to exaggerate his own importance, but it is nevertheless true that he was a most useful broker for Loring.[89] And the more the agent came to rely on Morice, the less willing he would be to challenge him.

The same held for Morice's relationship with the third member of the ruling triad, the chief factor. Indeed, by 1895 Morice believed that he was so indispensable that he began to make unreasonable demands. These requests were usually linked to the priest's increasing preoccupation with his literary pursuits. Isolated from other scholars, libraries, bookstores, and publishers, Morice relied heavily on the Royal Mail, and he became almost obsessively concerned with the arrival and departure of the mail carriers who visited Quesnel. Although he could not get along with other whites on a "face to face" or intimate basis, Morice kept up a prodigious correspondence. In February 1894, one mail delivery brought him thirty-seven letters from seven countries. He was as excited as a child on Christmas morning.[90] Whenever his Indian carriers fetched him up a lot of letters, books, or, better still, acceptances from publishers, he was elated. But if items he was expecting, especially books needed for preparing papers, did not arrive, he was bitterly disappointed. On one occasion, he considered the preparation of the mail important enough to put off confessions "to a later day." Sometimes unpaid Indian messengers were sent down to Quesnel when the need to send books to the binders or to collect letters did not coincide with the regular mail trips.[91]

But eventually and inevitably Morice asked Murray to change the mail schedule to suit his needs. In the early months of 1895, he was working on the manuscript of the story about his missionary adventures which was published in 1897 under the title of *Au pays de l'ours noir. Chez les sauvages de la Columbie Britannique.* The Kodak camera he had ordered to take pictures for it had to arrive in time for him to take it on his last summer tour before he was to leave for France, where the book was to be published. But the pack train that was to bring the mail in the spring of 1895 was not scheduled to arrive in Fort St. James until after Morice had left on tour. This news threw him into a dither, and he begged Murray to send down a boat which could bring up his camera and the two church bells (including the previously mentioned Babine thanksgiving bell) that were awaiting shipment at Quesnel. Morice expected the camera and the heavy bells to be shipped free of charge.[92] But the Hudson's Bay Company was now bringing in its bulky goods via the Skeena-Lake Babine route and had built a small schooner for that purpose. Consequently, Murray was reluctant to hire two boatmen at $45 each just to oblige his eccentric neighbour. Yet he was prepared to do so if Morice would pay six cents a pound in freight charges for the bells; the camera and the other mail would be carried free. Murray insisted that the trip would cost twice as much as the mission was willing to pay for it, but Morice made a counteroffer of three cents and said that if that was not acceptable, he would leave the bells until the fall. It was his camera that he was so anxious to have, and he could send a rider for that.[93]

However, when Murray refused to accept the three-cent rate, the peeved Morice changed his mind and resorted to his usual threat. If the company did not transport the bells and the camera on his terms, he would send the Indians down with "several craft." They would take down their furs and Morice would of course be "unable, this year, to dissuade them from trading at Quesnel."[94] This menace, which could have provoked a rupture in the good relations between the mission and the fort, reveals Morice's obsessional nature. Ostensibly, the object of the blackmail was to procure his camera, but Morice had himself admitted that a lone rider could do that. Getting the bells to the Indians who had paid for them was certainly not a priority. What was important was that everyone submit to him, and the threat was the only way to force Murray to bend to his will. It worked. The freight rate was not lowered, but Murray informed Morice that he would give him another "donation" of $50, provided "you induce the Indians to trade at home [and] to pay up their debts here." Furthermore, the $50 contribution would henceforth be made every year.[95]

Morice graciously accepted the offer, and he agreed to deduct the freight charges from the contribution for 1895.[96] No doubt Murray believed Morice was ruthless enough to carry out his threat. The prospect of a mass trek to Quesnel so endangered his career that he was prepared to pay the $50 from his own pocket, although he did not think that a missionary should need bribing in order to keep his Indians away from a town where they acquired both whiskey and the "loathsome disease of syphillis." In 1893, Joseph Prince had reported to him that some of the young Indian women at the fort were "rotting above ground" because of the scourge.[97] When this was brought to Morice's attention in the course of the Kodak negotiations in the early spring of 1895, he seemed surprised. There was, he said, no medicine for the treatment of the disease at the Mission, and in any case he would not give out such medicine "except possibly to an innocent party." At any rate, once the $50 was paid, he promised Murray that he would do his best to stop trading at Quesnel. The matter ended there, except for a conciliatory gesture on Morice's part. He sent Mrs. Murray some artificial flowers and charged her just the Montreal price instead of adding on the freight cost as well.[98]

It was the act of an aspiring king who lacked the regal virtues of magnanimity and generosity. But he did not lack power, though people outside the Northern Interior did not appreciate the extent of his dominion. In the midst of his conflict with Murray, the Hudson's Bay Company manager at Victoria expressed his sympathy for the chief factor, but he felt sure that "with tact and discretion," it would not be difficult to keep the priest "in his place."[99] Murray knew better. Morice's power as a patron-priest made him a valued broker for both the company and the Indians. He served both sides. The company asked him to get the trappers to trade "at home" and to pay their debts, and it threatened to report them to Morice if they did not return pilfered goods. The Indians wanted him to persuade the company to sell them hay when it was in short supply or to favour them when jobs were assigned. Also, Morice took it upon himself to complain on their behalf, for example, when an Indian packer was overloaded by a company official.[100] In effect, with his knowledge of the native language and his personal and religious authority he had taken over the role of the traditional fur-trade Indian chief.

The same attributes made it possible for him to reduce his dependence on Chief Taya. Since he could operate in both cultures, Morice needed no native brokers. Taya and the watchmen were only instruments of repression. And since the company now used Morice as a broker, it no longer needed Indians either. The Indian agent had taken advantage of Morice's services from the start of his tenure, and he was scarcely able to operate among the Carrier without the missionary's help. In other words, non-Indians who wanted something from the native people felt obliged to approach them through him.[101] Other missionaries have used their linguistic expertise to make themselves indispensable cross-cultural brokers. An Oblate missionary in Labrador virtually duplicated Morice's role in the 1960's, replacing the chief as the native community's intermediary with white authority figures.[102] But that priest used the influence gained from ties of dependence upon him to further his spiritual mission rather than to gain personal power.

In the new order of things at Fort St. James, the big loser was the trapper-chieftain Taya. But he put up a fight. In 1895, he again defied Morice and antagonized the company by taking his furs to Quesnel. He thus demonstrated his independence, but it did not help him to regain power. Whatever power that was left for any Indian seems to have passed to his rival, Joseph Prince. Joseph understood the language, work habits, and authority structure of the whites, and he aspired to their status. Murray admired his "great force of character," regarded him as "an excellent man," and frequently employed him; Morice relied on his advice and information and rewarded his loyalty with mail-carrying jobs.[103] Loring chose Joseph Prince, not the chief, as was customary, to be his constable at Fort St. James. Because this appointment was made before the agent visited the fort, it is likely that Morice had recommended Joseph, whom he regarded as the most influential Indian at the fort.[104] Given his aspirations, Joseph was no doubt prepared to defer to Morice, especially since he probably expected to succeed Taya in the near future.

For different reasons, Murray was also prepared to defer to Morice. As a fur trader, his principal concern was profit. It was safer to buy Morice's co-operation than to risk a potentially ruinous confrontation. After the dispute over the transportation of the Kodak and the bells, relations between the mission and the fort were once again marked by collaboration and even cordiality. Apart from the big favours of the free mail service and the annual $50 donation, the company often delivered Morice's horse to distant posts and did its best to supply him with good quality ink and the food he liked. Shopping lists were taken over to the fort by Indian "bearers," old men who served as the priest's messengers and language instructors. Requests for "fat thick bacon" were quite frequent, but dried peaches—"if good quality"—rice, coffee, beef, and fruit salt were in demand too. Members of Morice's church were sent over to the fort when they needed a potent medicine like laudanum, a painkiller made by steeping powdered opium in alcohol.[105]

While the renewed fraternization between mission and fort was influenced by Murray's dependence on Morice, the company's officers, even at the height of the conflict between Murray and Morice, continued to have an affectionate regard for "Good old Blanchet." Father Blanchet always had Christmas dinner at the fort and apparently took no part in Morice's political intrigues or indeed in any other important mission activity.[106] Had he been stronger and Morice's egotism less impregnable, perhaps the saintly old man might have been able to get Morice to think more often of the feelings and welfare of others or even of what other people thought of his behaviour. But that was not to be. To realize his dream of conquest, Morice had pursued two distinct but complementary power positions—missionary patron and cross-cultural broker—with ruthless determination. Simultaneously, he applied himself with equal force to the satisfaction of his other great ambition: to be an acclaimed explorer and scholar.

5

SAVANT OF THE WOODS, 1885–1896

As well as gaining personal power, Morice wanted to achieve fame as an Americanist—an expert on America and its native peoples—through his life with the Carrier.[1] Such recognition would extend his influence back into the white man's world from which he had fled.[2] He expected his invention of a syllabic script for Carrier to bring him widespread acclaim as a linguist. He made extensive use of it himself in conjunction with the knowledge of printing which he had acquired over the years. From his little print shop at Fort St. James, Father Morice began to crank out books and even a newspaper in the Carrier language. He started the operation with the rudimentary outfit he had used for printing Bishop d'Herbomez's pamphlet at St. Mary's, but later he ordered a more sophisticated and expensive press from Montreal. The Indians paid the considerable cost of producing the special type. The first item to come off his new press was a thirty-two page reading primer. Later in the same year, 1890, he ran off a fifty-six page catechism.[3] But his most ambitious syllabic printing venture was an eight-page monthly paper. Called *Test' les nahivelnek (The Paper Which Tells)*, each issue contained news of the locality, North America, and the Old World, as well as a text from the scriptures, the life of a saint, some aspects of natural history, geography, and other items. There was also a "Letters to the Editor" section which included Morice's responses.[4]

The paper first appeared in October 1891; by February 1892, Morice was able to report to MacFarlane that it was "taking" among the Carrier.[5]

He was justly proud of his latest literary venture, and in 1893 he sang its praises in the *Petites Annales,* an Oblate journal.[6] Some recognition came from other quarters too. A group of English "sporting gentlemen" had visited Fort St. James in the fall of 1893, and on their return to England one of them wrote a travelogue called *The Land of the Muskeg.* In the book, Henry Somers Somerset described his surprise encounter with "a savant and a man of learning" at his isolated mission station. Somerset quite incorrectly attributed the Carriers' log houses and knowledge of English to this "prince of missionaries," but it was the syllabic newspaper which the author admired the most.[7]

To Morice's great disappointment, this praise was no match for the acclaim afforded Father Lejeune's shorthand publications in the Chinook jargon, the most popular of which was the newspaper *Kamloops Wawa.* The idea of using stenography to write the native language was conceived in June 1890 when a number of Oblates who had gathered for a retreat began to discuss Father Morice's syllabic script. They all apparently agreed that it would be too difficult to adapt it for use with other Indian languages, and Father Chiappini, who had travelled from France with Morice, suggested that shorthand be tried. It was much simpler, and as Bishop Durieu pointed out, it had the added advantage of being universal, which would allow the Indians to write in a number of languages.[8]

The challenge was taken up by Father Lejeune. Regarded as a talented linguist himself, Lejeune was promised funds if he could manage to use stenography to write Chinook, the lingua franca of most of the province's Indians.[9] He succeeded, much to the delight of his Indian charges. Some members of the Thompson tribe who lived around Kamloops learned to read Chinook after just four hours of instruction, and a few months' study enabled one young man to read fluently in Thompson and English. By 1894, two thousand Indians could read and write shorthand, and thirteen hundred copies of a reading manual had been printed. Learning stenography was seen as an excellent steppingstone to learning English in shorthand and then finally to mastering the Roman script. These additional stages distinguished Lejeune's writing system from Morice's syllabary. Though Lejeune's stenography was intended for wide use, he was probably surprised when a priest wrote from Esquimalt to ask for copies of the *Wawa* for some poor whites who wanted to learn shorthand but could not afford a teacher. The great success of the *Wawa* aroused interest well beyond the borders of British Columbia.[10]

Morice greeted Lejeune's work with scornful condemnation. Obviously piqued because it was eclipsing his own efforts, in 1894 he bitterly attacked Lejeune's system in the preface to the new edition of his Carrier primer. According to him, the Duployé stenography could not correctly render the sounds of either the Indian languages or the Chinook jargon. Durieu was astonished by this "unspeakable" diatribe and wondered if one's brain did not have to be mixed up to write such a thing. He promptly sent a reprimand to Morice, along with an order to cease printing the polemic and to cut out the offending page before the new work was distributed to the Indians. But Morice defied his bishop and proceeded to print and distribute the new primer—complete with his preface. He was especially careful to send copies to partisans of the Lejeune system.[11] Although a definite rivalry now existed between the two writing systems, Morice's adversaries did not waste their time with polemics. Instead, they launched a linguistic invasion of Morice's mission district and encouraged the Fraser River Carrier to abandon Morice's syllabary in favour of the shorthand. At first the Indians rejected the new system, but by the beginning of 1895 Father Lejacq was able to report to Lejeune that at Fort Alexandria and Quesnel the stenography was dethroning Morice's script. At about the same time, Durieu learned that the Fort Alexandria people had instructed Morice not to bother sending his newspapers any more because they now had something better. The bishop was delighted and wrote excitedly to Lejeune that he could proclaim victory. This defeat infuriated Morice, and he sent a nasty letter to the people at Fort Alexandria.[12]

Morice's self-imposed and egotistical alienation from his colleagues naturally provoked hostility. Obsessed by his desire to dominate his environment and to realize his dreams of fame, he was unable to enjoy their fellowship or share their goals. The encroachment of the shorthand script was, however, peripheral to his major interests, though Morice regarded Lejeune's success as a slap in the face of the only real linguist among the British Columbia Oblates—himself. Henceforth, he neglected his syllabic publications and devoted more time to his research and writing in Indian linguistics and anthropology. His preoccupation with literary production, both writing and printing, had always been an important means of asserting his individuality and attracting approval. Now it became so more than ever. With no supervision from above, and with his paramount position at Fort St. James well established, he could freely indulge himself.[13]

Prior to 1895, Morice's major scholarly publications were in the field of anthropology. The first of these was a 165-page article on "The Western Dénés: Their Manners and Customs." It appeared in the 1889–90 volume of the *Proceedings of the Canadian Institute* and described the aboriginal culture of the Carrier, Chilcotin, Sikani, and Nahani. Based on years of personal research, the article indicates that Morice dedicated a good deal of time to his scholarly pursuits even in his early years at Fort St. James. In 1894, this first article was superseded by a more extensive study of the same kind. Although written for the Smithsonian Institute, the "Notes Ar-

cheological, Industrial and Sociological on the Western Dénés'' ultimately appeared in the less prestigious journal of the Canadian Institute,
as did his ''Three Carrier Myths; with Notes and Comments.'' A short but
provocative piece on the origins of the Carrier sociology and mythology
was published by the Royal Society of Canada in 1892.[14]

One of the principal merits of these works was Morice's use of linguistic evidence. In 1896 he admitted that despite his publications in sociology, archeology, and other fields, his preferred subject had always been
linguistics. Language alone, he believed, provided invaluable clues to the
origin and diffusion of cultural traits in pre-literate societies which had no
imperishable monuments.

Father Morice's great emphasis on language was inspired by his own
personal tastes and by the work of Horatio Hale, the brilliant analyst of the
languages of the American northwest.[15] Perhaps the obsession with racial
origins which he inherited from Petitot attracted Morice to Hale's theory
about the link between race and language. Hale believed that in the absence of written documents, language was the only acceptable evidence of
the affiliation of two groups; language could attest to a racial connection.
Morice agreed, though he called the affinity ethnic rather than racial.
Race, he believed, was the concern of physical anthropology; his preoccupation was with ''ethnological questions.''[16] In fact, Morice's reference to language proving that two groups had ''the same blood'' indicates
that his distinction between race and ethnicity was specious.

He dismissed the then-fashionable resort to head measurements for
such purposes as unreliable. Morice even questioned the efforts in this
field of so eminent a figure as Dr. Franz Boas, the German-born founder
of the American school of cultural anthropology. Since man was a rational
being and not merely an animal, Father Morice argued, it was
''unscientific'' to study him as animals are studied.[17] This laudable stand
reveals Morice to have been, at least as an Americanist, a thoroughly
modern thinker.

Perhaps the best example of his able use of language in the study of cultural diffusion was in his ''Are the Carrier Sociology and Mythology Indigenous or Exotic?'' In his usual politely combative manner, he set out to
refute the opinions of Boas and G. M. Dawson, the courageous handi-
capped geologist and Americanist,[18] to the effect that certain social institutions and myths of the Indians of the Northern British Columbia coast
were borrowed from the inland Déné tribes. According to Morice, the re-
verse was true: the naturally imitative Carrier had picked up the potlatch,
the rank structure, and some myths of the Tsimshian and Gitksan in the
course of the longstanding trade relationship with those tribes. For him,
the Carriers' rapid adoption of white technology and social forms proved

that they were inherently imitative and therefore that they must have imitated the Tsimshian and Gitksan. The fact that the Tsimshian had rejected Catholicism demonstrated to Morice's satisfaction that they and the Gitksan were naturally conservative.[19] To prove his case, Morice pointed out that important terms and chants used in Carrier potlatch rituals were of Tsimshian origin. For example, the hereditary song recited by a man validating his newly inherited noble title at a potlatch was a badly pronounced "Tsimpsian air."[20] In his study of the origins of Carrier mythology, Morice relied on careful textual analysis rather than on language, though without a thorough knowledge of the Carrier language, he could not have detected the subtle clues with which he made his case. In an important myth about the subterranean journey of two young men to the land of the dead, for instance, Morice noticed that the houses described were made of "board"—split cedar. Now cedar grows in abundance on the coast, where it was widely used for house construction. But inland, where the Carrier lived, split-cedar was not used.[21]

Morice's early anthropological writings had other strengths apart from his investigative use of language. For one thing, they contained little of the "noble savage" romanticism that sometimes marred his popular works, especially those written for French Catholic readers. When writing in English-language scholarly journals, he was more empirical and less likely to take potshots at European secular civilization.[22] Morice presented a balanced, if ethnocentric, picture of the Carrier personality. Their "relative morality, great honesty, intense fondness of their offspring, and a general gentleness of disposition" were attested to, but so too was the fact that they were "prone to lying, addicted to gambling, naturally selfish, cowardly, and at times very lazy, especially the stronger sex."[23] An observer better able to see these traits within their cultural context might have accounted for both the gentleness and the alleged cowardice as a preference for co-operation and conflict avoidance. Morice himself noted elsewhere that Carrier men were not afraid to do battle with bears.[24] Likewise, the men's supposed laziness was probably no more than an aversion for work traditionally performed by women. On the other hand, he subjected the potlatch, whose paganism and pride he condemned and outlawed as a priest, to a much more dispassionate, functionalist analysis. As a means of validating inheritance and the economic and social status that went with it, the potlatch was crucial to Carrier culture. To understand the ceremony, Morice insisted, one must realize that the "strictest point of the Carriers' moral law is nothing for nothing."[25] Later research on the subject by professional anthropologists has shown that this emphasis on reciprocity and legitimating of status was not misplaced.[26]

Turning his attention to the acculturation of the Carrier, Morice was equally judicious. Implicit in his treatment of this theme was a conviction that their new material culture combined the best of the native and European worlds: they could enjoy the comfort of log houses and the supplementary food obtained from vegetable gardens and cattle without forsaking their more traditional and still profitable economic activities—hunting and fishing. The chase, in particular, yielded meat to eat and furs to be traded for European goods, such as steel traps and guns, which rendered life easier and more secure. The Carriers' admiration for the products and ways of the whites was such, Morice claimed, that they had given up many of the pagan practices—cremation, for example—before the missionaries arrived; by the 1890's, they were loath to be called Indians. Unaccustomed to thinking in racial terms, they believed that "a person of Caucasian descent is no more a white man than the red-skin who conforms to European social notions."[27] This progressive image contrasts markedly with the pictures of simple and conservative natives which he painted in his missionary adventure books.[28] The Carrier Indian who emerges from the anthropological writings conforms more to reality, though Morice probably exaggerated his imitative propensity to lend weight to his thesis that the Carrier had copied the culture of the coastal Indians and not *vice versa*. Central to the economic order which grew from the contact with whites was, of course, the Hudson's Bay Company, to which Morice gave unqualified praise for its paternalistic concern for the destitute and for its refusal to sell liquor.[29]

This magnanimity towards his white rivals was matched by a knowledge of classical literature which allowed and encouraged Morice to put the Carrier society into historical perspective. The Indian's preoccupation with the significance of dreams, for instance, was something he shared with all of pagan antiquity. Likewise, the great feasts mentioned in the Bible and in the *Iliad* and the *Odyssey* fulfilled the same function as the potlatch. The resemblance between the myths of the Carrier and those of the ancients was even more striking. The adventures of the legendary Indian lads who journeyed to the land of the shades presented "remarkable analogies with those ascribed by the Greeks and Latins to Theseus and Hercules, Orpheus and Aeneas." Morice compared the Carrier creation myth to Genesis and identified Oestas, its hero, with Christ, since both figures were reputedly born of virgins. More mundane aspects of the Carrier culture, like the manner of wearing the hair, were also subjected to crosscultural analysis.[30]

But this concern for comparisons was often taken too far, and it became one of the weaknesses of Morice's scholarly writing. He continually used the existence of similarities in the languages or customs of two groups to build a case for ethnic affinity. He was not alone in this frequently fanciful search for racial origins. Many of his predecessors and contemporaries in the field of anthropology and linguistics dedicated themselves almost entirely to this quest.[31] Morice did not. The theory of ethnic affinity he put forward was an unwarranted and unfortunate by-product of his thorough research and exposition rather than the raison d'être of that research, as was apparently the case with Petitot.

Morice's boyhood hero had been passionately committed to combating the atheistic theory that mankind was made up of different species, each with its own distinct origin. Combining this aim with the traditional desire of Catholic missionaries to identify their beloved converts with the Christian tradition, Petitot came up with the not very novel idea that his Dénés were one of the lost tribes of Israel.[32] Morice came to the same conclusion, but he was more circumspect. In his works published before 1896, the Dénés-Israelite link was only alluded to in footnotes. His reticence was no doubt a result of his less religious turn of mind and his greater familiarity with the more scientific work now being done by English-speaking Americanists like Boas.[33]

Morice was less inhibited in his claims about the general relationship between language and race. His attempt to increase the use of language in ethnology constituted both the greatest strength and the major weakness of his work. The notion that language was the only acceptable proof of racial origin became his favourite hobby-horse, and he rode it with the same gusto and reckless abandon which marked his other exploits. As far as he was concerned, the fact that two groups spoke the same language made it "certain" that they were of common ancestry. This held true even when the groups in question had distinctive physiques and personalities, as he claimed the various Dénés tribes had. He rejected as invalid the common theory that similar myths and customs established ethnic affinity, because many myths were either universal or learned from neighbours. As well, ethnically distinct groups with no history of contact often had identical ritual observances.[34] He conveniently forgot this wise stricture, however, when he wanted to argue that a ritual which accompanied the sequestration of pubescent Carrier girls might be a "vestige" of a Jewish ritual of the same kind.[35]

A more important inconsistency was his failure to realize that language was not a constant—that it could be abandoned or learned just like myths and customs. Much of the deductive logic Morice so proudly applied to other areas of research was similarly flawed. Like most of his contemporaries, Morice lacked a genuine awareness that his ethnocentric biases led to racial stereotyping. His faulty logic and fondness for stereotypes are clear in his study of the influence of the coastal tribes on Carrier culture. The weakness of Morice's use of such stereotypes is obvious, and in this particular case, the linguistic evidence supporting his thesis made it redundant. Morice's tendency to generalize and to tackle major ethnographic problems rather than to concentrate on smaller, more detailed studies has been criticized by a later student of the Dénés. But, on the basis of an analysis of all Morice's writings concerning the Carrier, the same critic admitted that he was

> impressed by Morice's abilities. He was not a trained observer . . . but he was . . . less anthropologically naive than are most people in comparable situations. He combines excellent reporting, born of his intimate knowledge and extended observations of the Carrier, with anthropological interests and approaches.[36]

Although his academic writing was a serious undertaking, it was also a recreation. Writing is a solitary pursuit and had natural attractions for a withdrawn and unsociable man like Morice. The kind of writing he did was also well suited to his personality. It was the literary counterpart of his successful search for an exotic earthly haven far from the constraints of his own civilization. A scholarly dedication to the enchanting language and alien culture of the Carrier reinforced his physical marginality, yet at the same time, it was a way of obtaining recognition within his own society.

Success in his homeland would, he hoped, be guaranteed by the publication of his massive French-Carrier dictionary. The meticulous compilation required for this work began as early as 1884 when Morice taught at the Oblate school at Williams Lake. Serving as his principal reference book, the dictionary constantly grew, and in February of 1894 Morice had received an assurance that it would be published in Paris by the same prosperous patron who had backed Petitot. The printing was supposed to begin in 1895, but Morice felt that he needed more time. He applied to Bishop Durieu for permission to journey to France to supervise the printers, as Petitot had done.[37] Obviously hoping for the same honours that had been bestowed on his predecessor—Petitot's shortcomings as a linguist and anthropologist were by now subjects for footnotes in Morice's articles— Morice was extremely happy when permission was granted for him to leave in May 1896.[38] That gave him two writing seasons to perfect his work. Although he was away most of the spring and summer on his protracted tours, his sedentary fall and winter gave him plenty of time for academic activities.

This need to write and to succeed as a writer was incompatible with his vocation. There can be little doubt that Morice neglected his priestly duties and that the Indian chiefs and their watchmen were expected to keep things in order with their whips. When he was at his desk, he did not appreciate being "disturbed" by Indians in need of counsel or medicine. Yet, he did not mind bothering Murray with requests for ink erasers, "fine pointed" pens, and, when his ink was not to his liking, "for a little of yours."[39] Despite Morice's tendency to spoil pages, the dictionary was nearing completion early in 1896. Then doubts about its publication began to be expressed. His patron apparently lost much of his fortune in the Panama fiasco, and he had either withdrawn his backing or was thinking of doing so.[40]

Fortunately Morice's literary bow had a second string. Simultaneously with his linguistic efforts, he was working on a "popular volume" which described his missionary journeys and adventures. Titled *Au pays de l'ours noir. Chez les Sauvages de la Colombie Britannique,* the book's main claim to academic merit was to be its map. Morice contended that he would probably not have undertaken his geographical explorations without the requests for information sent by a member of the *Société de géographie de Paris.*[41] This is hard to believe. Petitot had been honoured as an explorer and cartographer, and Morice must have wanted to emulate and surpass him in this as in other fields. Perhaps of equal importance, however, was Morice's zest for exploration. The desire for power and reputation was what drove this British Columbian Livingstone. Like the English explorer, Morice loved both the thrill of being the first white to see a lake or mountain and the glory to be gained from that discovery. To satisfy it, he battled cold winds and snow to discover the beautiful Lake Morice and scaled the precipitous flanks of Mount Morice. These conquests were physically demanding, and Morice was not endowed with Livingstone's extraordinary strength and stamina. The Indians regarded him as a poor walker, and he never mastered the art of snowshoeing.[42] His determination and courage compensated for this physical ineptitude, and, in turn, they were to some extent the result of his desire to overcome it.

Yet despite its hardships, Morice enjoyed exploring. To plunge into unknown territory in the company of his loyal Indian guides and porters was an adventure and the most complete of all his escapes from the trammels of civilization. He was intoxicated by the landscape, particularly the austere beauty of the mountains, and he soared to the heights of rhetorical extravagance when describing them:

> Et quelles montagnes! Forteresses aux remparts crénelés, cathédrales gothiques ou byzantines avec vigoureux contre-forts, scies colossales qui fendent les nues, gigantesques pyramides qui ont peut-être l'âge de ces étoiles vers lesquelles elles portent leurs blancs sommets.[43]

The mountains were another and wilder world inhabited by ferocious bears and fickle spirits. In this world, the Indians' skills and superstitions came to the fore and became essential parts of the epic adventure. Their keen eyes spotted bears and other prey that Morice would never have noticed, and they were sure that rain fell on them because the mountains were disconcerted by the presence of strangers. If they blackened their faces with charcoal, they told their priest, the mountain spirits would let them pass unmolested. Naturally, he ignored this advice, though in more mundane matters Morice sometimes had to comply with Indian judgments. On one occasion, the exhausted and limping priest was forced, after a long day's march above the tree-line, to push on until they reached the trees again because his guide, the Sikani chief Karta, refused to camp without firewood.[44]

For most of the time, however, it was Morice who was in charge, and from time to time he had to assert his authority to prevent desertions from his expeditions. It is a wonder that there were not any mutinies, for he expected the Indians accompanying him to transport, feed, and guide him free of charge, as they did when he travelled on church business. Instead of being lucratively engaged in trapping, fishing, gardening, or wage labour, these men found themselves packing heavy loads, building rafts and canoes, poling or paddling their craft while Morice sketched the course of the rivers, hunting his food when he slept in late in the mornings, carrying him across waterways, and helping him with his cartography — sometimes from atop a mountain. The Indian, according to Morice, was "a born topographer" with a "wonderful capacity" for identifying features of the terrain he had traversed.[45] Later in his life, he acknowledged the great debt he owed to his Indian guides. They helped him even though they neither understood what he was doing — his perennial sketching was a source of amusement and the butt of witty remarks — nor stood to gain in any way from their exertions. Some of them came with him unwillingly and frequently needed to be reminded of their promises to keep them from turning back.[46]

As well as taking up the Indians' time, Morice's expeditions caused him to further neglect his missionary duties. To begin with, his trips were limited in scope and involved nothing more than finding a new way to return to Fort St. James from his summer tours. In 1893, for example, he made his way back from Hazelton via Takla Lake and Middle River rather than by the usual Babine Lake route. But in the spring of 1895, his Kodak camera arrived, and he was determined to explore in order to take pictures for his book and to collect data for his map. Hence he made plans for two expeditions, one to the north in July and the other to the southwest in September.[47] He refused to postpone or abandon his fall expedition even though Loring had sent a letter to Natléh to request his aid in settling disputes at Stuart Lake. The Indians too wanted him to come, but since it was his last chance to explore before leaving for France, he chose to ignore their appeals.[48]

He was not so pressed for time on his first expedition of the 1895 exploring season. Begun in mid-July, he undertook this trip with the intention of mapping the northern part of his district and at the same time visiting the northern Sikani. In May, two of his "best Indians" from Stuart Lake agreed to be his guides and porters, and they promised to meet him at a village on Lake Takla on 13 July. Arriving from his annual summer mission at Babine, Morice found that Duncan Paquette, a métis, and Robert, an Indian, were as good as their word. But that did not mean that they were enthusiastic. In fact, on the very first day of the journey, a Saturday, Robert announced that he had had enough and would return home on Monday. During the Sunday rest, Morice had a private chat with the fickle young man, and on the following day he was still with the party as it entered the Driftwood River.[49]

Robert and Duncan had to paddle their dugout against the current to the river's source near Bear Lake. The log dams and swarms of mosquitoes made the job laborious and tedious. The one consolation was that the mosquitoes tormented the animals as well as the men and provided the explorers with their first kill. Pestered by the insects, a bear fled to the river in full view of Morice's hunters. Once they had dispatched it, he stood them on either side of the trophy and proudly took his first photograph. Unfortunately, Robert moved his arm and spoiled the shot; but this was just the beginning of Morice's photographic headaches. He wanted some pictures of older Indians, especially the labret-wearing Babines, but they feared that the "mysterious box" would capture their second souls. The removal of this second soul or life force was believed to be a major cause of illness. Generally, it was purloined by an evil shaman or the spirit of an animal, and unless it was restored by elaborate shamanistic rituals, death would ensue. Since the curing rites were not always successful, it is not surprising that some natives did not want to court disaster. Whenever Morice broached the subject, they laughed, as much as to say, "We are not so foolish as you think we are." This fear was not shared by Duncan and Robert, probably because they were younger and came from the more acculturated bands of the Fort St. James area.[50]

Three days after the bear was shot and photographed, the group was joined by a member of the tribe which Morice considered to be perhaps the most primitive in British Columbia. Morice's party spotted the snow-capped mountains surrounding Bear Lake on 17 July. In the morning of the next day, they encountered a trio of ragged Indians. One of them, a man of about twenty, eagerly shook the priest's hand and identified himself as Baptiste, a member of the Sikani band at Bear Lake. The other two kept their distance, which was enough to tell Morice that they were "Atnas"—Gitksans—and probably Protestants to boot. His constant recourse to ethnic stereotypes combined with his romantic attachment to the various Déné tribes to reinforce the implicit division of spheres of influence between Protestant and Catholic missionaries. Father Morice never attempted to convert non-Déné Indians he came across. Indeed, he seems to have despised them, and he was glad to see Baptiste leave his Gitksan companions in order to travel with him.[51]

As his little party approached Bear Lake the next day, they heard the horn calling the faithful to evening prayers. For Morice, the Sikani seem to have been the "noble savages" par excellence—honest, generous, and naive. The Bear Lake Sikani had been temporarily joined by a group of Nahani—known also as the Takltan, a Déné people who lived to the north in the Stikine Valley. Morice was pleased with their participation in his five-day mission, but he was most disappointed when they refused to lend him two guides to add to his party for the long overland trek from Bear Lake to Fort Graham on the Finlay. They had heard that the priest was a poor walker, and the terrain was so difficult that they feared that they might have to abandon him en route. Their gloomy descriptions and predictions discouraged Duncan, and he decided to turn back; naturally Robert wanted to follow suit. As it turned out, however, they were more cowed by the reality of Morice's firmness than by the alleged hazards of the mountains to the north.[52]

Undaunted by the Nahanis' pessimism, Father Morice persuaded Karta, the Sikani chief, whose name meant "the eye of the hare," to be his guide. He would be assisted by a young man named Thomas. The true exploration was now to begin. On 26 July, the five-man, two-dog expedition left Bear Lake, the Indians and dogs bearing loads while Morice contented himself with his camera. They ascended from the lake to a height of 6,000 feet and onto the snow fields. Stopping at the tree-line on the opposite side of the mountain for the night, they continued their descent the following day. Nearing the headwaters of the Omineca River, they found themselves wading through bogs covered with fine grass and dotted with grizzly bear tracks. Once they reached the river, Robert was obliged to carry Morice across the torrents that ran into it. On 30 July their climb out of the Omineca Valley began. The criss-crossing of fallen tree trunks made for hard going, but things got worse at the higher elevations. Between and underneath the tree trunks lay jagged rocks and holes hidden by moss and bramble bushes. But for Morice at least, this penance was more than compensated for by the beauty of the ocean of mountains he could now see. The Indians usually hunted groundhogs while he sat and contemplated the mountains. A good hunt boosted their spirits and prompted them to jump cheerfully from rock to rock with their heavy loads.[53]

Their attitude towards the mountains was diametrically opposed to that of their priest, and it reveals the enormous cultural ravine that separated them from him. The Indians were content to propitiate the spirits of the mountains and to be free from hunger. But Morice's ambitions were of a different kind—of a different world. He sought an absolute transcendent freedom, perhaps even from his own troubled spirit. Yet, he could not escape his will to power. Instead of feeling impotent before nature and trying to appease it as his guides did, Father Morice was determined to conquer it. Mountains were there to be climbed and lakes to be sounded and measured; the naming of each was a mark of their conquest and possession. These names on the map would immortalize him, perpetually setting him apart. And whereas the Indians constantly sought spiritual cooperation in their struggle for survival, the conquering priest seems to have turned to God only rarely.[54]

He certainly needed a little divine assistance at times. Karta was now following a hunting trail, and as usual Morice was straggling behind. Since the "trail" was nothing more than an occasional axe mark on a tree or a bent and dried-up willow branch, Morice had to keep looking ahead. So he frequently tripped and fell. Disorientated when he got to his feet, he would go the wrong way and have to shout for assistance. But he was most at the mercy of the Indians at river crossings. On 31 July for example, the party was following a river, which Morice had named after his guide Duncan, when the way was blocked by another river flowing into it. The waters were deep and swift, and all the Indians refused to carry Morice across. Finally Robert put one of the dogs' leather packs on his shoulders to ensure that the water did not reach Morice, hoisted him up, and waded in. The mosquitoes quickly zeroed in on the immobilized priest, who instinctively began to defend himself. At that point, Robert gravely warned him to sit still or risk a soaking. He submitted on that occasion, but a few days later he refused to heed Duncan's appeals for caution as they approached a rapids. When they heard the thunder of water in the distance, they brought their two rafts to the shore and sent Duncan ahead to reconnoitre. Convinced that shooting the rapids would endanger their lives, Duncan recommended that they unload and portage. But Morice and the others were enjoying the restful ride with the current after a long arduous march, and they preferred to risk the rapids.[55]

Fortunately, the raftsmen came through with just a soaking, and they continued on towards Fort Graham at what seemed like the speed of an express train. Leaving the newly baptized "Raft River"—probably modern Pelly Creek—as it swung south, the party once again took to the land for the last leg of their journey. At about three o'clock on the afternoon of 5 August, they spotted the Finlay River. Descending into its valley, they reached Fort Graham that evening. Morice had planned to meet the Sikani band which traded at the fort; it was to be the climax of the exploration. But apart from Billy Fox, the métis in charge of the fort, there was only one Sikani family in residence. For the next few days, they searched the neighbourhood and, in spite of the torrential rain, tried to send smoke signals. Alas, contact was not made with the band of forty or so which was hunting in the nearby mountains, and on 10 August Morice borrowed a boat from Billy Fox and left with Duncan and Robert to return to Fort St. James via the much travelled Finlay-Parsnip route. Karta and Thomas prepared to retrace their steps back to Bear Lake.[56]

Morice must have felt like a conquering hero as he descended the Finlay. Everything had gone so well, and in the evening of the first day on the river, he finally encountered a band of Sikani. The next day was a Sunday, and so he decided to camp with them. They lived up to their reputation for generosity: the women prepared his camp, the youngsters fetched firewood, and the men presented him with mocassins and such delicacies as caribou tongue and moose snout. When he bid them adieu on Monday morning, they provisioned the party with bear, caribou, and moose meat in exchange for a few trifles, which made the last leg of the water-borne journey particularly carefree. On 17 August, Morice arrived at Fort McLeod just a few minutes ahead of Donald Prince, who was bringing his horse from Stuart Lake. Donald arrived exactly according to the plan made four months before. The next day, a Sunday, Morice spent sounding McLeod Lake and chatting until after midnight with Mr. William Ware, the Hudson's Bay Company clerk. Taking a letter from Ware to Murray with him, Morice rode out of Fort McLeod on the morning of Monday, 19 August. His companions were provided with horses too, though Duncan probably wished that he had not been. After posing as an experienced horseman in the presence of the Sikani, who had no horses, he was so fearful once in the saddle that he tied himself on. But they all reached Fort St. James safely on 24 August, more than five weeks after their journey began.[57]

Following a week's rest at the fort and an eight-day mission at Natléh, Father Morice planned to set off on his second and last expedition of the season. It was a frantic affair. Anxious to add more places and names to his map before leaving for France, he watched the snow fall while waiting at Natléh for his messenger to return from Fort St. James with a new sounding line. On the evening of 11 September, Morice's courier arrived back with a message from Loring appealing for assistance. But it fell on deaf ears, and Morice began his journey to the headwaters of the Nechako

River before darkness. By morning they had reached Fond du Lac, at the far end of Fraser Lake, where they borrowed a large canoe. They portaged it a few miles to Lake François and hoisted sail. Heading in a north-westerly direction, they passed a good sized encampment of hunters. But despite the hunters' beckoning fusillade, Morice disappointed his companions by ordering them to pass the hunters by. Curious about the identity of the discourteous voyageurs, the hunters gave chase and caught up with Morice when he stopped for the night. From them he learned that the camp he had passed was made up of about twenty Babines, including Denys, who was famous for having stared down a grizzly bear. His compatriots imagined that he had great magical powers. Morice claimed Denys as a friend, and in the morning they departed together after prayers.[58]

At about ten o'clock the canoe was beached, and Morice and three of his men began the walk to Cambie Lake—the modern Ootsa Lake—where they expected to find a canoe for their use. The other two Indians in the party returned to Fond du Lac with the big canoe. The three who remained were, Morice claimed, canoemen and porters rather than guides. They were not familiar with the terrain and were therefore dependent on the compass or "the box which directs the walk," as they called it. While they frequently got lost and were soaked by rain, they were less prone to discouragement than Duncan and Robert. As far as Morice was concerned, his companions were the most obliging imaginable.[59] The most stalwart of this loyal trio was Thomas Thautil, who ten years before had ridden to Fort St. James to bring Morice to the bedside of his dying brother, Isaac Qasyak. Perhaps Isaac's recovery put the brothers in the priest's debt; they certainly attributed his survival to Morice's intervention. In any case, Thomas had become Morice's regular sacristan and Mass server, and both he and Isaac helped with his explorations. On this occasion, Thomas was accompanied by Isaac's son, John Stené, and his nephew, William Khétloh. The fact that all his helpers from Natléh, both in 1895 and on future trips, were related to Isaac further suggests that the family felt a special loyalty towards Morice. This would explain why Thomas and the others obliged him without the pressure he exerted to keep Duncan and Robert going.[60]

The exploration from Natléh did not, however, require the long over-land treks that had characterized the slog from Bear Lake to Fort Graham. The walk from Lake François to Cambie Lake was the longest of the whole journey. They should have covered the fifteen or so miles that separated the two lakes in one day, but they got lost, wasted a day, and then had to travel on a Sunday to make up the time. On reaching Ootsa Lake, which Morice named Cambie after the surveyor who had visited it in

1876, they could not find the canoe that was supposed to be waiting for them. Morice never explained why he expected a canoe to be at this remote spot. They certainly needed one, and Thomas was therefore sent to catch up with Denys. But his only canoe belonged to a 'pagan' Hotsoten from Rocher Déboulé, who explained to Morice that it was the only one his party had. They were just beginning their fall hunt, Nakon pointed out, and if they lent Morice the canoe, they would have no way of getting it back. Morice had no choice but to get his men to fell a poplar tree and carve a dugout of their own. Once again their efforts were dogged with bad luck. Thomas gashed his foot with an axe and had to rest. Finally, as the canoe was near completion, the forcing in of a cross-piece split it in two.[61]

Taking pity on the hapless Christians, Nakon gave them his canoe. With their food supply depleted by the constant delays, they headed across the lake to its western outlet. After they left the turbulent waters of Cambie Lake, Morice and his companions entered a wide river he called the Dawson after a correspondent in England. (Today it is known as Whitesail Reach.) When the river seemed to turn into a small lake after a short distance, Morice named it Lake Sinclair, after the Hudson's Bay Company clerk at Fort Fraser. This discovery and naming process continued, and on 19 September, he named what was apparently a small lake in honour of his Indian companion Thomas.[62] But "Lake Thomas" turned out to be a bay which opened out into a magnificent expanse of water surrounded by glaciers and peaks covered with perpetual snow. Surely, Morice thought, such beauty would draw tourists. It would also attract attention, and, consequently, the lake soon found itself submitting to a new baptism—as Lake Morice. In one book Morice claimed that Thomas, realizing that the lake was "altogether too important," had immediately insisted on the new name.[63] Elsewhere, he attributed this insistence to all the Indians.[64] When he was drawing his big map in 1904, he claimed that he had not changed the name in 1895. Supposedly he finally put his own name to the lake because the Indians had persisted in calling it "Morice" when talking to whites. Thus, he was simply recognizing "le fait accompli" and thereby avoiding the confusion that would have resulted if he had reverted to Thomas.[64] Yet the lake bore Morice's name on the map he included in his *Au pays de l'ours noir* in 1897.[66] What probably happened was that Thomas was coaxed into suggesting the name change as soon as Morice realized the lake's impressive dimensions. Almost certainly, the Indian cared more about returning home safely and quickly than he did about what the egocentric explorer called the big lake he knew as Oeteauh Youtsou. The notion of naming places after people was foreign to the natives. Their geographical nomenclature was more descriptive and utilitarian.

The large island in the lake was, for instance, called the isle on which the bear eludes us, which eloquently described its size in terms a Carrier hunter understood.[67]

After much sounding and sketching, they left Lake Morice behind in the evening of 20 September. From now on they would be heading toward Natléh and home. The first leg of this return journey was a short portage around the rapids that led to yet another lake, which Morice named for Father Lejacq, perhaps to forestall criticism of Morice's use of his own name. Further on, a smaller lake was given the name of Chief Factor Murray.[68] On future expeditions, Morice honoured the Indian agent and the Indian affairs superintendent at Victoria. Morice undoubtedly expected these influential men to be flattered, and in a sense his geographical baptisms became a kind of prestige patronage. In this doling out of honours, the Indians who made the exploration possible were left with the consolation prizes. When Morice's map of the Northern Interior was completed, the bay which opened out into Lake Morice was marked as St. Thomas Bay. Ironically, this is the only name which Morice applied on that expedition which has survived. Today, Lake Morice is known as Lake Eutsuk, an abbreviated and corrupt version of the native name.[69]

The string of smaller lakes to the north of Eutsuk flow into the Nechako River, and when Morice's men saw its fast flowing waters, they knew that the journey was nearly over. Since leaving the big lake they had been tired, cold, and hungry. Although they did all the hard work, rations were not pooled; Morice fared better than they did. On Sunday, 22 September, all they had to eat between them was a fish which they had found floating dead on the water. To add to their difficulties, the next day they discovered that the rapids on the Nechako were too dangerous to shoot and too long to portage with Nakon's canoe. They had to abandon the boat, hoist its cargo onto their backs, and continue on foot towards the village of Pelkatchek at the eastern end of Cheslatta Lake, known to the Oblates as Lac Ste. Marie. Once again, Morice had arranged to end his exploration by visiting a group of natives who lived beyond the limits of his missionary tours. They were expecting him and fêted the explorers like heroes when they learned that they had traversed lakes Dawson and Morice, the depths of which they believed to be inhabited by enormous marine grizzly bears.[70] No wonder the men from Natléh had wanted to hug the shore-line!

On 25 September, Morice heard the public confessions of the whole village, blessed the tombs of their dead, and then departed in the large but rotten canoe which they lent him. The next day his companions were home, but Morice had to spend another two days on the trail between Natléh and Fort St. James. He arrived there on 28 September. Except for a short stopover in July, he had been travelling since 13 May.[71] Yet despite the rigorous terrain and climate, the wandering priest was in excellent form. The isolation from contact with other Europeans and the constant physical activity which wilderness travel provided had the same therapeutic effect on Morice as they had on David Livingstone, who was depressed, morose, and withdrawn when he was forced to live in one place with other whites. Morice also shared with Livingstone and Petitot their preference for the company of natives; none of these missionary explorers could establish or maintain amicable relations with their white colleagues.[72] But both Morice and Livingstone had an uncanny ability to command loyalty and great physical effort from their native guides and porters.[73]

In Morice's case at least, the Indians were perhaps more tolerant than loyal. They were not prepared to risk the upheaval that would inevitably result from the frustration of his domineering drive. Not only was conflict abhorrent to them, but the material and spiritual benefits they received from contact with the white men could be jeopardized if the requests of a powerful priest were refused. In particular, his supernatural and secular intercession might no longer be available to them. Similar motives aided Livingstone, who was provided with porters by African kings and chieftains who believed his promises to help them against their enemies and to establish remunerative trade links with Europe. But among Livingstone's most devoted African helpers were men who owed him great personal debts; he had rescued them from slave traders and treated them with more kindness than he ever displayed towards his European companions.[74] And the relationship was comparable to that of Morice with Isaac Qasyak's relatives.

Now that his exploration was over, Morice applied himself to the presentation of his findings. The snow had fallen steadily as he and his companions made their way back from their geographical tour, and during the ensuing winter, he recorded these and his other adventures and prepared his map. At the same time, he completed the final draft of his French-Carrier dictionary. All these manuscripts were to be ready for his long-awaited return to France. Although Morice claimed that his French sojourn would provide him with a physical rest, this need was far from urgent.[75] Apart from the occasional lung trouble that followed his accidental overdose, his health, particularly his mental health, had actually improved since his arrival at Fort St. James.[76] His main purpose for the trip was official recognition.

On 4 May 1896, Father Morice left for France. As the bishop had nobody to replace Morice, the elderly Father Blanchet was sent down to stay with his old friend Father Lejacq at Williams Lake.[77] Murray was a little anxious about the departure of the two priests. He told the company manager in Victoria that since he had become chief factor, both priests had influenced the Indians to trade at home, and he feared that their absence would adversely affect business.[78] When he passed through Natléh and Quesnel on his way south, Morice was confronted with fears of a different kind. At Natléh he found the whole band crying fretfully because a giant as big as a mountain had been seen walking on snow-shoes in the woods. Having calmed this hysteria, he arrived at Quesnel only to be overwhelmed with questions about an apocalyptic rumour that was circulating in the area. The Quesnel Carrier had heard that the Pope was predicting three days of complete darkness from which only those who possessed holy candles would emerge alive.[79] While they might not have liked Morice, as Murray contended, the Indians naturally turned to him in such times of anxiety. As a priest, he was the representative of the Pope and of God, both powerful entities. They, like Murray, had come to rely on him, and like Murray, they were prepared to tolerate his egotistical and domineering ways.

6

"KING OF THE COUNTRY"

Father Morice spent a busy and fruitful year in France. Although his Carrier-French dictionary was not published, *Au pays de l'ours noir* was. Apart from seeing this work through the press, he travelled to the Juniorate at Sion and the college at Nancy, where he seems to have taught English for a while.[1] But he could not live at ease in the France of the Third Republic or, indeed, in any essentially European community. Morice was never more than a sojourner among whites, and he was always happy to return to what he called his "element Indian life and environment"[2] on the shores of Stuart Lake.

On 26 June 1897, Morice arrived back at Fort St. James—just in time for the 1 July horse races and tug-of-war contests. The white participants were no match for the Indians, who made a clean sweep of the prizes. Among the white merrymakers was a party of prospectors down from the Omineca mines to collect provisions, and at least three other groups had passed through in June. Since Morice's departure in the spring of 1896, there had been a revival of interest in these mines. Consequently, the number of whites and Chinese in the area had increased, and Indians began to work for them as miners, guides, and packers. Most of these Indian workers were Gitksan, since the miners tended to come in via the Skeena. Some ten whites and sixteen Chinese wintered at Hazelton between the 1896 and 1897 mining season. Few, if any, stayed in the Fort St. James area, though a number did pass through.[3] But when the 1898 Klondike rush began, this transient trickle was to become a torrent which threatened to wash away the props of Morice's power as a priest and broker.

But in the summer of 1897, these storm clouds were just appearing on the horizon. Morice's traditional rivals, the Hudson's Bay Company officials, were probably glad to have him back. As Murray had feared, the departure of Morice and Blanchet was followed by an increase in the number of furs taken to Quesnel. Despite poor prices paid there in the summer, Taya and another senior trapper and their respective followers had taken down their fall hunts in mid-October 1896. Taya had had a "magnificent" beaver hunt, Murray recorded bitterly in his journal, and he wanted to "show his spleen with the Coy."[4] Murray was apparently unaware that Father Blanchet was returning early to the fort and that Taya might have been asked to fetch him from Quesnel. But even so, it was no excuse, for Taya took with him all but the few furs he had traded at the fort to get provisions for the trip. Powerless to stop the morose chieftain, the trader angrily confided to his journal his hope that Taya would get "cinched" by low prices and frozen in to boot. His first wish came true, and the Hudson's Bay post at Quesnel ended up buying most of the furs. The trading done, Taya returned to the fort with Blanchet on 7 November.[5] Murray was no doubt happy to have the popular Blanchet back; he might help to keep the Indians trading at the fort.

But Blanchet could not help with another trading problem linked to Morice's absence. The fur intake at Fort Fraser—and probably at other posts located near Oblate meeting places—was down, and Sinclair, the clerk there, attributed it, in part at least, to Morice's absence.[6] With no gatherings at nearby Natléh for the customary missions in the spring, fall, and Christmas, some trappers presumably took their furs elsewhere. Indians from the Fort Fraser area sometimes travelled as far as Bella Coola in search of better prices and superior goods. They would take with them the furs of their confrères, together with "memos" written in syllabics listing the goods they desired. The Bella Coola trade so worried the Honourable Company that it took the trouble of having one of those lists deciphered by Fort St. James' Indians—only to be disappointed when it revealed no trade secrets.[7] Ever fretful about keeping their trappers "at home," the company's officers obviously appreciated the value of the regular missions given at their posts by itinerant missionaries like Morice.

Morice's visits were always recorded by Sinclair in the Fort Fraser journal, and when the priest made his first visit to Natléh after his return from France, Sinclair noted that he looked "well and hearty." That was in early September 1897, and Sinclair's entries show that Morice quickly took up the routine he had developed before he left for France: he spent a week on his mission, during which time an Indian was dispatched to Stuart Lake for supplies, and at the conclusion of the mission he left for a week on

what Sinclair was told was an "Exploratory Survey."[8] As well as record-
ing Morice's comings and goings, Sinclair noted many incidents in the Indians' economic and social life, including potlatches and gambling. It is
not clear whether or not Morice was apprised of these activities. He would
certainly have been interested to know that during his absence in France
the Chislata people had visited Natléh for "Cemetery Ceremonies" organized by the chief following his wife's death and that Stuart Lake Indians who came to buy salmon had played "Naras," the traditional game
of chance, with the local menfolk.[9]

But even if Sinclair did keep such things to himself, Morice must have
heard about the potlatches from his various agents at Fort St. James and
elsewhere. Yet he did not confront the Indians who dutifully gathered for
the mission at Natléh with these "public faults." Loring too chose to ignore the potlatch. He justified his decision to his superiors by pointing out
that the enforcement of the anti-potlatch law would disturb his agency; it
was better to let the custom die a natural death.[10] Possibly, Morice permitted the "Cemetery Ceremonies" because they were not traditional potlatches. The house-like tombs were a fairly recent innovation, and though
their erection was accompanied by a potlatch, they were also blessed by
the priest. It is more likely, however, that Morice had decided that since
the Fraser Lake people were in other respects humble, obedient, and generous, there was no good reason to expend effort combatting the potlatch;
there were more important things to do. Morice was interested above all in
power and acclaim, and having established himself as a feared patron in
the Indian society and as an indispensible broker for the whites, he increasingly directed his energy toward exploration and publication. Indeed, he spent as much of his fall tour exploring as in giving his Natléh
mission.

He should have hurried back to Fort St. James as soon as the mission
was over. Father Blanchet had been ill for some time, and in an article
written for the *Petites Annales* in 1898, Morice explained that because of
his fears about the old priest's condition, he made his absences from the
fort as short as possible. This hardly accords with the entries in Sinclair's
journal reporting him off exploring "towards the Mud River" between 15
and 22 September.[11] At that time the ailing and partially blind Blanchet
was alone at the mission, waiting for a boat to take him down to live out
the rest of his days with Father Lejacq at Williams Lake. Morice clearly
felt some attachment to his socius and he later complained of loneliness.
Yet his obsessive egotism—in this particular circumstance, his desire to
acquire more information for his future map—prevented him from re-
sponding to his companion's need. When Father Blanchet left on 11 October, he was, according to Morice, accompanied by the good wishes and

the affection of the whole Indian population.[12] In 1974, old people at Fort St. James still had pleasant memories of Father Blanchet. John Prince, son of Joseph Prince's younger brother, Louis Billy, recalled Blanchet's frequent visits to people in their homes and his carpentry work. Indeed, Georges Blanchet seems to be remembered more as a church builder than as a cleric.[13] This no doubt reflects the fact that he was less prominent as a religious figure after Morice's appointment as mission director in 1888. From then on, Morice's spiritual direction of the Fort St. James mission and the various meeting places went unchallenged.

That was about to change. Some two weeks after Blanchet left, the Fort St. James journal notes that Father Marchal had arrived to take charge of the Mission.[14] Marchal had been director of the mission in the early 1880's, and since he was to be the resident priest at Stuart Lake, it is not surprising that he was put "in charge" once again. Similarly, it was no shock to those who knew Morice's history to learn that the appointment of a superior sparked a fiery conflict and led quickly to his rebellion. Marchal was himself an authoritarian person who had disapproved of Blanchet's fraternization with the Indians.[15] Consequently, he would not resign himself to serving Morice as Blanchet had done. Probably, however, the mutual resentment at the priests' house just smouldered until after the 1897 touring and festive season was over and Morice settled in at the mission for a winter of writing and printing.

All Saints and Christmas were important feast days for the Catholic Carrier. "Big Sunday," as they called All Saints' Day, was celebrated most extravagantly at Fort St. James. People travelled to the fort from all directions, and Father Marchal was likely brought up by a group of pilgrims from Fort George. Naturally, many trappers brought their fall hunts with them, and in 1897 the new chief factor, W. E. Camsell, noted with pleasure that much fur was being traded.[16] Sinclair made similar entries in his journal at Christmas time, when Indians braved the weather to travel from Fort St. James, Fort George, and elsewhere to witness the Christmas pageant at Natléh. Things were busy at Fort Fraser for days before Christmas, and on Christmas Eve there was a flood of requests for cash to be offered to the Church for a look at the wax Jesus figure. Fur-trading was carried on even on Christmas Day, and Sinclair seemed happy enough with the impact that the feast had on his business affairs.[17]

Potlatching was another matter. According to Sinclair's journal, for much of the month of November and the early part of December 1897, the Natléh Indians and their potlatch partners from nearby Stella were "making [the] night hideous" with the feasting, dancing, and singing that accompanied their "Cemetery Work." When the Stella people first arrived, Jack Sutherland, one of the leading men and the chief's main rival, slaughtered a bull in their honour. Sinclair would probably have been prepared to put up with all the noise if more furs had been brought in exchange for potlatch supplies, but few were. Instead, many potlatchers came to pawn what Sinclair contemptuously called "their *trash,* which they seldom redeem."[18] Apart from bringing in fewer furs than the large Catholic gatherings, which attracted people from the wider area, the potlatches consumed far more time and apparently led to more debt and pawning. Small wonder then that Chief Factor MacFarlane had damned the potlatch as "foolish" while giving the Oblates and their festivals his full support.[19]

Nor was it difficult, it seems, for traders like MacFarlane and Sinclair to reconcile themselves to the cash drain that contributions to the Church entailed. So long as the priests bought their provisions at the fort, much of the money would end up in company coffers. Similarly, furs donated by Indians were invariably sold to the company. However, Morice managed to accumulate a surplus of alms, which was not all spent locally. He used part of it, together with money from the sale of *Au pays de l'ours noir,* to purchase an excellent and sizable new press. Earlier on in his rule at Fort St. James, he had bought himself an organ; with his new press he could freely indulge his lifelong passion for literary reproduction. Now he was able to turn out, among other things, a two-toned Prayer Book, which sold for $3, as well as a collection of his essays, written in English.[20] Had he not been removed from Fort St. James in 1903, it is likely that he would have himself printed his *Carrier Language,* which he continued to work on throughout his missionary career.

Morice was so pleased with his new press that he confessed to being "in love with her!" And although he later claimed that the machine was used "almost exclusively, for the benefit of his Indian charge," such was clearly not the case.[21] Morice had a deep-rooted need to control his environment and destiny completely; he had to own all that played an important part in his life—hence his insistence on running the mission district without financial assistance from outside and his desire to buy a modern press. With it, he could produce all the works that he felt his Indians needed and print his own material. He gained particular satisfaction from the fact that he had personally composed and printed all the prayers, hymns, and everything else in the syllabic prayer book.[22] Morice's attitude could be interpreted as a good example to his Indians of the principle of self-help. But it was a very different kind of self-help from that preached by William Duncan and other missionaries of the Protestant Church Missionary Society, who tried to cultivate Samuel Smiles's ethos of individual economic and social improvement. And, unlike his fellow Oblates, with their industrial schools and model farms, Morice never used the funds at his disposal to finance economic or social development.[23] At Williams Lake he had rejected the dull role of schoolmaster, and he never changed his mind. He did not want to teach Indians English and help them find a place in the white man's world; he wanted to rule them. But he also wanted to be noticed and praised, and having a modern printing press at his disposal would help him to gratify that desire too.

Father Marchal was a threat to these ambitions. He particularly disapproved of Morice's preoccupation with writing and printing. The printer apparently stayed up with his beloved press until late at night and then stayed in bed in the morning. His non-conformist habits obviously had not changed since his days as a delinquent seminarian. Indeed, during his years with Blanchet he had indulged them. But it was Marchal's opposition to another aspect of his printing operation that precipitated the inevitable showdown between the two priests.

The Mission had a small chapel where the priests could say their daily mass when there was no Mass being celebrated in the church. Morice had turned the chapel into a print-shop, and he refused to comply with Marchal's wish to use it for Mass. A bizarre and sacrilegious contest ensued. Marchal said Mass in the chapel and left the Blessed Sacrament—the consecrated wafer—in the tabernacle, thereby rendering the chapel too sacred for the profane operation of Morice's press, which needed "kicking" because it did not come equipped with the motor for which it was designed. A past master at passive and active resistance to authority, Morice knew exactly how to neutralize this clever coup; he said a Mass himself and consumed the Host put in the tabernacle by Marchal. This freed him to kick his press into action again—until Marchal said a second Mass and once more locked the Blessed Sacrament in the tabernacle. Naturally, Morice repeated his desanctification procedure, a procedure which again raises the question of his religious commitment. The battle of Masses continued for some time until finally, "in one of his holy inspirations, Father Morice threw the key of the tabernacle into the lake."[24] That presumably settled the matter. In any event, Marchal conceded defeat and was so anxious to flee Fort St. James that he left before the spring thaw. He was the first of a number of priests who fled from the Stuart Lake Mission because they could not tolerate Morice's behaviour. Among the Indians of Fort St. James, Father Marchal was remembered for his habit of sitting at the door of the priest's house drumming on a tin dish and singing "La Marseillaise."[25]

Although Marchal's winter retreat was a victory, Morice did not like the solitude to which it condemned him. He wanted a white companion, but one who would be totally subservient, as Miranda had been to her father, Prospero. Henceforth, he was to live without a white *socius* at the

Mission, except for two brief periods when Oblate confreres were sent to assist him and to keep him company. Morice expected these men to be his servants; they could be of no use as missionaries because, unlike him, they would spoil the Indians. This was so, Morice argued, because they had no knowledge of the Carrier language and culture.[26] Like the dictatorial William Duncan, Morice was evidently afraid that his colleagues would erode his monopoly of authority.[27] He waited in vain for a second Blanchet, someone who would do the menial work that took up his valuable time— he especially resented being his own cook[28]—while providing him with non-competitive companionship. It is hardly surprising that he found no priest willing to accept this demeaning position. What is more difficult to understand is why the bishops in New Westminster (d'Herbomez had died in 1890, and Bishop Dontenwill was consecrated as Durieu's co-adjutor and heir in 1897) tolerated Morice's cavalier treatment of Marchal and those who succeeded him. No doubt the shortage of missionaries, especially those who spoke the native language, had something to do with it.[29] Perhaps of greater importance though was the difficulty of dealing with a character like Morice, who was as incapable of recognizing his aberrant behaviour as he was of contrition and reform. He was bound to disrupt any Oblate community to which he was transferred. Durieu was probably conscious too of Morice's reputation as a missionary-savant and of his facile pen; to discipline him might provoke an embarrassing scandal. That possibility had certainly occurred to Martinet in the days when Morice was first sent to Stuart Lake.[30] The Oblate bishops found it convenient to keep Morice isolated at Stuart Lake, where he caused them no serious inconvenience. When he submitted his annual report for 1897, Bishop Durieu said very little about the Stuart Lake district because he had not been able to correspond with the Mission for six months.[31] Clearly, Morice's exile was as mutually satisfactory as ever.

But if Morice's rule was threatened by neither Marchal nor Durieu, it was to be challenged by the rush to the Klondike and by the increased mining activity on the Omineca River. The *Klondike Official Guide* published by the Canadian government in the winter of 1897–98 had exaggerated the advantages of the route from Telegraph Creek on the Stikine to Lake Teslin and thence to the Klondike. At the same time, the Telegraph Trail route from Ashcroft to Telegraph Creek was being promoted by certain newspapers, particularly the *Ashcroft Journal,* and by others who stood to gain from the opening up of this "Poor Man's Route."[32] The Telegraph Trail had been cleared in the 1860's as part of an ambitious attempt to link America and Europe via the Bering Strait, but it was abandoned after the laying of the Trans-Atlantic cable. The Trail passed through Quesnel, Stoney Creek, Natléh, Moricetown, and Hazelton, and throughout the summer of 1898, a steady procession of men, women, and pack animals trudged slowly northward. Few of them made it to their Eldorado; most returned home via the Skeena, Nass, or Stikine rivers.[33] Although the Klondikers usually by-passed Fort St. James, it was on the north-south route to the Omineca mines and therefore did not entirely escape the effects of the gold fever.

Both the Telegraph Trail and the Omineca route were long and arduous, and many travellers experienced misfortune and even disaster while traversing Morice's district. In the regular articles which he sent to the Oblate journals, Morice described the grim end met by some of them. But he was not sympathetic towards them, for he feared their effect on his district. When impoverished and disenchanted prospectors told him of their losses, which in one case included seventeen out of twenty-two horses, he chuckled to himself and thought "there's one anyhow that will not come back." Morice despised the miners because he perceived them as corrupting his Indians and spoiling his paradise.[34] In the fall of 1898, he had to admit that the description of his mission district contained in his *Au pays de l'ours noir* was no longer true: now there *were* depraved whites to hinder the missionary and Indians who thought they were civilized because they drank liquor and could speak a few words of English. The miners— rarely the cream of the race and often both lawless and Godless, as Morice put it—needed the labour of the Indian men and the companionship of the women. Their ample supplies of liquor helped them to obtain both. The Carrier men proved particularly susceptible to the temptation, whereas most of the women seem to have resisted.[35] Rape was frequent, especially at Hazelton, where the Omineca miners wintered. Drunken whites invaded the adjacent reserves and broke down doors in their quest for women.[36] In the spring of 1899, women at Rocher Déboulé—also known as Hoquel-get or Agwilgate—were made drunk, stripped, and "outraged." Their assailants further amused themselves by photographing the scene and displaying the women's underwear on sticks. The debauchers had such a hold on Hazelton in January 1898 that "pandemonium" reigned for weeks and a "pair of female under garments, stained in every conceivable manner" were run up the Hudson's Bay Company flag pole. Loring regarded such events as part of a plot to "deride" him and to undermine his authority.[37]

Morice too felt directly threatened by the miners, some of whom set out to win the Indians away from his influence. But Morice was happy to report to the readers of the *Petites Annales* that the robust faith of even the least fervent of his flock prevented them from falling into this atheistic trap. Though tempted by liquor and money—conducting pack trains made theft all too easy—they were not all attracted by the miners' free-thinking materialism. Louis Billy Prince, who seems to have replaced his older brother Joseph as Morice's principal aide, quickly rebuffed an American miner's claim that life after death was a lot of nonsense invented by the priest to keep the Indians subjugated. Since the Carrier Indians had believed in a land of the dead long before the whites arrived, this represented a double challenge. Louis Billy met it head-on: if the miner thought that he was no more than an animal, then, when he died, people would shrug and say "one dog less."[38] That apparently ended the debate.

The mining frontier also brought more insidious challenges to the status quo, and these were harder to combat. In the fall, every adult male at Fort St. James was engaged to take miners down to Quesnel in canoes. They returned with liquor, which stimulated outbreaks of violence. The very existence of new economic opportunities probably aggravated the chronic factional rivalry. It certainly led to a neglect of what Morice regarded as the Indians' proper occupations—trapping and fishing.[39] The coming of the miners accelerated the trend for many Fort St. James Indians to become a "Home Guard" of wage earners and petty contractors. In 1900, a Hudson's Bay Company inspector commented on the impact of this change at the fort:

> The Post was established in 1806 and until recently had been one of the old class. The passing of Miners, Government Officials, and Prospectors has had some effect upon the Indians, and they are getting more independant [sic] and tricky, and exorbitant in their demands.[40]

A new kind of society was emerging. The "old class" of Hudson's Bay Company fort was the centre of an aristocratic society where the chief trader, the chief, and the trappers were linked by strong bonds of mutual dependence. In return for loyalty, the company officials dispensed gratuities and charity with a sense of *noblesse oblige*. The coming of the Oblates did not destroy this society but rather led to the creation of a second and parallel aristocratic structure, with the priest at the top of the new hierarchy. The erosion of the Hudson's Bay's monopoly had begun with the growth of Quesnel during the Cariboo gold rush of the 1860's; the Klondike and Omineca rushes completed it. The mining frontier's economic individualism and its multiplicity of economic relationships meant that the Honorable Company's monopolistic and paternalistic aristocracy was replaced by the democracy of free enterprise.[41] The company officials at Fort St. James reconciled themselves to the change: they no longer expected loyalty from the chief and trappers and regarded the provision of welfare as the government's business.[42]

The gold rushes also threatened the Oblate's aristocracy. But unlike the fur traders, Morice was not prepared to relinquish his prerogatives; he counterattacked. In the fall of 1898, on his return to Fort St. James from his summer travels, he began a determined assault on the evils introduced by the miners. Towards the end of October, the bands from the villages around Stuart Lake, together with groups from further afield, began to gather at the fort for All Saints.[43] To get the people to repent and atone *en masse,* Morice had to enlist the collaboration of the chiefs and watchmen. They would enforce what Morice called the return to God.[44] But, unfortunately for the priest, their "ardeur" had cooled considerably, owing both to the temptations of the summer of 1898 and to Morice's neglect of administration in favour of exploration and writing. Having gained paramountcy, he had confidently left the repression process to his Indian aides. Disdain for the mundane routine of any assignment was a prominent feature of Morice's personality. It had rendered him a reluctant and not very successful pupil, seminarian, and schoolmaster; eventually it would lead to the loss of his missionary kingdom. He had delegated most policing and judicial functions to Indians, and the influence of the mining frontier's ethos of democratic individualism—the independence and trickiness noticed by the Hudson's Bay Company—probably made it difficult for the chiefs and watchmen to reassert their authority after Morice had rekindled their enthusiasm.

Morice designed the 1898 All Saints' *réunion* as a revival and a reconquest. He preached an eight-day retreat, the climax of which was the imposition of public penances.[45] Morice does not mention what these penances were, though they probably included whipping—usually with a blanket placed over the prone penitant—the tying of hands, and kneeling in various uncomfortable and humiliating positions. In other Oblate mission districts, sinners had to kneel at the church door, sometimes with a rope around their necks.[46] Such practices may have occurred at Fort St. James, but oral evidence suggests that Morice preferred more active chastisements. One informant, who had felt the sting of the chief's rawhide horsewhip as a young man, reported that Morice "Gave penance [to] people too much, too much whip, too much tied-up."[47] The people rarely resisted these punishments when the priest ordered them personally, but "one or two" men were reluctant to be humiliated before all those assembled for "Big Sunday." These men were probably prominent fort Indians. They assumed a rebellious stance, but when Morice refused to relent, they submitted. The missionary had emerged victorious from what was obviously a serious confrontation. By 15 November 1898, he felt confident enough to report that the Indian community at the fort had returned to its former Christian life and its trapping and fishing economy.[48]

Since this report was destined for publication, it is no doubt optimistic.

Yet it nevertheless reveals Morice's persistent opposition to the material acculturation of his subjects. Indians were suitable objects for his romantic fantasies only so long as they remained *"sauvages."* Being the curé for a sedentary population of miners, pack-train operators, and petty traders was no work for a hero. It was easier for a priest-king to exact obedience and deference from the trappers and fishers of an aristocratic fur trade society than from the wage labourers and entrepreneurs of the mining frontier. Fortunately for Morice, the Omineca mines made few fortunes, and he was able to reassert his authority after the miners departed.[49]

But many of the disruptive effects of the miners' presence remained, and pre-gold rush conditions were not easily restored. Some of the depredations suffered were more serious, if less dramatic, than Hazelton's drunken orgies. One Omineca company got a whole season of free labour from a number of Babine, Hotsoten, and Gitksan Indians. The unpaid payroll came to over $2,000, and Loring noted scornfully that it was "considered among the old time miners here [Hazelton], quite a feat, and without a parallel to have work done to such an amount without the actual outlay of a cent."[50] Loring had to provide for the duped and destitute Carrier and Gitksan, and he had to do the same for many Sikani, even though few of them had abandoned their traditional pursuits in favour of mining jobs. They were the victims of theft: miners had stolen sixty steel traps and quantities of food from their caches, something other Indians would never have done. And this had happened despite the fact that many lost or starving prospectors owed their lives to the hospitality of the Sikani. The larceny was compounded by disturbances to the hunting grounds caused by the bells of the pack animals and the tendency for campfires to become forest fires. By September 1898, Loring was concerned about racial tensions and was asking for 1,000 lbs. of flour, 200 lbs. of bacon, and equally large quantities of beans, rice, and tea to ward off the starvation of the Sikani during the forthcoming winter.[51]

These problems, together with the increased liquor traffic and factional violence at Fort St. James, meant that there was stepped-up government intervention in the Northern Interior. Loring was kept very busy, as was Mr. Ewen Bell, the Indian agent appointed to be responsible for an area which included the most southerly portion of Morice's district. The white police constable at Quesnel became much more active in Carrier affairs. On the Omineca fields, the gold commissioner, Mr. F. W. Valleau, was made a stipendary magistrate, and at Hazelton a Hudson's Bay official named R. S. Sargent was appointed a justice of the peace. The North West Mounted Police's famous Klondike expedition led by Inspector J. D. Moodie stayed for more than a month at Fort St. James in the spring of 1898. But the mounties spent most of their time hunting with the Hudson's Bay Company's officers or preparing for the next leg of their overland trek. Conditions at Fort St. James did not concern them. Similarly, Mr. Valleau, who was based at Manson Creek, eighty miles north of Fort St. James, seems to have had little to do with the maintenance of law and order in the lacustrine heartland of Morice's district, namely, Stuart Lake, Babine Lake, and Fraser Lake.[52]

The two Indian agents and Constable D. W. Anderson from Quesnel were responsible for that area. Their main concern was with the violence at Fort St. James and the liquor traffic to the fort from Quesnel. The fort's métis were the most active bootleggers. It was also they who violently resisted Chief Taya; both Joseph Prince and his brother Leon injured watchmen who tried to arrest them.[53] While they were as eager as Morice to end the liquor trade, Bell and Anderson resented the parallel police and judicial system operated by the Oblates. Like some other government officials, they seem to have regarded the spying and gossiping it involved as distasteful.[54] Loring did not share their misgivings, and he never criticized the Oblates' indirect rule system. Indeed, during the gold rush, he was so busy keeping order and trying to maintain his own power against the miners and new functionaries that he praised Morice and encouraged his superiors to allow Morice to manage things in the distant interior.[55] It was as if Loring saw his *modus vivendi* with Morice as more mutually beneficial than ever before; now they were both struggling against the onslaught of the new society of the mining frontier, which was destroying the progress toward a settled and "civilized" life as promoted by Loring and the ideal of the Christian *sauvage* cherished by Morice. Loring was just as fond of asserting his authority as Morice.[56] This trait, along with differences of opinion over the measures needed to suppress disorders, led to a bitter power struggle between Loring and Sargent, the magistrate, who was supported by a Protestant missionary and other whites.[57]

Yet instead of supporting his old friend and ally, Morice joined in the criticism of him. When he wrote to Indian Affairs Superintendent Vowell in October 1898 concerning the procurement of liquor at Quesnel, Morice complained that Loring's authority did not extend much beyond Hazelton. This assertion took Loring completely by surprise. Admitting that in emergencies his control was "less operative" in the interior, the agent nevertheless claimed that his influence was "paramount throughout this Agency."[58] But it was not true. The agency and its problems were too large for one man to handle adequately; besides, for a long time Loring had relied on Morice to cope with certain emergencies and with census-taking and welfare allocations in places distant from Hazelton.

Since Morice had always appeared happy to keep Loring away from Fort St. James, his criticism of the agent is puzzling. The most obvious explanation for it is the gravity of the liquor problem at the fort and the seeming inability or unwillingness of the watchmen to grapple with it. Morice knew that intervention by Loring would not threaten his own authority. Indeed, if the past was any guide, Loring could be counted on to bolster Morice and his indirect rule system, which was being criticized both by the Hudson's Bay Company and by the constable at Quesnel. Even after Morice's criticism, Loring was as fulsome as ever in his praise of the priest. He reported to Vowell that Morice had the Indians of the interior "well in hand."[59]

Morice's relationship with Indian Agent Bell and Constable Anderson was not so satisfactory, and his most telling criticism was reserved for them and other unco-operative officials. In a long letter written in early January 1899, Father Morice bitterly denounced the incompetence of the officials responsible for the maintenance of law and order among the southern Carrier. The well-documented brief persuasively argued that their lack of familiarity with the Indians' language and culture encouraged them to allow the innocent to suffer injustice while the guilty roamed free. Morice contrasted this ignorance with his own unique linguistic and anthropological knowledge and the bungling of legal administration with his judicious handling of Indian-white conflicts. Essentially, his letter was a declaration that given the influx of more whites, his ability to act as a broker between the two cultures should be given greater recognition; it was also a resentful and mocking attack on the pretensions of the tenderfoot functionaries of the mining frontier. He apparently wanted there to be no doubt about who was the most powerful white man in the Northern Interior of British Columbia.[60]

Morice deplored Constable Anderson's inability to stop the extensive bootlegging between Quesnel and the fort. This was not Morice's first criticism of Anderson, who, according to the priest, did not know what was going on under his nose. Despite an earlier denial by Anderson, Morice insisted that Indians got liquor "by the gallon" from whites, métis, and Chinese "middle men" at Quesnel. Some of this they then consumed in the town, behind two firewood piles known as the "Indians' Saloon." But most of the liquor was brought up to Fort George and Fort St. James on the boats of the Indian voyageurs, including Hudson's Bay Company vessels. These trips were marked by "sprees and rioting and immorality." Once they reached Fort St. James, the voyageurs cached the remaining liquor in the woods, and fighting flared up sporadically after they had recourse to it.[61] Oral evidence indicates that Indians expected each other to say "no, no, nothing" when asked if they knew anything about the bootlegging. But "pretty hard" men, presumably watchmen, would sometimes catch a drinker, "tie him up, whip him and make him quit."[62]

Morice was convinced that strict enforcement of the liquor laws at Quesnel was the real remedy. Yet he felt that Anderson's lack of experience and his reluctance to be guided by Morice militated against it. According to the missionary, Anderson rejected his information on the grounds that it came from "gossiping watchmen." As if this was not enough, Morice reported to Vowell that despite being new to the area, the policeman had had the audacity to imply that he knew its affairs better than a priest who knew by name "about all" of the Indians of the interior between the 52 and 56 degrees of latitude and whose ministry required him to learn all that happened amongst them. Morice dismissed Anderson's alleged claim as "simply preposterous." He then proceeded to present precise statistics concerning the number of fort Indians who had recently procured liquor at Quesnel. He gave no names, though he said he would provide full particulars of several cases if freedom from prosecution was promised. He asked Vowell to excuse him from the obligation of "turning informer against my own people."[63] This statement underlines the crucial fact that Morice regarded himself as part of the Indian society. In an academic paper written in 1898, he claimed to have "become, as it were, one of them."[64] He saw himself as their ruler, and the bonds that bound him to his subjects were much stronger than his tenuous links with the hostile white society that was encroaching on his kingdom. The complex relationship between the priest and his Indian charges was both spiritual and political; he could not risk losing their loyalty by wholesale denunciations. To alienate them would be to cut his only emotional lifeline to the rest of humanity and to condemn himself to loneliness, despair, and paranoia—his eventual fate after his removal from the district.[65]

Having demonstrated the gravity of the liquor problem, Morice directed Vowell's attention to the government's miserable law enforcement record. According to Morice, in the fourteen years that he had been in the area, only one fort Indian had been convicted of a liquor offence; Anderson had claimed a total of five such convictions. Furthermore, Morice boasted that the convictions of two of the three whites and métis found guilty of liquor offences were more his work than Anderson's. He then added, menacingly, "I pass over many damaging facts," presumably other examples of Anderson's neglect or incompetence.[66] But Morice could not resist digging the grave for the policeman's reputation a little deeper, and he went on to describe an incident which emphasized his own authority and the constable's floundering impotence when it came to dealing with non-white fugitives.

The suspect in this case was Morice's old acquaintance Jimmy Alexander, the métis who as a boy had been his first tutor in the Carrier language. In late October 1897, Jimmy had got into trouble while on a drinking spree with an American prospector. Offended by the Yankee "Colonel," Alexander had beaten and bitten him and then thrown him over a fence, inflicting injuries which forced the American to retreat to Quesnel. There he laid a complaint against Alexander, and Constable Anderson and two other white officers went up to make the arrest. With guns drawn, they surprised him at home. Yet he managed somehow to flee across the frozen lake. The police gave chase, but despite a bullet in his heel, Jimmy made good his escape. The shooting so angered certain local natives, Morice informed Vowell, that Anderson would have been fired upon if a Winchester had not been wrenched away from two young men. Apparently unaware of their hostility toward him, Anderson tried to enlist Indian help in what turned out to be a fruitless search for Alexander. While "feigning" sympathy for the enforcers of the white man's laws, the Indians "were really for Jimmy" and showed this by giving Anderson false leads.[67]

Morice stood on the sidelines. He did not offer to intercede with Alexander. Apart from an impulse to identify with a member of his flock, even a black sheep, in his contest with white authority figures, Morice was piqued by the failure of the police to pay him their respects and to seek his advice or active assistance. His prejudice against Americans may have reinforced this reticence. After four frustrating days of searching and questioning, the police were compelled to recognize their impotence and turned to Morice. In exchange for a promise of leniency for Jimmy, whom in his opinion the American should never have plied with drinks, the priest agreed to act as a broker. After the police had left for Quesnel, Morice wrote a letter to the fugitive and had it delivered by his aides — "gossiping watchmen are at times good for something," he added parenthetically in his letter to Vowell. Within two days, Jimmy was at Morice's door, and as soon as his injured heel was strong enough, he snow-shoed 130 miles to Quesnel to give himself up. He was fined $50.[68]

Morice's accounts of this incident show that he relished the policeman's discomfiture and his own command of the situation. Although he did not hide his attitude in his letter to Vowell, it comes out particularly strongly in his disguised autobiography, *Fifty Years in Western Canada*. In it he stressed the humiliating predicament of the "outwitted" officers and identified himself with the Indians, who for years afterwards amused themselves by mimicking the white policemen's "funny way of running." His knowledge of the Indians' language permitted Morice to be one of them, but more importantly it helped him to make them *his* people in a possessive way. He boasted in *Fifty Years* that his ability to persuade men like Jimmy Alexander and the Babine chief, Alec Typee, to abandon their resistance to white laws illustrated his "unlimited power over his charges." Its tone was more tempered, but Morice's letter to Vowell hinted as much and implied that the possibility of racial friction would be reduced or eliminated if his power was recognized and put to good use.[69]

In the early part of 1899, Father Morice again proved his ability as a cross-cultural broker between the Carrier Indians and the white authorities. Late in October 1898, a teenage boy from Natléh had been arrested and taken to Quesnel after the shooting death of his hunting companion. After hearing the details of the case, the local magistrate sent him down to Clinton to stand trial for murder. Morice regarded this as a flagrant miscarriage of justice, for he knew that the shooting had been an accident. Much of the important letter he sent to Vowell on 10 January 1899 was devoted to gaining the release of the boy, Edward, who was then awaiting trial. The fatal accident had taken place while Morice was giving his September mission at Natléh, and he had tended the wounded boy for a week and was with him at the moment of death. When Joseph Prince, in his capacity as a special constable, was instructed to arrest Edward, Morice sent word for the boy to go peacefully. The priest also took the trouble to inform Constable Anderson that as far as the Indians were concerned, the matter had been settled by the payment of compensation to the dead boy's parents.[70]

Both Anderson and Indian Agent Bell interpreted this as an attempt by Morice to obstruct the white man's judicial process and to perpetuate the settlement of such cases according to tribal custom. Worse still, the magistrate apparently chose to regard the compensation paid by Edward's parents as tantamount to an admission of their son's guilt. This misunderstanding, compounded perhaps by faulty court interpreting, led to the murder indictment. Thirty years later, when the ex-missionary Morice was an ardent supporter of the anti-semitic *Action Française,* he presented the murder charge as a vengeful conspiracy on the part of a Jewish magistrate determined to victimize a Catholic Indian and his priest, though there was no mention of this alleged plot in Morice's detailed letter to Vowell.[71]

In 1899, Morice's concern was to clear Edward's name and his own. He wrote down all the pertinent testimony, including the victim's often repeated assurance that the gun went off accidentally. At the end of his report was a statement signed by Louis Billy Prince, the court interpreter, who corroborated Morice's version of the affair. Morice did not fail to point out that he was the only white man who spoke the language of those involved in the case; *ipso facto,* he was the only white man capable of preparing this kind of report. He went on to demonstrate that even an elementary knowledge of Carrier customs on the part of the police and the magistrate would have avoided all the injustice and bad feeling. Of course, in doing so he did not miss a chance to poke fun at Anderson, Bell, and the magistrate. Bell apparently claimed that Morice had "strongly objected" to Edward's arrest because such issues were settled by compensatory gifts according to "customary law".[72] For the benefit of all his badly informed white adversaries, whether they were policemen, Indian agents, or justices of the peace, Morice succinctly explained the Carriers' traditional response to murder and fatal accidents:

> The "customary law" among the Indians was that you *killed* in return for killing or, when the cause was *evidently* accidental, that you marked your sympathy for your involuntary victim's relatives by making them presents.[73]

This being so, what the magistrate interpreted as an indication of guilt should have been recognized as proof of innocence.[74]

But it was not. And now, in addition to losing their only horse, which was part of the compensation they paid, Edward's parents had lost their son. They were poor people, Morice stressed in his letter to Vowell, who, as the Indians' protector, was asked to intercede with the court in order to obtain Edward's release since he was their only means of support in old age. Finally, reverting to the question of his alleged opposition to Edward's arrest, Morice pointed out to Vowell the "irony of fate" whereby a missionary who had spent his whole career opposing Indian customs, including perfectly legal ones, should have been accused of defending one which ran counter to Canadian law. While there is no reason to believe that Morice tried to obstruct the legal process in this case, he did resent the activities of the officials at Quesnel. Unlike Loring, they had adopted a critical attitude toward the Oblate policing system in general and to Morice in particular. Morice's letter to Vowell was a defensive counterattack designed to prove that he was better at law enforcement that they were. But it was also meant to gain Edward's acquittal—and not just for humanitarian reasons, though Morice made much of the plight of "the poor defenceless boy" and his family.[75]

A larger issue was at stake. The conviction of an innocent Indian whom Morice had advised to trust the white man's court would seriously undermine the missionary's influence. His success as a broker in earlier cases had rested on his assurances that the magistrate would never condemn an innocent party. If Edward was convicted, the Indians would no longer listen to him. Instead they would settle matters according to the old revenge laws and would resist white lawmen. This last point had budgetary implications bound to impress themselves on Vowell, and Morice spelled them out: if Edward was found guilty, "the enforcement of the law throughout the whole district will be well-nigh impossible, unless accompanied by very high expenses."[76]

Having appealed to Vowell's heart, to his responsibility as the Indians' guardian, and to his bureaucrat's desire for peace and parsimony, Morice rested his case. It could not have been better advocated by the Dominion's leading lawyers. And, of course, he won. Edward was freed and British Columbia's attorney general, Joseph Martin, wrote to Morice to express the government's gratitude.[77] This kind of recognition and implicit support must have helped to free Morice from the danger of having the government's local representatives interfere with his rule. Of equal importance, his successful intercession on Edward's behalf was, in his own words, "calculated to augment his prestige with his flock." Indeed, Morice believed that such "interventions . . . gained for him such a tremendous power over the whole North that he literally had its inhabitants at his beck and call." His preoccupation with his power and his desire to flaunt it are reflected in his frequent use of the word "power" in his autobiography. In the space of six pages he refers once to his "unlimited power" and once to his "tremendous power"; the police, that symbol of white authority, are described as "powerless." And as though to reassure himself and to leave the reader with no doubts about his paramount power, he quotes—within the same six pages—a Hudson's Bay Company inspector's reference to him as "the king of the country."[78] There is no record of this statement in the extant company inspection reports, but Mr. E. K. Beeston, who inspected the fort in 1900, described the local Indians as being "altogether under the control of the Roman Catholic priest, Father Morice."[79]

Beeston's assessment is corroborated by oral evidence. John Prince, who served Morice as an unpaid "house-boy" and as a voyageur, stated that "long time ago . . . Indian treat priest like king. They thought he big, big, big man." Mr. Prince's father, Louis Billy Prince, Morice's longtime assistant in linguistic and anthropological research as well as in geographical exploration, told his daughter that Morice "had to have everything done for him." The daughter, Mrs. Lizette Hall, and her brother, John Prince, both remarked on the regal treatment accorded Morice when he travelled. Each January, five or six Babine men came with two toboggans or *carrioles* equipped with a wedge-shaped box on top. Wrapped in furs and covered with a bear robe, Morice would spend the whole journey nestled in the box. Upon his arrival at Babine, he was carried from the carriole into a house. That was not an easy task, John Prince recalled jocularly—"Big fat fellow, you know." The same pattern was followed when Morice made his Christmas visits to Natléh, and on one occasion, a reluctant porter is supposed to have "pretended to stumble and dumped Morice into the snow." Though this kind of covert resistance and even open "run ins" were not unknown, they were exceptional. Deference and compliance were the rule. Somewhat at a loss to explain this attitude, Mrs. Hall concluded that "the majority of them [the Indians], well, they just had to do these things for him."[80]

Some of the things Morice expected required little effort and were even amusing. For example, when he arrived at a village, he was always accorded a splendid gun salute. The Fort George Indians fired more than two hundred rounds in his honour in May 1899; by October of the same year Simon, the carpenter, who had visited the Lower Mainland with Morice, had made a wooden cannon whose detonation produced clouds of smoke.[81] A few of Morice's other expectations were more exorbitant. Anxious to return promptly to the fort—probably in order to resume his writing and printing—at the end of his Babine visit in January 1898, Morice asked his men to travel for two days and nights without rest. They were so exhausted by the time they reached Lake Tremblé that it took them fourteen hours to cover the approximately fifteen miles from one end of the lake to the other. Their zigzag tracks looked like those of a party of drunks.[82] And all this enervating effort was given freely for God.

Clearly, Morice's religious status goes a long way toward explaining his ability to command such loyalty and service. John Prince said that the people regarded Morice as such a "big, big, big man" because he was "closer to God. They know him work for the God."[83] For a profoundly religious people like the nineteenth-century Carrier, who feared epidemics sent by spiteful Protestant ministers and believed that holy candles could save them from cataclysmic darkness, the priest's intercession with God was as important, if not more so, than his role as a broker in their relations with fur traders, Indian agents, and policemen. In 1898, Morice said that the Hotsoten of Rocher Déboulé regarded him as a "sorcerer par excellence, the great doctor who cured or killed by his own will or at least by the effect of his prayers."[84] That his authority and influence depended to a great extent on his mastery of the Carrier language was frequently emphasized by Morice, and it is confirmed by oral testimony. His linguistic skill impressed and puzzled the Carrier, and they remember and admire him, above all, for his knowledge of their language. John Prince's response to a question about the Carrier syllabic prayer book is instructive:

> Yes, that's funny . . . Father Morice he's a white man, he came from, I don't know where he came from. Then he start to make book, and he know my language a hundred per cent better [than I do]. He mention

everything. . . . But, you know, I talk to myself lots of time[s] [while] I sleep "How do he do it, who told him?"[85]

Some of their own leading men, like Joseph Prince, for example, spoke English, French, Carrier, and perhaps Sikani too; yet this does not seem to have detracted from Morice's unique achievement. Related to the Carriers' appreciation of his linguistic skills was a persistent reference to Morice as being "smart," a quality much respected by the Carrier Indians of his day. He noted himself that they "craved knowledge." The older people interviewed expressed disappointment that they had been unable to receive a good education. They seem to have wanted to equip themselves to compete successfully with the whites, and in the days before schools the priest was the only potential educator.[86] These expectations would have inclined the natives to tolerate his autocratic ways.

But while the Carrier had reason to continue to defer to Morice, the Hudson's Bay Company's officers were becoming increasingly antagonistic towards his methods. A. C. Murray had left to take over Fort Simpson just before Morice returned to Fort St. James from France in 1897. His replacement, W. E. Camsell, was himself superseded by A. S. McNab in the fall of 1898.[87] Morice was never able to develop with either Camsell or McNab the kind of relationship that he had with Traill and Murray. Both of the new men, but especially McNab, resented Morice's interference in company affairs and were hostile to the Oblate system of indirect rule. Although Traill and Murray had regarded spying and whipping with distaste, neither of them had actively opposed it; Camsell and McNab did. The old *modus vivendi* between the fort and the Mission was over.

The conflict began in January 1898, when both Morice and Marchal were in residence at the Mission. It was sparked by an attempt on the part of Taya's watchmen to "arrest" and tie-up Joseph Prince. Some of his brothers had come to the rescue, and the watchmen came off badly in the ensuing melée.[88] Joseph, who was the government's Indian constable at the fort, protested to Constable Anderson, and Camsell supported him. Joseph seems to have been an important Hudson's Bay Company employee, probably a sort of foreman, and this, together with his métis status, no doubt explains why he enjoyed what Camsell called "the privileges of a white man." This being so, the fur trader insisted in a letter to Anderson that Joseph was "entitled to the rights of one," meaning that he should not be tied and whipped. Camsell was convinced that the priest was behind the affair, which suggests that a power struggle was going on between Joseph and his former mentors.[89] It could have been either Morice or Marchal who instigated the attempted arrest, though it was probably Morice. After his return from France, there is no evidence of the co-operative relationship that had previously existed between him and Joseph. Louis Billy, his brother, seems to have taken over Joseph's role. Until 1897, Joseph was praised by Morice as an influential aide; afterwards, he is only mentioned as Loring's constable.[90] The latter's knowledge of English and of the skills and practices of the whites must have boosted his importance when the mining boom began in 1897. And it may have prompted the "conceited Joseph," as an anonymous fur trader writing in the fort journal called him, to rebel against subordination to the priest.[91]

Since Camsell also resented the priest's power and pretensions, he was willing to do more than just plead on Joseph's behalf. He used the incident to argue for the end of "priest rule" and the appointment of an Indian agent at Fort St. James. Far from contributing to the betterment of the Indians, Camsell was convinced that the Oblate system of spying watchmen provoked conflict in the community, especially when force was used. He asked Anderson if the repressive apparatus was sanctioned by law.[92] It is worth noting that neither Joseph Prince nor Camsell complained to Loring, the Indian agent responsible for Fort St. James. Possibly, Loring's preoccupation with the Skeena region accounted for this, though his special relationship with Morice could well have inhibited complaints. The coming of the mining frontier brought men like Anderson, who owed nothing to Morice, into the picture; it made sense to enlist their support against "priest rule."

But Camsell looked to Victoria too for some check on the Oblates. In January and in April 1898, he communicated his concerns to R. H. Hall, the company's manager for British Columbia. The company's men at the fort were not on good terms with Marchal, who had forbidden Indian women to come to the New Year festivities. This kind of interference annoyed Camsell, and he believed that the appointment of a resident Indian agent would cause the priests to lose much of their influence.[93] Hall shared Camsell's opinions, and he complained to the Indian Affairs Superintendent Vowell about the whippings in the Stuart Lake area. The man Vowell held responsible for investigating this matter was, of course, Loring. And Loring said he would consult Morice when the priest came for his summer visit. In the meantime, he played down the problem. No Indian had ever complained to him about being flogged, he told Vowell, and he strongly implied that the priests no longer resorted to whipping.[94] Loring was obviously protecting the Oblates, for whippings were regularly and openly carried out until well into the twentieth century. Although Vowell goaded Loring into visiting the fort in the summer of 1898, no Indian agent was stationed there and "priest rule" was not overthrown.[95]

To judge from the way he treated the man who replaced Camsell in September 1898, Morice was still as powerful as ever. Or at least he acted as though he was. McNab failed to call on him after he took charge of the fort, and angered by what he evidently regarded as discourtesy, if not disrespect, Morice wrote a letter reprimanding and threatening the fur trader. That letter has not survived, but it is apparent from McNab's reply that Morice had alluded to encouraging a free trader to operate at Fort St. James if McNab did not adopt the compliant attitude which Morice had come to expect from the chief factors. But McNab was not going to be bullied or scolded. On the contrary, he gave the French priest a few pointers on manners; in America, it was the new resident who was called on and welcomed by the others, not vice versa. Nor was he willing to countenance intimidation: "threats I do not like," he firmly told Morice.[96]

Thus began the longest and most bitter of Morice's duels with Hudson's Bay Company officers. The "king of the country" could admit no equals, and McNab would not subordinate himself. There was no rational, material reason for Morice to declare war on McNab. The hostility was based entirely on Morice's need to assert his paramount power. Although the two strong personalities co-operated quite well in the distribution of government financed winter welfare supplies, their antagonism heated up with the coming of the thaw. The first spring supply boats from Quesnel brought Morice a shipment of watches—probably surveyors' chronometers—from France, but by the time they reached the Mission one was missing. Having somehow heard that McNab had held the package, Morice penned what was virtually an accusation of theft and sent it to him. McNab responded calmly. He confirmed that the seal on the package had indeed been broken, probably by the customs officer, but he denied that the watch had been removed and "forgotten to be replaced," as Morice had suggested.[97] A few days later, Donald Prince—once again the Princes are seen acting as a link between the Mission and the fort—told McNab that the wife of a company man at Quesnel had informed Morice that the watch was missing when the package arrived there. Immediately, McNab wrote to Quesnel to seek confirmation. In his letter, he roundly condemned Morice for not having the "common decency or manliness to visit me and apprize me of the information." This, he confided to John Boyd at Quesnel, "is the kind of man this priest is, and he is a curse to the place, after all that is done for him by the Company to almost accuse us of being thieves are the thanks we get."[98] It is no wonder that McNab was angry and perplexed, for Morice's behaviour was like that of a frustrated child.

When his will was thwarted, he instinctively lashed out with no thought for the consequences. And whenever he was proven wrong, he refused to apologize.

His decision to support a free trader who would compete against McNab exemplifies this compulsive mentality. To vent his spleen and to regain an ascendancy that was irrelevant to the success of his missionary duties, Morice was prepared once again to sacrifice the considerable benefits that he and the Oblate mission gained from peaceful co-existence with the company. Like his former protégé, Frank Guy, the new free trader was a Frenchman. Known locally as "French Joe," his real name was Castillion.[99] He was associated with a trader named Marion at Quesnel, and Marion was apparently on good terms with Morice. This and other bits of intelligence about the new "opposition" convinced McNab that Morice had organized it. Consequently, McNab proposed to his boss in Victoria that they cease to provide him with free services, referring specifically to the free delivery of his mail, including heavy parcels, and to the favourable prices paid for furs donated to him. McNab also told Hall that it was "intolerable" that the company's officers should have to consult Morice concerning the hiring of mail carriers. McNab refused to do so and suggested that a showdown with Morice was inevitable and even desirable:

> The time is coming when the Company will have to make a stand, and defy this man or allow him to interfere in matters that does [sic] not concern him, just to show his power to whoever is in charge at Stuart's Lake.[100]

McNab obviously realized that his conflict with Morice was not a result of an inherent incompatibility of fur trader and missionary or of irreconcilable religious or ideological differences; it was a personal power struggle in which he was defending his professional prerogatives and pride against Morice's drive for dominance. But the decisive confrontation that McNab wanted did not occur. Probably Hall recommended caution, and McNab reluctantly continued to carry Morice's mail and to buy furs from him. There is no evidence, however, that McNab capitulated entirely and allowed Morice to hire the mail crews. Consequently, a state of chronic hostility continued, and the company's senior officials no longer regarded Morice as a useful ally. Instead, in the 1900 Inspection Report, Morice was described as being "not altogether well disposed towards the Company."[101]

For the first time, Morice had not emerged as the victor from a contest with the factor in charge of Fort St. James. Two facts may account for this.

First, NcNab seems to have been a stronger personality than either Traill or Murray; he was not as ready to sacrifice his self-respect for the sake of the company's ledger. But the question of character may have been less important than circumstance. The coming of the miners had changed the economy of Fort St. James in a way that caused Morice to lose much of his leverage as a broker. Formerly, he could dictate to the company because he alone was able to keep the trappers from taking their furs to Quesnel. But with the Omineca gold rush, the fort Indians were engaged to transport the miners to and from Quesnel. It would have been difficult, if not impossible, for Morice to have forbidden this large-scale and apparently lucrative enterprise. And, surprisingly, though the Indians visited Quesnel more than ever before, they did not take their furs down with them, except a few that were sold in order to buy provisions — and booze, no doubt. Obviously, the voyageur work became such an important economic activity that taking furs to Quesnel was no longer worth the trouble. These changes took away Morice's major leverage with the company. Even Castillion's "opposition" represented no real threat. His stock was small, and the Indians only gave him enough fur to encourage him to stay and thereby keep up the prices paid by the Hudson's Bay Company. Since the company made a $4,878 profit on its Fort St. James's area operations in 1899, its officers were not too concerned about Castillion or the higher prices. What pre-occupied McNab was getting an "attractive" range of goods to get the Indians to spend their cash at Fort St. James rather than in the Quesnel stores.[102] The more the chief factor became a provisioner and storekeeper, the less power Morice had. Although he resented the intrusion of the policemen, magistrates, and other officials who accompanied the gold rushes, by 1899 Father Morice's greatest source of power now lay in his ability to act as an intermediary between them and the Carrier Indians.

7

BACK TO BUSINESS:
EXPLORATION AND ITINERANT PREACHING
IN 1899

Despite the important place that Father Morice made for himself as a broker on the mining frontier, he was indissolubly wedded to the old order. He made no attempt to adjust his missionary methods to the new conditions. Elsewhere, missionaries reacted to the corrupting influence of miners by encouraging their converts to withdraw into segregated communities. William Duncan, for example, moved his neophytes from Port Simpson to Metlakatla, and to keep them from the temptation of employment with miners and other whites, he helped develop a diversified and lucrative economy for them.[1] At St. Mary's (Mission City), the Oblates had built a school and a model farming village, complete with saw and grist mills, in the hope of providing the Indians with an alternative to employment in New Westminster. But Morice was not inclined to follow the example of either his Oblate colleagues or his Protestant enemies. He had already created for himself a way of life which conformed to his adolescent dreams and which was in harmony with the activities of Carrier trappers and fishermen. The material improvement of his flock was too mundane to warrant his attention, though there was a need for it. In 1899, Mr. R. H. Hall, the Hudson's Bay Company manager, remarked that the Fraser Lake people "seemed to be an unhealthy lot—always sick and generally blind," and a year later Mr. F. K. Beeston, the inspector, reported that the Fort St. James Indians were "somewhat degenerate." Both of these senior company officials linked the Carriers' sorry state to the priest's authority over them. Hall suggested to Sinclair at Fraser Lake that the "priest's good offices may save their souls, but their poor bodies appear to have suffered under the influence of prolonged religious training."[3] While this judgment is unfair, since Morice's presence did not cause a decline in Carrier living standards, it is nevertheless true that Morice did little to mitigate the deleterious social effects of the mining frontier.

Indeed, the missionary method to which he remained so attached—the giving of missions at the various meeting places—depended on the Indians' ability and willingness to cease their labours for religious instruction and for the regulation of disputes and disorders. Morice regarded the summer meetings at Natléh as perfect missions, for they demonstrated the compatibility of his missionary objectives and the Indians' traditional occupations. He arrived when the area's four bands were at Natléh for the annual salmon fishing. The fish were caught in the traps at night, and in the morning they were collected without much effort. Unlike most Protestant and Catholic missionaries, Morice apparently did not regard work as intrinsically good.[4] Neither did he wish to change the Indians' semi-nomadic life, and the mission meeting system meant that they could be converted to Christianity without any threat either to their trapping and fishing economy or to the commercial interests of the fur traders.

It also had another, more important advantage for a missionary like Morice. Since most of the missions were held in the summer, he was able to spend much of the rest of the year as he wished. That time could have been spent running a school, if only a rudimentary one, at Fort St. James. But despite the Carriers' desire for instruction, especially in English, Morice refused to provide it.[5] This further differentiates him from the bulk of his Oblate confreres as well as his Protestant rivals, who invariably regarded schools as the most effective way to convert the natives. Influential Oblates thought that itinerant missions were a virtual waste of time; they preferred to devote most of their time and resources to schools.[6] In a mission district as vast as Morice's there was obviously a need for the missions, and he enumerated their advantages when he described his work to the readers of the *Missions*. He noted, for example, that the gathering of the various bands permitted the missionary to encourage devotion by comparing one group to another; it also helped him to find marriage partners who were not closely related. The priest acted as a broker between bachelors, on the one hand, and maidens and their parents, on the other.[7]

Of course, the meetings were less important as marriage marts than as occasions for religious and ritual instruction. Each day of Natléh's summer mission in 1898 included a Mass, a sermon, and one or two catechism classes. But the public confession, which was held at the church door, was perhaps the most important event. Morice jogged memories by listing sins, and the confessions were followed by public penances and appeals for contrition. Church members deemed worthy were rewarded with scapulars, cloth "medallions" worn next to the body on the chest and between the shoulder blades.[8]

At Natléh the idea of collective guilt was instilled by the ever popular Stations of the Cross, a pale reflection of Bishop Durieu's Passion Play. Both in the format of his missions and in his emphasis on emotional rituals, Morice followed Durieu, who in turn was inspired by the famous "exercises" of St. Ignatius. The Jesuit founder's lurid image of hell's horror and pain was intended to purge sin through fear. He used "little dramas" and paid attention to details which would have an impact on the senses.[9] Following St. Ignatius, Durieu recommended a sensual rather than an intellectual approach to religious instruction. Oblate itinerant missionaries should not give theology lectures; instead, dogma must be brought down from the mysterious realm of revealed truth so that the Indians could identify themselves with the sinners described.

The Oblates' calculated use of sensuality, their cult of the Eucharist, and the importance they attached to the Passion Play and similar dramas were in sharp contrast to William Duncan's vehement opposition to emotionalism and ritual. Duncan, the Victorian Englishman whom Robin Fisher considers to be "in many ways typical" of British Columbia's other Protestant missionaries, preferred to convert by intellectual persuasion and economic progress; Morice followed Bishop Durieu in relying on the methods of the Counter Reformation.[10] But unlike d'Herbomez and Durieu, who established schools to impart the useful skills of European civilization, Morice's acculturation programme was concerned exclusively with the spiritual and with the creation of a new social hierarchy.

The difference between Morice and his Protestant rivals was reflected in the architecture of their respective churches. In 1898, the Protestants built a church for their Gitksan converts at Hazelton. Always eager to use rivalry to keep up the fervour of his own flock, Morice persuaded the Babines to rebuild their dilapidated church at Hwotat. They must not be humiliated by Protestants. With the help of two Fort St. James' carpenters, the Babines' church was rebuilt with such features as a double floor and a sky blue interior. Now when the Gitksan mentioned the minister's church, the Babines could reply disdainfully that it could not compare with the Catholic church. Morice obviously regarded the Protestant churches as utilitarian and uninspiring, and he referred to the one at Hazelton as "une maison bourgeoise."[11]

In his articles in Catholic journals, he liked to ridicule the Protestant ministers and to laud his own efforts. In a letter sent to the *Petites Annales* in 1898, for example, he quoted a Hazelton storekeeper's wife, a Protestant, who apparently marvelled at his ability to "bewitch" the Hotsoten. Even though the natives were visited frequently by a Protestant minister and accepted his medicine and other aid, the lady told Morice, when it came to religion, they turned to Morice and laughed at the Protestant. And if his Hotsoten clients became troublesome, the storekeeper just had to threaten them with Father Morice to calm them down quickly. Such stories were probably exaggerated, but it nevertheless seems to have been true that the Hotsoten feared him as a sorcerer and that he could command loyalty from them. But, as he readily admitted in 1898, they were still essentially traditionalists.[12] With them, and to a lesser extent the Babines, Morice was still engaged almost exclusively in the first, repressive stage of the Durieu missionary method. His major targets were potlatching and shamanism, and by the summer of 1899, he felt that the Babines were making progress. The band chiefs were chastizing the delinquents, and most of the people had been baptized. Morice was particularly pleased when one of the noblemen finally abandoned his attachment to the potlatch and submitted to baptism.[13]

The Hotsoten shamans were more obdurate, and most of their clients continued to believe in traditional healing methods. Among the Bulkley Carrier, sickness was usually attributed either to the stealing of a person's "shadow," or vital force, by a shaman or to its imprisonment in the world of the animal spirits. Whether the attending native physician diagnosed the first or second condition, the treatment was the same. His shadow was sent to retrieve the patient's for temporary safekeeping in his own body. Then, accompanied by the requisite drumming, dancing, chanting, and rattling, the shaman "vomited the errant shadow into his cupped hands, and laying them on the patient's head blew it into his body. Thus he restored the vital spark . . . and set the patient on the road to health."[14] Herbs were also used in the treatment of certain illnesses, and the priest, like the shaman, was considered to be a doctor whose remedies were both material and magical. Medicine was the first thing that people asked for when Morice arrived at a meeting place, and the stronger the potion and the more frequent the dose, the more it was appreciated. Scapulars, baptism, and the other sacraments were all no doubt seen as part of the Catholic healing cult. With the constant threat of devastating epidemics, the Hotsoten and other Carrier sub-groups naturally wished to make use of both traditional and Catholic medicine. But Morice continued to reject such syncretism. The Carrier regarded the blessing of a tomb, for example, as a most important ritual, but Morice refused it without pity if the deceased had had recourse to a shaman during his or her mortal illness. The shamans obviously resented this competition, and in the summer of 1899, those at Rocher Déboulé tried some coercion of their own. Not long before

Morice was due to arrive, they wanted to prove their power by curing a chronically sick and mentally unbalanced woman called Cécile. But she fought them off, declaring that she belonged to the priest, who alone could cure her. When she set out to meet Morice, the shamans brought her back and forcibly subjected her to their insufflations, incantations, and other devices. Alas, in Cécile's case these well-intentioned efforts were in vain, for she died on the morning after the treatment.[15]

This was just the kind of opportunity Morice needed to launch an attack on the Hotsoten shamans. His duels with the shamans were at the personal level, and Morice gives the impression that he enjoyed them, especially when fate dealt him a good hand. Cécile's death was the trump card. He assured the shamans that in the eyes of God and of the law they were her executioners. He ridiculed their methods as ineffectual and denounced their claims to have supernatural powers as sinful and absurd. Wherever traditional methods had been abandoned in favour of God, Morice assured those gathered for the mission, the population had increased and the rare cases of sickness that did occur were cured by prayers and the white man's medicine. In support of his dubious thesis, he cited examples known to them, including perhaps the Babines' escape from the influenza epidemic which had ravaged the Hotsoten in 1894. Morice thundered, and for the first time, he felt that he had inspired the Hotsoten to doubt the efficacy of their "superstitions."[16]

This feeling was strengthened two days later, when one of their most renowned shamans asked to be delivered from the dangerous spirit which possessed him. The man, Yoes'en, promised to prepare for baptism if Morice succeeded. Among the Carrier most shamans were people, usually men, who claimed to have been possessed by a spirit while they were gravely ill. Their recovery was believed to indicate that they had developed a special relationship with the spirit, a relationship which conferred healing powers on them. Morice surmised that Yoes'en now doubted the effectiveness of his spirit and therefore wanted to be rid of it. It is likely too that he wanted to acquire some of the priest's magical power. Morice's response to his request probably disappointed him, for instead of resorting to holy water and Latin incantations, the missionary tried to exorcise the demon as a psychiatrist would. Suddenly the learned anthropologist took over from the awesome black robed priest, and Yoes'en was asked to explain how he came to believe that he was possessed. He dutifully related how, following a fruitless hunting expedition, he roamed the forest in a state of exhaustion, relieving his hunger pangs by continually smoking. Eventually he collapsed and experienced convulsions and temporary paralysis which he attributed to spirit possession. From the time of his recovery he had lived as a shaman. Father Morice explained to him that these symptoms had been produced by hunger, exhaustion, and nicotine intoxication; he had never been possessed. Although seemingly unconvinced by Morice's diagnosis, Yoes'en nevertheless reaffirmed his desire to quit shamanism and presented Morice with a magnificent marten skin. This gesture suggests that Yoes'en regarded himself as Morice's patient and pupil, because traditionally a shaman was trained and initiated into the profession by the man who had cured him of a serious affliction, and the novice paid with skins.[17]

After finally making some progress with the people of Rocher Déboulé, Morice made his usual summer call at the Hazelton home of Mr. Loring. There he was always assured of a comfortable rest. Located on a plateau, the Loring property was neatly fenced and had a sidewalk, steps, an impressive flower garden, and mountain ash and hops planted for decoration. There was also a stable, pig and chicken houses, and an orchard. Loring, who wanted his Indian charges to emulate him in his "civilized" pursuits, had invited the "most deserving Indian couples" to settle on the plateau and thereby to escape the "heathenish nuisances" of the Indian village. Mrs. Loring took it upon herself to teach the natives to cook and to sew, and she regularly acted as nurse and midwife. One of the things which caused Loring to dislike miners was that their drunken rampages had prompted some of the settled, "respectable" Indians to abandon their homes. Inevitably, when he and Morice met in early August 1899, they talked of the Klondike gold fever of the previous summer; both seemed relieved that the "rush" to the diggings had almost ended and that as a result the associated problems were less severe.[18]

The change allowed Morice to devote more time to the exploration needed to complete his map of the Northern Interior. In the period from 1897 until he left Stuart Lake in 1903, the map was one of his major preoccupations. Even under the seige conditions of 1898, he had found time for a small mid-summer expedition, and if it had not been for the shooting accident at Natléh, he would probably have organized a fall survey as well. The Indians who guided Morice on these "outings" continued to do so without wages, although Loring and other whites now paid them $3 per day for similar services, and the fur traders had told them that the government would "richly remunerate" Morice for his map.[19] Because they continued to donate their services, Morice assumed that the Indians did not harbour resentment. But some did. Louis Billy Prince, for example, aided Morice without expecting remuneration, but later on, after the priest's map and Carrier dictionary were published, he came to feel that Morice had unfairly benefitted from his help in the fields of both geographical exploration and linguistic research. Morice should have expected this, for he was aware that Indians shared neither his scientific curiosity nor his desire to conquer nature and thereby win recognition; when they undertook an arduous journey it was for material gain.[20]

Father Morice's principal guide on the trip which began in August 1898 was the first and the only Indian to desert him in the course of an expedition. The man, named Isaac, together with two other Babines, Soesradou'as and Johny Hol, had agreed to guide him from Takla Landing across the mountains to the source of the Nation River. After crossing the highest point in the mountains, Isaac insisted on returning home, and his pack was divided between Soesradou'as and Johny. The expedition was a long detour whose objective was to collect data for Morice's map. Henceforth, the same motive frequently inspired him to forsake the established and well-trodden routes between the meeting places in favour of unmapped and often circuitous alternatives. These detours probably helped Morice forget the painful fact that the highways of his kingdom were being tramped by the invading miners. As usual, he named the lakes he "discovered," one of them after the premier of British Columbia, John H. Turner. From Nation Lake he rode home on his beloved horse Bobby, which Louis Billy Prince had brought with him from the fort.[21]

The expedition of August 1898 was small compared with those mounted in the following year. For Morice, 1899 was the year of exploration *par excellence,* and the bulk of the surveying for his map was completed by October. He lost no opportunity to explore. While giving his usual spring mission at Fort George, he received a telegram asking him to officiate at the funeral of a river boat captain, a Frenchman, who had died suddenly at Soda Creek. He rode down on the forest trail, but on the way back to Fort George he turned west at the junction of the Blackwater Nazko and the Fraser, and he then headed north toward the Mud or Chilako River, which he charted. After the completion of the spring mission at Fort George, Morice left for McLeod Lake via the Fraser, Giscome Portage, and the Crooked River. He recruited four Fort George men to paddle against the Fraser's spring current to Giscome Portage.[22] Later, in August, at the end of the summer visit to the Babines, he undertook a gruelling eight-day trek through the dense forests and across the steep ravines of the Nilkitkwa Valley to Bear Lake. At Bear Lake, Morice blessed the tomb of Karta, the Sikani chief who had been his guide.[23] While his guides did not usually share the exhilaration Morice derived from the conquest of nature, he did occasionally manage to impart some of his pleasure. His new Sikani guide, Jean-Marie, for example, came to share his enthusiasm for mountain-climbing. Beginning the ascent of the highest peak in the Bear Lake area reluctantly, Jean-Marie ended by scaling the seventy-foot column of rock at its summit and then pulling up Morice with a rope. As the vertigo-stricken priest lay prostrate at his feet grasping the rocks, Jean-Marie laughed heartily and proclaimed that he could see the whole world. Morice named the mountain after himself.[24]

A month-long expedition in the Autumn of 1899 culminated in another mountaineering exploit. With his usual Natléh guides, the brothers Isaac Qasyak and Thomas Thautil, and Isaac's son, John Stené, Morice set off from Natléh towards the Coastal Range and the highest peak in the region. But an ascent by Morice, Thomas, and John failed when Morice became exhausted and the Indians lost their nerve. Morice then asked a local mountain dweller, Louis, to climb the fog-bound and wind-swept mountain with his instruments. Louis obliged and was rewarded by having the mountain named Mount St. Louis in his honour; it is known today as Atna Peak.[25] On the return journey, he charted the shore and islands of Morice Lake. Ending with the falling of the first now, on 11 October, this exploration provided Morice with most of the remaining data he needed for the map of the northern interior published in 1907.[26] Modern surveys have revealed Morice's map to be, in the words of the former head of British Columbia's Geographic Division, "a remarkable achievement" and more "thorough and accurate" than the work of government surveyors.[27] In 1954, the province's chief cartographer, G. S. Andrews, particularly praised Morice's ability to show "with astonishing fidelity the countless lakes, their shapes, with soundings, and drainage relationship."[28] It was a great irony, but one of which Morice was seemingly unaware, that his map would aid miners and other whites in the penetration of his mission district which he so resented.

During the winter of 1899–1900, Morice intended to keep busy with his other major hobby, the Carrier dictionary. Far from being discouraged by his failure to publish it in French, Morice continued to compile data and analyse the language. He intended to combine the dictionary, which was being prepared with English-speaking Americanists in mind, with a Carrier grammar.[29] These works, together with the composition and printing of his Carrier syllabic newspaper, had occupied much of his time in the winters of 1897–98 and 1898–99. Though he was not yet ready to publish any new material himself, he carefully scrutinized the works of other Americanists and frequently found them lacking. Consequently, he kept his name in the academic journals, principally the *Transactions of the Canadian Institute,* by penning long, combative, and convincing rejoiners. He maintained his strong interest in the Déné language group as a whole and in the use of language to establish racial origin or affiliation, so it is not surprising that he reacted to an article entitled "The Dénés of America Identified with the Tungus of Asia."[30] In it, Professor J. Campbell, a Protestant clergyman, dared to venture into Morice's academic domain and to criticize him. For this, he was mercilessly pilloried. Campbell had proved to his own satisfaction that the Déné and the Tungus of Siberia and Manchuria had a common origin. Morice believed that the reverend gentleman's "unscientific carelessness" and "hasty writing" had produced "such pitiful results" that they should be contemptuously dismissed: "From such writers deliver the comparative philologist!" While Morice still laboured under the illusion that language was a "safe criterion of ethnological certitude," his scholarship was infinitely more rigorous than was that of Campbell, whom he called "my opponent."[31]

In the second of the two articles directed against Campbell, Morice also criticized Petitot for committing the same sins as the Protestant professor. His former idol's "inordinate love of linguistic assimilations," Morice said, tempted him to distort evidence and to use dubious logic in "the interest of the thesis."[32] In Petitot's case, the outlandish thesis was, of course, that the Déné were one of the lost tribes of Israel. Campbell's "flights of imagination" had produced an even more bizarre "history of the Déné," which took them from their native land in East Asia to Troy, then on to Alexander the Great's conquests; they returned to devastate Rome as the Huns and eventually moved to North America.[33] Morice's exposure of Campbell and Petitot's preposterous theories and cavalier use of evidence was as ruthless and sarcastic as it was necessary. It is to his credit that he preferred long and laborious linguistic research to the facile fantasies so popular among his fellow amateur Americanists.

Morice confined his story-telling to the pages of the Oblate journals, for which he continued to write articles regularly. On 6 November 1899, when he sat down to describe his summer and fall explorations, he was pleased to be able to begin on a dramatic note. His side was riddled with stab wounds, though they were not, he told his presumably disappointed readers, a result of a "pagan" attack. Rather, they were the work of native surgeons to whom Morice had had recourse to relieve the pain that resulted from yet another drug overdose. His health had not been good since he had returned from France, and while he usually came back from his wilderness tours in better health than when he left, such was not the case in October 1899.[34] Perhaps the harsh weather and meagre rations account for his condition. In any event, a chronic ailment, probably a respiratory difficulty, flared up, and he decided to try an American medication reputed to be an effective remedy. But, characteristically, the impetuous priest took a triple dose and ended up in such agony that he could neither work nor sleep. After suffering for two weeks, Morice explained, he submitted to the traditional bleeding process, which involved darting the painful flesh.[35] The operation had dangers, not the least of which was the possibility of severing a major blood vessel. But Morice believed that the relief it brought him was worth the risk. Since there were no white doctors and the rivers would soon freeze and cut off the usual links with the Lower Mainland, it was either Indian surgery or no treatment at all.[36] However, Morice was probably less apprehensive about this therapy than other whites would have been. During his many years with them, he had observed the Carriers' surgical techniques and discovered that they could successfully operate to correct prolapsed wombs and remove cataracts. Using moose sinews and swan bone needles, they also managed to suture bad cuts.[37]

Despite the efficacy and sophistication of some procedures used in traditional Carrier medicine, the bleeding Morice underwent provided a respite rather than a cure. For that he had to leave the rigours of the Northern Interior for the doctors and the temperate climate of the Lower Mainland. On 12 November, he left for New Westminster, where he was to spend the winter recovering from pneumonia. While there he had plenty of time to complete a long letter for publication in the *Missions* and to write an article called "Déné Surgery."[38]

But if the winter sojourn at New Westminster was convenient enough for Morice to endure it without complaint, it was positively welcomed by Chief Factor McNab. He took advantage of the priest's unscheduled departure to send a letter with him to Mr. Hall in Victoria. In it, McNab explained that Morice was leaving for the winter and confessed that "his presence will not be missed by me, and his influence will not be used against us in our trade."[39] His words reveal that the missionary and the fur trader were still at loggerheads and that McNab continued to believe that Morice was in league with Castillion, the free trader. McNab's reaction to Morice's departure was in sharp contrast to Murray's apprehension when the priest had left for France in 1896. Murray and Traill had needed and feared Morice; McNab regarded him as an irritating nuisance. Things had changed. The new economic opportunities brought by the miners had cost Morice his leverage.

8

A KINGDOM LOST, 1900–1903

By June 1900, Father Morice had recovered sufficiently from his lung ailment to return to Stuart Lake for what were to be the last years of what he regarded as his reign as the king of the Carrier. Only three more years remained of the liberty and power that made his missionary career the only happy part of his life. But it was this very autocratic freedom which was to be his downfall, for in the few years after 1900, he increasingly neglected his priestly duties so as to spend more time on his map and various printing and literary projects. Yet when young assistants were sent to him, he refused to permit them to practise their ministry; they were only suited to be his cooks and servants. Morice was certain that he alone knew the Indians' language and ways well enough to be their priest. Similarly, his confidence in his indispensability as an effective broker between white and Indian encouraged him to flaunt his waning power and thus to deepen the antagonism between himself and certain officials of the Hudson's Bay Company and the federal and provincial governments. No king can make so many enemies and survive, especially when his subjects come to believe that he is not providing the services to which their deference, loyalty, and generosity entitled them.

Upon his arrival back in the north country, obliging Indian travelling companions awaited him at Quesnel. Mounting the horse they brought for him, Morice headed northwest along the Telegraph Trail toward Blackwater Crossing and Stoney Creek. Despite the rain and the mosquitoes, he was happy to have left behind the train, the stagecoach, and the steamboat which had conveyed him to Quesnel. He claims to have preferred the primitive simplicity of his mission district, and he was delighted when, towards the end of their first day on the trail, he smelled the welcoming aroma of a bivouac fire. The camp was on the north shore of the Blackwater or Nazka River, and it was inhabited by a lone nomadic hunter, James. He was as pleased to see Morice as the priest was to meet one of his humble flock. Was it true, James anxiously asked Morice, that the anti-Christ had just arrived and that the end of the world was fast approaching? When exactly would it come, he demanded, and had Morice, as people claimed, discovered Noah's ark on the summit of Mount St. Louis? Once James had been disabused of his fears, he asked Morice to hear the confession of his dead brother. Just before he died, the man had confided his sins to James and asked him to tell them to the first priest he met. Instead of absolution, Morice could only offer James a catechism lesson. This encounter seems to have been typical of many he had with his scattered neophytes, who were frequently agitated by rumours of cataclysmic upheavals. The deep and pervasive spirituality of the Carrier was such that even a professional anthropologist like Jenness could not discuss it without raising the possibility that they were "somewhat unbalanced mentally."[1] Much of the religious anxiety reported by Jenness and Morice was of course generated by Christian beliefs, and it seems inappropriate that Morice should have treated it in so patronizing a manner.

Still, he did reassure James, and the next day the party pushed on through the rain to Stoney Creek. The local natives had gathered to wait at the traditional meeting places, even though a white construction contractor was soliciting their services. The Telegraph Trail which had been cleared in the 1860's was now being used for the erection of a cable to the Klondike, and the line was approaching Stoney Creek. Apparently, the Indians' desire to receive the sacraments was stronger than the lure of cash wages. But the mission was soon interrupted by the arrival of two messengers from Fort St. James. They bore the news that Nisitan, a man who lived in isolation in the forest around Tremblé Lake, had been brought to die at the Stuart Lake Mission. As he had not been a practising Catholic, Nisitan's need for the priest was urgent. Consequently, Morice quickly heard the confessions of the people assembled at Stoney Creek and galloped off at full speed toward Stuart Lake. The Indian couriers and travelling companions who formed his entourage ran along behind. The swarms of mosquitoes were the worst Morice had ever seen, and it was not safe to open either eyes or mouth. The gasping Indians screamed with rage, rolled around on the damp grass, and then ran on. But during their first day out of Stoney Creek, a young man from the fort brought them news of a tragedy that must have made their discomforts seem trivial: the Babines had been stricken by a dreadful epidemic and twenty-seven of their number were already dead. Some of their still healthy compatriots had arrived at the fort to fetch Morice.[2]

Spurred on by these sad tidings, the priest reached the fort the following day. The Carrier from all the villages around Stuart Lake—the two at the fort, those at Pinché, Taché, and Yoekoutche—welcomed him extravagantly, for word of the Babines' fate had spread quickly among them, and now they clamoured for baptism and confession. "Oh!" Morice thought, "what a good preacher is sickness!"[3] But as the Stuart Lake people were not yet sick, Morice felt obliged to minister first to Nisitan. Fear of the eternal anguish of Hell had turned the independent hunter into a grovelling and pathetic penitent, which is not surprising, since the prayers Morice composed for the Cárrier described Hell's fire in graphic, horrible detail. One of them translates roughly as follows:

> Hell, our fire is but smoke compared to it.
> If I go to Hell, fire only shall I see.
> I shall eat [it], I shall lay on [it].
> My flesh shall burn.[4]

Nisitan appreciated the ministrations that saved him from such a fate, and with his feeble hands, he grasped the priest's narrow stole, which he kissed as he muttered interminable *"mercies."* Lacking a word equivalent to "thank you" or *"merci,"* the Carrier incorporated the French word into their language; they pronounce it *massé.*[5] Soon after receiving the sacraments and blessing the priest who had saved him from Hell, Nisitan died. The ability of epidemics to frighten Indians into conformity with the demands of Christian missionaries had been underestimated by Robin Fisher, the most recent historian of culture contact in British Columbia. He tends to regard the encroachment of the "settlement frontier" as the *sine qua non* of missionary success. In the case of the Carrier, it was not so much the demoralizing presence of the miners and the few settlers which boosted the priest's power and influence, as it was the panic provoked by plagues which the shamans could not control. Gibson reports the same decline in shamanism and interest in Christianity among the Tlingit following the 1835–38 outbreak of smallpox. Since the Carrier frequently regarded disease as the retribution of the white man's God, recourse to the priest was to be expected.[6]

They looked to confession and the other sacraments he dispensed for salvation. But the district's only priest could not hasten to their assistance without first ministering to the apprehensive Stuart Lake folk. For four days, he did nothing but confess and baptize, and once that mission was over, he hurried off home with the Babine canoe men to begin a more sad but satisfying one.[7] Two days before Morice's arrival on 14 July 1900, Charles French, the clerk at Fort Babine, recorded in his journal that his medicine had run out and that the ''people are in a very bad way.'' Yet the same journalist reported that the Indians summoned the strength and enthusiasm to give Morice ''a great reception'' when he arrived.[8] As usual, the Old Fort band had journeyed up to Hwotat with him. The 'flu had claimed most of its victims, including the chief, before Morice's arrival, and his first duty was to listen to people describing the last moments of their dead relatives. Many of them had left messages for Morice, and this touched him. The chief bequeathed to Morice a written confession; someone else had confessed to a Catholic image. Obviously, the ravages of the disease had whipped up a wave of religious fervour, and most of the dead had expired holding a holy candle in their hands and murmuring a plea for divine mercy. One of them claimed to have had a vision of the bliss awaiting him in Heaven.[9]

Inspired by these tales of humility and faith, Father Morice began all his regular mission exercises, sermons, catechism lessons, confessions, and Masses. The gathering of all the congregation in the church must have helped to spread the contagion. About half the population was already infected, but this did not prevent them from attending services. Those who could not walk were brought on blankets; those who could, supported themselves with hefty staves. It was customary for sick Carrier to arm themselves with such a baton, from which they refused to be parted. On the day that Morice chose to summon the Babine women for the collective examination of conscience that preceded the public confessions, the church looked like a forest of little trees stripped of their branches rising above the women squatting on the floor. The Indian churches of the Stuart Lake Mission district had no pews. Whether they were coming for morning prayers or a sermon, the congregation just ''flopped'' down on the floor, as a former free trader has described it.[10] They probably knelt for Mass. Now, because of the epidemic, the people vied with each other to get Masses celebrated for themselves and their relatives. Naturally, Morice favoured those who paid the fee promptly. Yet despite the Masses, benedictions, and prayers, five more people died during the week-long mission. The final toll probably reached fifty, about 15 per cent of the Babine population.[11]

The Hotsoten of Rocher Déboulé were more fortunate. When Morice arrived from his trek over the mountains that separate the Babine and Bulkley valleys, he found few 'flu casualties. But news of his presence soon spread to stricken Moricetown, and a contingent of its sick inhabitants walked the approximately thirty miles to Rocher Déboulé to see the priest. Some arrived on their knees.[12] The fact that they undertook this painful journey suggests that Morice had ceased to visit Moricetown on a regular basis. His earlier plans for a model community had certainly been forgotten, and in all probability the Hotsoten meeting place had been moved from Moricetown to Rocher Déboulé, perhaps to cut down on his travelling time. Loring's records indicate that Morice held an annual gathering there, and the agent chose to visit the people at the same time in order to enlist the priest's support and services as a broker and interpreter.[13]

Such aid was especially needed in 1900. In January, the Hotsoten had questioned Loring's authority and attacked his Indian constables when they tried to determine the source of illicit liquor. Loring believed that this revolt was indirectly inspired by Hazelton whites with whom he was still locked in a bitter power struggle. Ranged against him were Mr. Sargent, the J.P., and the Church Missionary Society's Mr. Field, backed up by other whites and some Indians. According to Loring, "secret councils" were held at which Sargent promised that if Loring were ousted the chiefs would "become real chiefs whilst the Agent kept them down as slaves." On one occasion, Loring's authority was openly challenged: Sargent, Field, and six other whites demanded the release of a white man whom Loring had sentenced to two months in jail for assaulting an Indian. Because the group seemed prepared to "rescue" the prisoner, Loring reluctantly conceded.[14]

Naturally, those Hotsoten who did not wish to submit to the agent's authority took advantage of his weakness. His constables, who were probably Oblate "watchmen" recommended by Morice, were "taunted" with the remark that there was now "another law aside of that of the Indian Agent's." Opposition to them became so violent that Loring told them to remove their badges in order to avoid being injured. He chose to regard this abdication as a tactical retreat; he would counterattack when Morice arrived for his summer visit. The agent was apparently impotent just a few miles from his Hazelton headquarters, but he claimed that the priest from far off Fort St. James would be able to get twelve reliable Hotsoten "publicly sworn in to do their duty, one and all without a flinch and without pay, except when actually rendering services."[15] While Loring probably exaggerated Morice's power in order to allay the worries of his superior, Mr. Vowell, he was obviously confident that the missionary could bolster his sagging prestige and authority. The anticipated arrival of settlers in the Bulkley Valley during the summer of 1900 made the re-establishment of the agent's law and order all the more important. Loring and Vowell hoped that successful settlement would be followed by a railway, since they had both engaged in speculative land purchases along what they anticipated would be the path of the future track.[16]

Possibly the outbreak of 'flu so preoccupied Morice during his 1900 visit to Rocher Déboulé that he was not able to muster the forces which Loring needed. There is every reason to believe, however, that he continued to co-operate with the man who had consistently praised and supported him. At other times during 1900 he helped Loring to settle disputes and translated government forms into Carrier for him.[17]

Father Morice was certainly kept busy when he returned to the fort from the Bulkley Valley. Virtually the whole of the adult population was laid up with the 'flu, which they probably caught from the Babines who had come to fetch Morice a few weeks before. Since many of the sick had only little children to tend them, Morice became their nurse as well as their priest. Despite being "on call" night and day, Morice's health remained excellent, and as usual he was pleased with the reviving effect that sickness had on his flock. There were many "returns to God," and one consistently refractory woman finally submitted to him. This was a particularly gratifying *coup*, and Morice's account of it once again reveals his apprehensive attitude towards Indians who aspired to white status. During her youth, the old woman, whose name was Pass, had lived with various whites and métis, from whom she had learned to speak what Morice regarded as atrocious French. Yet she was so proud of her linguistic virtuosity and of her former adventures with whites and métis that she looked down on her compatriots and refused to embrace their religion. Instead, she had had herself baptized by a Protestant minister who was passing through en route to the Skeena. This "uppity" and rebellious attitude infuriated Morice, who believed that there was nothing as ridiculously vainglorious as an Indian who had left his or her proper station in life.[18] For him, Pass must have represented the antithesis of his ideal noble Catholic savage, who should be humble, devout, obedient and, above all, subordinate. There would be no place for a priest-king who spoke the natives' language and printed prayers and newspapers for them if all the Indians learned to speak the Europeans' languages and adopted their economic and political systems. An upstart like Pass was a reminder of the constant danger that contact with whites represented. Fear of the sickness that infected and often killed Indians yet left the priest unscathed finally brought about her submission. She learned the catechism and was baptized a Catholic.[19]

Happily, she and most of the other sick Stuart Lake people survived. But as the late summer salmon catch had been poor and rabbits and deer were unusually scarce, they all faced a lean winter. McNab believed that there was even a possibility of starvation, and he therefore advised Mr. R. H. Hall, the Company's manager at Victoria, to request government aid. In the event of a dire emergency, McNab planned to communicate the area's need via the telegraph office at Fraser Lake. As for issuing government rations, McNab insisted that the company and not the priest be responsible. He obviously did not want Morice to have any patronage with which he could enhance his waning power. Castillion was still at the fort, but since his activities did not threaten the Company, the chief factor regarded the "miserable creature" with contempt.[20]

Embittered by his inability to humble McNab, Morice used the outbreak of drunken brawling on New Year's Day 1901 to accuse the trader of illegally providing liquor to Indians. As had been the custom for many years, a supper and dance had been given for the Indians and métis. The Indians were given tea and lime juice to drink, while the métis and white Hudson's Bay Company servants got the "usual" two bottles of port mixed with rum to divide amongst themselves. What Morice complained about to Vowell was the fact that the "Indian family," the Princes, was allowed to have liquor as though its members were métis. The priest also intimated that the company was selling liquor to Indians.[21] The tone of his letter indicates that the Oblate missionary was still alienated from his former aide, Joseph, as well as from his brothers, except for Louis Billy, the youngest. The "Prince boys," all of whom had strong ties to the Hudson's Bay Company as employees, were "rather given 'to play the white man,' " and these pretensions, like those of Pass, could never be tolerated by Morice.[22]

Although the available evidence makes it difficult to trace the exact evolution of the fascinating relationship between Morice and the Princes, it appears that in the days before the gold rushes he enjoyed their support. Both Joseph and Francis were appointed Indian constables by Loring, and it is extremely unlikely that either of these appointments had been made without Morice's approval. Yet by 1900 the brothers had apparently aligned themselves with McNab. A new-found desire to escape the discipline and humiliation to which the Oblates subjected the Indians is one obvious reason for this; the ability of those accepted by the traders as "half-breeds" to acquire liquor and other perquisites is another. Perhaps, too, the Princes wanted to avoid the stigma that was increasingly being associated with Indian status. From the mid-1890's onward there were more references in the Hudson's Bay Company journals to "siwashes"—the derogatory Chinook word for Indian. And more frequently than before, the natives were being criticized for laziness and stealing.[23] Presumably, both the Indians' behaviour and the fur trader's attitude towards them was being modified by the encroachment of miners, telegraph contractors, policemen, and others.

While the individualistic ethos of the settlement frontier probably stimulated the Princes to rebel against Morice, one of them at least had a personal grudge against the Church. According to local tradition, Francis

Prince withdrew from the Indian community and the Church after he had been wrongfully whipped, presumably on the orders of either Taya—his family's archenemy—or Morice. But the eruption of factional violence seems to have been an inherent by-product of the Oblates' attempt to combine indirect rule through chiefs and watchmen with the coercive repression process. Even in the priest's absence, the watchmen called the people to prayers every morning. At Fort Babine the church bell was rung at sunrise and then again a little later to hurry up the heavy-eyed congregation. As all the dogs of the village felt obliged to bark in accompaniment with the bell-ringing, few slumbered on after the second bell. This included the Protestant free trader, who later bemoaned the "terrible" howling of the dogs.[24] The journals of the Hudson's Bay traders show that on Sundays the chiefs lectured the people and sentenced delinquents to the usual public penances. But the condemned parties did not always accept their chastisement meekly. There is more evidence concerning resistance from 1900 onwards, though it undoubtedly occurred earlier too. Twice in the early months of 1900, fighting broke out at Hwotat. In the first fracas, guns were used, and in the second, knives. The clerk at Fort Babine noted that such "rows always happen at the church door after they come out from their prayers," and the account of a massive Sunday mêlée at Fort George in February 1902 mentions that it was sparked by an attempt by the "Indian Police Department [the Watchmen]" to arrest offenders as they left church. In the Fort George case, friends of the delinquents tried to rescue them, and the result was a free-for-all involving men, women, children, and dogs. The combatants, human and canine, used teeth, feet, fists, knives, and clubs.[25]

The fighting that broke out at the fort on New Year's Day 1901 was not, however, of this kind. In all likelihood, the circulating alcohol inflamed the smouldering hostility between the Prince and Taya factions. It also, of course, brought Morice and McNab into open conflict again. The fur trader was a total abstainer, and he was incensed at the priest's suggestion that his allegedly illegal doling out of liquor was responsible for the violence. It was not, he insisted, the two bottles he gave that caused the trouble; rather, it was a much larger quantity brought up from Quesnel in the fall by Francis Prince and cached until the New Year's festivities which did the damage. McNab told James Thomson, the company's new manager for British Columbia, that Morice had deliberately misrepresented the facts in order, once again, to lay all the blame on the company.[26] As it happened, Morice gained nothing by his accusations. Indeed, they irritated Vowell, who apologetically assured the company that he was confident that it conducted its affair in conformity with the liquor laws.[27] With the exception of Loring, Morice had by now succeeded in alienating all the company and government officials with whom he had regular dealings.

His estrangement from his fellow Oblates was more complete. Despite regulations that forbade missionaries to live alone among the natives, Morice had been without a colleague since Marchal had fled early in 1898. Though clearly responsible for his own solitude, Father Morice complained to the bishop about it and begged to be sent a companion. Durieu died in June 1899, and in September of the following year Morice journeyed down to see his successor, Bishop Dontenwill, at Williams Lake, where he was visiting.[28] Morice hoped to return to Stuart Lake with an assistant, but the bishop had not brought anyone with him, presumably because Morice was such a notoriously difficult person to live with that nobody wanted the job.[29] His Oblate colleagues and his bishop must have known that what Morice really wanted was someone to replace Blanchet—a housekeeper, cook, and deferential human presence. Although he was unable to oblige, Dontenwill promised the disappointed Morice that he would tour the Stuart Lake district the following summer. It would be the first such visit to the Stuart Lake district since Morice had been dumped there in 1885, and it indicates that the new young prelate was going to be more active in the Northern Interior than the old missionary pioneers, d'Herbomez and Durieu, had been. While the projected tour momentarily cheered Morice, it did not compensate for being condemned to return to his hermit's existence at the Stuart Lake Mission.[30]

But Father Morice did not live alone. From oral evidence it has been possible to establish that he requisitioned the free services of an Indian boy, who stayed with him in the priest's house over the winter.[31] At the turn of the century, his native servant was John Prince, the son of Louis Billy. He came to live with Morice when he was about sixteen, and he remained on and off for about two or three years. His principal duty, it seems, was to cook, and he was given a room next to the kitchen. Unfortunately, he did not know how to prepare the food and Morice was not willing to devote much time to instructing him. Consequently, John had to proceed by "trial and error," and the errors did not please his busy master. Later in his life, John described how he learned to cook brown beans on the priest's big Dutch oven:

> I stay the whole day boiled beans, boiled beans. Pretty soon no more water; I put some more water in. Father Morice come, say: "How are the beans? Oh, Oh I get it alright. What kind of water you put 'em on? Oh, pretty near boil 'em out I put cold water on. John! you crazy [Morice retorted]. You spoil the beans altogether, throw them out." I didn't say much, you know, but he went out. [Then] put more fire,

more fire, pretty . . . [soon] beans come to the soup like. Then they get black. [Morice] come out again: "Oh John, you cook beans too much [laughter]."[32]

Though John Prince could chuckle as an old man when he recalled his adolescent service with the priest, at the time he was not always happy. On one occasion he ran away, no doubt in order to escape the drudgery and confinement as well as Morice's admonitions. When he was asked if he remembered Father Morice, he replied:

Oh yes, that's why I am a good man, you see. He used to keep me. But one time I run away, sneak away from him. Then he send big talk, you know, to chief, Indian chief: "You find him, give him a good penance because he fooling the priest . . . Whip him." They did. So they whip, no blanket on me. Now they do that they put 'em in jail, son of a gun. Yeah, that's Father Morice.[33]

According to Mr. Prince, the priest was prone to fits of temper, and sometimes in church, "he talked so loud, you know mad."[34] A Kamloops man, a white Catholic who met Morice after he was withdrawn from Fort St. James in 1903, remembered that "he had a voice. You could hear that voice ten miles."[35] This voice and the chief's whip were most often raised in response to offences against the Catholic code of sexual conduct, although those successfully arrested by the watchmen were not always whipped immediately. Often their hands were bound together, and they were put in a cellar which served as a jail. The rope was sometimes tied so tightly that people's hands turned black. Before long this discomfort and the darkness of the improvised dungeon would cause the offenders to cry out for mercy, and at that point they would be brought to repent on their knees before the priest. The usual penance for both men and women was between fifteen and thirty strokes of the horse whip, the number depending upon the gravity of the transgression. In the majority of cases, the penitents had a blanket thrown over their backs before the lashes were administered. According to John Prince, only the worst offenders were flogged without the blanket. He presumably regarded his flight from Morice as a serious offence. The memory of his painful "penance" was still vivid more than seventy years later.[36]

Whipping was not the only punishment to which Morice resorted. Some "bad" people, possibly obdurate backsliders or traditionalists like Pass, were ostracized for periods of up to a year, and anyone caught speaking to them was whipped. Collective penances were also used. At Fort St. James, Morice sometimes refused to say Mass if the congregation

had failed to conform to his instructions.[37] In 1900, the Babines were subjected to a more severe punitive measure. Father Morice had promised to
break his tradition of spending Christmas at Natléh in order to be with
them, perhaps as a reward for the fervour they had displayed during the
'flu outbreak. But since they could not resist the temptation to potlatch for
several weeks after they came in from their fall hunt, he refused to go with
the men who arrived at the fort to fetch him. This must have caused great
disappointment, for not only did the Lake Babines gather for the Christmas ritual and festivals, but also about fifty Hotsoten came.[38]

Fortunately the bishop's visit in the following spring gave them a
chance to repent and to enjoy many Catholic ceremonies belatedly. Dontenwill and his assistant, Father Wagner, began their two-month visit in
late June of 1901. The bishop's presence made a great impression on the
inhabitants of the Northern Interior, and among the Indians it seems to
have inspired something of a reformation which henceforth facilitated the
work of both Morice and Loring. Guided by Morice, the bishop visited
each of the principal meeting places. The people who gathered at Natléh
were the first to greet him and they did so amidst ''great excitement.''[39]
Then he went on to the fort, where the houses had been scrubbed in his
honour and a chant was sung to welcome him. The Stuart Lake Carrier
were joined at the fort by most of the Mcleod Lake Sikani, which did not
seem to please the clerk in charge at Fort McLeod. Nor was McNab enthusiastic about the bishop's visit, for he knew that it would be difficult to get
anyone to trap while he was there.[40]

According to one report, however, the Hudson's Bay Company's representative at Babine saw the matter in a different light. Mr. Loring's stepdaughter, Mrs. Constance Cox, has alleged that with ''an eye to business,'' the Honourable Company's clerk told the Babine women that they
should be dressed in silk and carrying parasols when the ''Great Father''
arrived. According to the same informant, who was definitely hostile to
the Hudson's Bay Company, the bishop stepped from his canoe onto a red
''broadcloth'' which stretched from the lake to the house prepared for
him. The bolt of cloth used supposedly cost $200.[41] Even allowing for ex-
aggeration in this oral testimony, it is clear that the preparations for the
bishop's visit were long and costly. Apparently the Indians of each locality were trying to outdo each other in a new form of potlatch.

Combatting the traditional potlatch seems to have been a prime objective of the particularly big mission held at Rocher Déboulé. Present were
the Hotsoten of Moricetown and Rocher Déboulé as well as contingents
from throughout the whole mission district. When the bishop and the two
priests rode into Hazelton on 24 July, they were escorted by forty mounted
Indians, including some Sikani. Such scenes must have quickened the

pace of Morice's romantic heart. The Indian agent certainly was infected by the exhilarating pageantry of the tour. Following Morice's routine, the bishop took a two-day rest at Loring's "oasis." After this respite, the agent went with the party across the Bulkley to Rocher Déboulé. Loring felt that co-operation with the dignitary who was so influential among the Catholic Indians was good government policy.[42] He probably hoped that if he formed part of the bishop's white entourage he might enhance his own prestige among the troublesome Hotsoten. In any case, he remained with the bishop for the three days that he administered the sacraments to the approximately four hundred people gathered for the occasion.[43] The short mission reached its dramatic climax on the evening of the third day, 28 July. A huge bonfire was made of "pagan" paraphernalia, and pot-latching was formally proscribed. Loring was present and was somewhat awed by the sight:

> They stripped their houses and boxes of every vestige suggestive of heathen rites and burnt it [*sic*]. It was quite an impressive sight. The night was calm and dark, and by the column of glaring light the Indians were exhorted in the act, by Father Morice and Wagner, the Bishop's fine presence lending colour to the effect.[44]

Morice felt ambivalent about what he later called the "drastic nature of the proceeding." As a missionary priest he was duty bound to implore his people to reject "paganism"; as an Americanist he "felt a pang at the sight of the miniature museum going up in smoke."[45] Since events would soon show that he had become a far more dedicated scholar and printer than he ever was a devout and dutiful priest, it is fair to assume that he felt more than just a "pang" as he watched the Hotsoten burn their masks and other precious possessions. No longer was he fired with the evangelizing zeal that Bishop Durieu's work had inspired in him. The days when he took parties of Carrier to witness the Passion Plays and great meetings of the Lower Mainland tribes were over. From the time of his return from France he had become increasingly absorbed in the research for his map and in writing his dictionaries and other works. But for the duration of the bishop's visit, his old enthusiasm had perforce to manifest itself.

The Indians' eagerness to please and impress the bishop was less inhibited. While he was busy with the Babines and the Bulkley bands, the Fort George people rushed to repair and paint their church. A flag pole was erected and the Hudson's Bay Company's flag was borrowed for the occasion. On the day before the bishop was due to arrive, the Indians were "in a state of feverish excitement."[46] For nearly a week the natives of the Fort George area flocked to the mission exercises while the salmon swarmed up the river unmolested and the fur traders did little trading. Yet the company officials at Fort George bore no grudge. Indeed, on the next day, a Sunday, the fur traders attended a special Mass at which a new church bell was blessed. Here, as at the other big events of the tour, Morice spoke for the bishop. His linguistic skill together with the Carriers' extraordinary display of fervour, diligence, and propriety probably impressed the bishop and helped to counteract the bad reports about Morice circulated by Father Marchal and others. At Fort George and at Fort St. James, Dontenwill's principal preoccupation seems to have been to combat the illicit liquor traffic rather than the pagan vices of potlatching and shamanism. Solemn temperance pledges were extracted from those who gathered to see the "Great Father."[47]

The need for such promises and for the bonfire at Rocher Déboulé are a clear indication that Morice had not elevated his neophytes beyond the first stage of Bishop Durieu's system—the repression process. The number of communicants was small, and the cult of the Eucharist, the central focus of the moulding process, was weak. The repression of what the Oblates called public faults was still Morice's major concern as a missionary.

Naturally, there was a correlation between the duration and degree of white contact and the nature of the vices to be repressed. Drinking was a serious problem at Fort St. James and Fort George, where the inhabitants had experienced prolonged and close contact with fur traders and could easily visit Quesnel. Loring believed that the Stuart Lake people were the most materially progressive of the Carrier, and as proof he pointed to their planting of potatoes, fencing of fields, and harvesting of hay. Their attraction to digging and packing work for the Omineca mines also seems to have been seen as a sign of progress, as was the large number of cows that they kept.[48] Among these people, traditional potlatching seem to have been weak and possibly even non-existent. It was the more conservative and isolated Babine and Hotsoten branches of the Carrier tribe which clung to ancient practices. In 1902, Loring bemoaned the Hotsoten resistance to innovation; they preferred their semi-nomadic existence to the sedentary pursuits that many Gitksan and Stuart Lake Carrier were adopting.[49]

Yet the Indian agent was able to report that the bishop's ban on potlatching had been observed, as had the promises of the Fort St. James drinkers. The former development was what most pleased Loring, for as the Hotsotens' potlatch partners were Gitksan, the reform led to the decline of their potlatch too. With the heightened interracial friction that was accompanying the movement of settlers into the Hazelton and Bulkley Valley areas, Loring was relieved to see the weakening of links between Indian tribes. The conversion of the Gitksan and the Carrier to different Christian denominations had begun this process, and the apparent demise of the potlatch completed to Loring's satisfaction what he consciously regarded as a "divide and conquer" strategy. Since he believed that the Gitksan were quick to learn European ways and that the Hotsoten were naturally belligerent and cohesive, an alliance of the two tribes would have been "a great source of danger."[50] From his and the government's point of view, co-operation with Morice and the bishop had indeed paid handsome dividends.

In fact the Hotsoten were not as estranged from the Gitksan as the agent believed. Anthropological research conducted in the 1920's showed that the potlatch had continued and that the masks burned by the Hotsoten had been replaced by ones obtained from the Gitksan. However, the anthropologist concerned, Diamond Jenness, reported that "the acquisition and dramatization of the personal crests," which was the principal *raison d'être* for the potlatch, was "fast becoming a mere entertainment divorced from its old social significance." He noted also that the "very distinction between nobles and commoners has broken down."[51] Consequently, though the potlatch may have survived in secret after the bishop's visit, it soon became so politically and socially insignificant that it represented no danger to the interests of either the Indian agent or the Catholic missionary.

But as the potlatch was waning, the influence of Gitksan curing societies among the Hotsoten was increasing. The *kalullim* society was first introduced in the 1880's, but it was not firmly established until the turn of the century. Membership in the society was restricted to nobles who had suffered a minor attack of "*kyan* sickness," one of the symptoms of which was a craving for human flesh. Their recovery supposedly gave them the power to assist the specialist *kyan* doctors in the treatment of other victims. Since fees were paid to both the doctors and their assistants, joining the society brought wealth as well as prestige. When it came to combatting sickness, the Bulkley River Carrier obviously believed that an eclectic approach was wise, and in spite of all their promises to Morice and to the "Great Father," they neither abandoned the supernatural beliefs of their ancestors nor stopped borrowing those of their Indian neighbours. To these beliefs and rites, they simply added Christianity, which "increased life's complexity because its teachers and missionaries condemn the old principality and demand undivided allegiance to the new."[52] At times, such as the bishop's visit, enthusiasm for a true conversion to Christianity seems to have developed, and some individuals did persevere in their commitment to forsake the ancient ways.[53] But most people relapsed into traditionalism or syncretism, as had the people of Europe after their exposure to Christianity. What has been said of the long conversion process in Europe holds true for the Carrier too: it required "endurance" to maintain an orthodox Christian life "in the face of the ever-present loss of social amenities, club-life, and festivities."[54] It was at times of sickness that the Carrier faced their most trying dilemma. Failure to perform a traditional curing rite could, they believed, result in death, but disobeying the priest's injunctions would bring eternal damnation. Certain illnesses were thought to be caused by the imprisonment of a person's shadow by an animal spirit, during which time the person might learn a "medicine song." In order to be cured, it was necessary to sing this song, and the singing of medicine songs was strictly forbidden by the missionary. The Carrier were convinced that some people sickened and died because they were too frightened of the priest to release their songs.[55] Clearly, developing a satisfactory religious syncretism was not an easy task.

In order to help Morice in the constant struggle to suppress the old ways, Dontenwill at last sent him an assistant. He must have thought the need rather urgent, since the new man was dispatched soon after the bishop's return to New Westminster from his northern tour. Father E. C. Bellot, the young Frenchman assigned to this unenviable post, had not been in British Columbia very long, and he spoke English poorly.[56] Morice made no allowances for Bellot's linguistic shortcomings, and the young man's inability to "as much as pronounce" the sounds of the Carrier language was a convenient pretext for Morice to restrict him to cooking and housekeeping,[57] which gave Morice more time for writing and printing.

Like the Indian boy and the last priest sent to live with Morice, Bellot soon fled. He seems to have descended to Quesnel on the first spring boat, but he returned in June when Morice was away on a special mission to the Nahani who lived in the Stikine Valley.[58] Possibly Dontenwill reprimanded Bellot and instructed him to return to his post, or he may have been sent back temporarily to replace the absent Morice. All that is known about his activities in the summer of 1902 is that he spent the early part of July visiting the Sikani who gathered to trade at Fort McLeod. In doing so, he was assuming the former summer assignment of Father Blanchet. Unfortunately, the condition of the Sikani had deteriorated since the days when Blanchet ministered to the nomads, and the Hudson's Bay man who traded with them felt that they were being corrupted by the Stuart Lake Carrier as well as being exploited and robbed by them and transient whites. The Carrier were suspected of encouraging the Sikani to sell their best fur to the free trader Marion and of raiding their supply caches. In addition, a party of whites lost on their way to the Peace River refused to give the Sikani who had volunteered to guide them the food they had promised him for his return journey. The company clerk thought that this would be a "lesson learnt as to helping whites."[59] Yet despite his sympathy for the plundered Sikani, the fur trader harboured none of Morice's romantic ideas about them. He found them to be "careless and unthrifty" and paralysed with panic when struck by illness. Worse, they preferred gambling to trapping and paying their debts. And as far as the trader was concerned, "getting priest ridden" had reinforced these reprehensible traits. Consequently, he did not rejoice to see Father Bellot arrive, and when he noted the date of the Oblate's departure, he added a sardonic "good job too."[60] What Bellot did after his visit to Fort McLeod is unknown, but he had almost certainly left the district by the time Morice returned in mid-August.

Bellot had fled, but another white resident of Fort St. James had been forcibly removed during Morice's absence. On 16 June 1902, the store of Castillion, the local free trader, was "thrown down," and he was taken under arrest to Quesnel.[61] The man responsible for issuing the demolition order which led to the arrest was A. C. Murray. He had returned to the fort as chief factor in the summer of 1901, and early in 1902 he had been appointed a justice of the peace. Having confirmed that the trader's "shack" was erected on land owned by the company, Murray formally ordered Castillion to remove it in mid-May. Castillion did not comply. Instead, the fiery Frenchman threatened to chop down the company's building if he was not left alone; Murray feared that he might even resort to arson. In the face of this belligerent defiance of the law, the fledgling J. P. ordered Francis Prince, the Indian Affairs constable, and a white man whom he swore in as a special constable, to evict Castillion and to destroy his store. Castillion was arrested when he tried to scare off the constable with his gun; Francis and Leon Prince took him to Quesnel.[62]

Although Murray must have guessed that "French Joe" would resist and perhaps even resort to violence, he did not hesitate to take action against a competitor whom McNab had dismissed as inconsequential. The company probably changed its attitude toward Castillion because at the Easter *réunion* in April 1902 Chief Taya had told the Fort St. James Indians that all debts to Castillion had to be repaid.[63] Since the opposition trader had dispensed a large amount of "Jawbone" which had hitherto remained unpaid, such a massive repayment of debt might very well have suddenly made him a serious threat to the company. It is likely, too, that Murray's new judicial powers encouraged him to act. Whether Morice's absence influenced his timing is an intriguing question. Perhaps the priest resented Murray's elevation to the magistrate's bench and therefore prompted Taya to order the payment of debts to Castillion. One thing that this incident definitely does confirm, however, is that Murray feared

Morice's power to influence the fortunes of the company but was unable to counteract it effectively. Though Morice had interfered in both his business and private affairs, the chief factor had always tried to appease him, yet the eviction of Castillion indicates that Murray was not by nature a timid or indecisive man.

Against Morice he was simply impotent. The priest's pretensions and demands probably irked Murray as much as they always had, but after the trader's return to the fort in the summer of 1902, Morice seems to have re-established the old *modus vivendi*: the chief factor obliged the priest and, in return, expected him to use his influence in the interests of the company.[64] Since Loring continued to support and praise him, Morice must have felt that he had finally won back his undisputed supremacy over the other two members of the ruling white triad. Morice had not yet found a priest willing to replace Blanchet, but in other respects his life returned to the routine he enjoyed. In the late summer, he went to give missions to the people gathered to catch salmon at Stoney Creek and Natléh. He returned to the latter place at Christmas time, and in February 1903, he paid his annual winter visit to the Babines. A number of Hotsoten travelled all the way from Hazelton to attend the Hwotat mission, which indicates that the religious fervour whipped up amongst the Indians during the bishop's visit had not yet dissipated.[65]

Morice, on the other hand, seems to have been more and more preoccupied with his worldy hobbies—research and writing. During the winter, when John Prince probably moved in with him again, he turned his attention to a major new project. He decided to write what would today be called a culture contact history. It would describe and analyse the relationship between the Carrier and the whites, mainly the fur traders, who moved into their territory. The work was published in Toronto in 1904 under the title of *A History of the Northern Interior of British Columbia*. A year later, it was reprinted, and in 1906 it was published in Britain.[66] A new edition came out in 1971, at which time the publishers could justifiably refer to the book as "still a standard British Columbia History."[67] They should have added that the work was the result of a truly innovative synthesis of oral and documentary evidence. Morice was perhaps the first Canadian ethnohistorian, in that he realized that the methods of the historian and the ethnographer could be, and indeed had to be, combined if histories of Indian-white relations were to be written. He described the genesis of the work as follows:

> in the course of my [anthropological and linguistic] researches among them [the Carrier] I had found most interesting traditions referring to late enough events wh[ich], after proper control and critical compari-

sons, had proved to constitute the elements of genuine history rather than the more or less fabulous myths of American aborigines.[68]

His long experience as a missionary obviously facilitated Morice's collection of oral tradition and oral evidence—the former refers to stories passed down from generation to generation and the latter to eye witness accounts. Knowing the language and culture intimately, Morice had the ability to get informants to spend many hours relating their tales to him. A particularly valuable informant was old Julian Etê Tsaniya, the former native prophet who had rendered Morice such sterling service as a language teacher when he first arrived at Fort St. James.[69] In the years that followed, Julian, who was probably too old to trap, seems to have acted as Morice's messenger. This task, as well as being a source of linguistic and historical information, perhaps gave Julian a sense of purpose. The Carrier knew that Morice was some kind of savant—he was "smart," as they put it—and they were not reluctant to tell him their tribal lore. They seem to have accepted his assurance that he, unlike some whites, did not belittle them "behind their backs."[70]

In the *History of the Northern Interior,* it was whites, particularly important figures, who were debunked. If any hero emerges from its pages, it is Chief Kwah, who is shown overpowering and humiliating the impetuous young James Douglas, then a clerk at Fort St. James and later the first governor of British Columbia.[71] Morice had Kwah's wooden tomb engraved with the following epitaph:

Here Lie the Remains
of
Great Chief Kwah
Born About 1755
Died Spring of 1840
He once had in his hands the life of (future Sir) James Douglas, but was great enough to refrain from taking it.[72]

This English version was placed below the same inscription written in the Carrier syllables invented by Morice. The tomb still stands amid the undergrowth that lines the bank of Stuart Lake near the point where it flows into the Stuart River. The present writer was guided to it by a Carrier woman who was splitting and drying salmon after the fashion of her ancestors. The wording of the epitaph is yet another indication that in his relations with the white civilization from which he had fled Morice remained an anarchist individualist. In writing the *History of the Northern Interior,* he evidently relished the opportunity to reduce the stature of white dignitaries by contrasting their ignoble acts with those of such a "noble savage" as Kwah.[73] Since much of the book was written just after Morice was removed from his post—a move that was probably prompted at least in part by complaints from the Hudson's Bay Company—his uninhibited exposure of the public sins of the early fur traders was undoubtedly motivated to some extent by a desire for vengeance. That is not to say that he fabricated or distorted evidence; there is no reason to believe that he did. He simply was not willing to "pull his punches."

The company resented this, particularly since it had provided Morice with so much of the incriminating information. Finding oral history data inadequate for his purposes, the priest had sought reliable written accounts of early Indian-white contact. Hearing of this search, Murray mentioned that there were numerous old papers in the attic of the fort. To his amazement and joy, Morice found that though some of the documents were in a bad state, they turned out to be "a veritable treasure." Among these precious papers were sections of the journals of Simon Fraser and his assistant, John Stuart, as well as hundreds of letters.[74] Naturally, Morice wanted to peruse the whole collection, and Murray allowed him to take the documents. It seems, however, that Morice never did return them. The only other condition which Murray imposed on Morice's use of the company papers was that his book would not mention "what would be considered as family affairs or facts of [a] strictly personal character."[75] Morice agreed and went to work combining the documentary evidence with oral testimony, using one to verify and/or augment the other. This was exactly the method later used and recommended by such professional ethnohistorians as Oscar Lewis, whose 1942 study of the effect of the fur trade on the Blackfoot is a more dispassionate product of the same methodology.[76]

Although it was Murray's generosity which had provided him with the documents indispensible for the writing of his *History,* Morice did not hesitate to threaten the chief factor when he was unwilling to grant unreasonable favours. Entirely unintimidated by Murray's magisterial powers and his eviction of Castillion, in April 1903, Morice demanded that the company send a canoe to fetch "his things," presumably the mission's provisions or his books and other mail or perhaps both, from Quesnel. And reverting to his old tactic, he said that he would dispatch his own canoe and crew if Mr. Murray refused. The blackmail worked, but it was with reluctance that the chief factor once more conceded victory to his ungrateful neighbour. He explained his decision to oblige Morice to the company's new manager at Victoria:

> The Indians whom he would send would be some of those with good hunts, and could afford to go, for he does not pay them a cent for

freight. I know these fellows so well it is a great thing to prevent any of them from making the first start. If they have a start, it is almost a sure thing that everybody else who can afford it will follow.[77]

Murray expected to make a "good profit" in 1903, and he obviously was not prepared to jeopardize it by confronting Morice as McNab had done.[78] The decline of river freighting between the fort and Quesnel which accompanied the decreased flow of miners to the Omineca gold fields probably meant that trapping was regaining its traditionally predominant position and that trips to Quesnel were once again associated with higher fur prices rather than lucrative freighting jobs. Murray's decision might also have been influenced by the high prices being paid by the local "opposition." In February 1903, the company's clerk at Fort Fraser, Mr. E. S. Peters, was forced to raise lynx prices because of the presence of a free trader at Stoney Creek, and when the area's Indians gathered for the spring mission at Natléh, Peters paid $105 for a silver fox pelt. In an effort to get an even higher price, the trapper had tried to make the fur seem darker by rubbing it with charcoal.[79] Notwithstanding this constant search for higher prices, it does not seem as though the Fort St. James trappers were planning to go to Quesnel. Consequently, if Morice had carried out his threat, he would have been initiating the very anti-Hudson's Bay Company move which he had originally volunteered to help curb. So long as the fort people wanted to try to get higher prices at Quesnel and Morice stopped them, the chief factor obliged and humoured him. But when the missionary declared his intention to precipitate a rush to Quesnel by trappers who would otherwise have traded "at home," Murray must surely have come to regard him as a dangerous enemy whose continued presence was undesirable.

One thing is certain: Morice remained obsessed with flaunting his power and maintaining his independence, financial and otherwise—hence his desire to force Murray to carry his freight free of charge. He continued to assert his paramount position vis-à-vis other potential competitors too. When in May 1902, a Fort George Indian was arrested and confined to the company's house after murdering a "Chinaman," Morice demanded that the prisoner be handed over to him.[80] He resented the exercise of power by any other group or person. This included of course Constable Anderson at Quesnel and Indian Agent Bell from Clinton. In the summer of 1902, both men complained to Superintendent of Indian Affairs Vowell about Morice's "undue interference."[81]

Such conduct would be understandable or even excusable if Morice had devoted himself to the welfare of his flock and if the actions of the Hudson's Bay Company and the federal and provincial governments' officials had been consistently inimical to the Indians' spiritual and material progress. But this was not the case. Morice had so neglected his priestly duties that the Stuart Lake Indians complained to Bishop Dontenwill. It is impossible to find out whether these complaints were relayed directly to the bishop or were conveyed via Father Bellot or the Hudson's Bay Company. In any event, it is likely that Morice was reprimanded and warned to mend his ways when he visited the Lower Mainland in the spring of 1903. Probably the main objective of this trip was to go to libraries in Vancouver and Victoria to consult books and documents for his *History*. Dontenwill also responded by assigning Morice a new and energetic young assistant, Father Pierre Marie Conan.[82] Conan seems to have journeyed to Fort St. James late in June 1903.[83]

Father Conan had offered to go to Fort St. James even though he had heard about Morice's behaviour from Fathers Marchal and Lejeune. He was working with the latter at Kamloops at the time of his transfer to Stuart Lake. A powerful ox of a man, Conan was also pious and intelligent. He seems to have enjoyed wilderness travel as much as Morice did, and soon after his arrival, Morice took him along on his 1903 summer trip to Lake Babine and Rocher Déboulé. But at the conclusion of the Rocher Déboulé mission, Conan parted company with Morice and returned to the Fort via Babine Lake. Morice now considered himself to be "free" for a few weeks, and he planned to map the source of the Bulkley River.[84] This entailed travelling up what is known today as the Morice River. As neither of the Sikani bands had been visited that year, it is hard to see how Morice could have thought himself free to explore in the opposite direction from their summer camps. He had not gone to Bear Lake since his exploration of the Nilkitkwa River in August 1899, nor to McLeod Lake since he mapped the route from Fort George to Fort McLeod via the Crooked River in June of the same year.

It is quite clear that Morice's desire to complete his map was greater than his sense of duty as a missionary. A short expedition undertaken in September 1901 had enabled him to draw a map of the Nechako Basin and a section of the Stuart's Lake Valley. After that, all he needed was a few extra journeys to permit him to prepare a map of the entire Northern Interior.[85] His explorations were part of his compulsive need to control his environment. He wanted to be the area's geographer, historian, linguist, and ethnographer as well as its priest-king. But no man, not even one as gifted and driven as Morice, could do it all; therefore, he neglected his converts.

While Morice was still on his expedition, Father Conan had returned to Fort St. James in a state of despair, and he decided to quit the district. On 22 August, he wrote a long letter to Father Lejeune, who seems to have been his confidant, in which he explained his reasons for abandoning his post without the bishop's permission. It seems that Conan's two month stay at Stuart Lake had been enough to confirm the truth of the stories about Morice which he had heard from Lejeune and Marchal. The Carriers' veteran missionary had made it perfectly clear that he wanted Conan to be his cook rather than an assistant in the holy ministry. The aspect of Morice's behaviour which most shocked and discouraged Conan was his monarchical manner. The young priest refused to conform to this way of treating Indians. Morice, he told Lejeune, "from the height of his grandeur treated the natives like slaves," and consequently many of them were discontented. And while Morice demanded to be treated as a potentate, he seemed not to know what was going on in the villages.[86] He must, in fact, have been aware of the flouting of the prohibitions on gambling and potlatching, which indicate that he was content with a public acceptance of his authority. Father Morice's commitment to religious acculturation was less important to him than his personal prestige. The tacit toleration of the Carriers' syncretism was certainly not motivated by philosophical reflexion; in principle, Morice was in favour of a total conversion. But to have achieved it, when he had either no assistants or assistants to whom he refused to delegate any religious authority, would have taken too much time from his exploration, writing, and his broker role. Grant has suggested that by stopping halfway, as it were, Morice made of the Durieu System "precisely the police activity that Durieu had sought to avoid."[87]

The consequences of Morice's negligence were all too clear to his new assistant. Comparing the Indians of the Stuart Lake district to Father Lejeune's Shuswaps, Conan reported them to be more immoral, lazy, and far behind in their spiritual development. The Sikani were not visited at all, and the Babines of the lake and those of the Bulkley Valley seemed to Conan to be quarrelsome. Moreover, those of the Hazelton area were influenced by Protestantism, and among them nobody had received Communion. The Carrier of Stuart Lake and those further south, whom Morice visited more often, were scarcely better disposed or more spiritually advanced, particularly those who lived around Fort George and Stoney Creek. Conan further claimed that a majority of the men in one of the two Indian villages at Fort St. James wanted a new priest.[88]

The lamentable state of affairs throughout the Stuart Lake mission district obviously scandalized the young man assigned to assist the mission's director. Yet it was Morice's attitude towards him which most discouraged Conan. Notwithstanding the Indians' need for instruction and surveillance and their pastor's blatant negligence, this same pastor nevertheless believed that any other priest would spoil them.[89] Conan therefore left, passing through Fort George on his way south on 31 August, just about the time when Morice would have been returning from his mission at Natleh.[90]

Although Father Conan was later removed from the ministry because of mental illness—he treated an Indian as a saint—his observations concerning Morice and his flock seem reliable enough.[91] The existence of Indian malcontents, for instance, is corroborated by oral testimony. Some, like the Princes, rebelled against Morice's autocracy; others believed that he did not do enough to prepare them to compete with the white man. In particular, they noted that he did not establish a school and refused to teach them to read and write English. In 1974, Mr. Justa Hansen, an elderly Stuart Lake Carrier, showed the present writer his copy of Morice's *History of the Northern Interior of British Columbia,* and then with a touch of bitterness, he explained that Morice's opposition to teaching English meant that he could not read the book.[92] John Prince, Morice's former "house boy," also recalled the priest's negative attitude to English-language schooling. Neither of the two Indian informants understood the priest's motives, though both questioned his sanity. Mr. Hansen described Morice as being "like [a] crazy man," and when John Prince was asked why Morice opposed English education, he replied: "I don't know. He [was] crazy anyway."[93]

For men of John Prince's generation, literacy in English represented an escape from what they regarded as ignorance, an ignorance which condemned them to watch whites monopolize good jobs.[94] Their reaction to Morice's negligence and to his opposition to their acquisition of the whites' secular culture tends to support Elizabeth Graham's contention that Indians threatened by the settlement frontier were most inclined to support a missionary who seemed capable of helping them to adjust to the new conditions. And Clarence Bolt has shown that in the 1870's, the Tsimshian of Port Simpson wanted to westernize and expected the Methodist Thomas Crosby to facilitate their assimilation.[95] Like the Tsimshian, the Carrier seem to have felt they must quickly learn the white man's language and ways. Yet their missionary gave them no assistance whatsoever. Being a broker with white officials was his only important secular service. Far from being in conformity with official Oblate policy directives, Morice's refusal to teach English contravened explicit instructions from French-speaking Oblate leaders to promote the use of English, which would be a better medium than the native languages for the communication of Christian concepts.[96] Father Morice himself had an impressive command of English, and he used it to great effect in his scholarly writing. If the Carrier had acquired a better knowledge of English and hence a greater ability to deal directly with whites, Morice's influence would surely have declined. Already some of the most acculturated Indians had broken away from him and were themselves becoming cross-cultural agents for the Hudson's Bay Company, the magistrates, Indian Agent Bell and Constable Anderson. In other words, a new intermediary system was being established in direct competition with Morice. He had taken over the powerful broker role from Taya, the fur trade chief, and now the senior Prince brothers were undermining his power by siding with and serving his white rivals. In April 1903, when Francis Prince, the Indian constable who had disarmed and arrested Castillion, wanted some information, he wrote directly to the province's Indian Affairs superintendent, bypassing both Morice and Loring.[97] Perhaps Murray or some other company man helped him compose his letter. Morice could have better maintained his influence among his Indian charges if, like William Duncan, he had helped them to achieve the social and economic change which many of them wanted.[98] But his personality and the nature of his ambitions meant that he was not suited for such a role change.

The only person who still regarded Morice as a useful ally was Loring. Consequently, he continued to support the priest while other white officials became increasingly irritated by his threats, and the Indians and his Oblate assistant complained about his negligence and his dictatorial demeanour. Loring made one of his infrequent visits to Fort St. James just as Conan was leaving. The trip was inspired in part by a letter from Vowell which implied that Loring was neglecting his duties in the Carrier section of his agency. In the spring, Morice had written directly to Vowell complaining about the impoverished state of the Sikani, which to some extent was the result of destructive trapping by a man named Henri Varice. Loring had promised to confer with Morice about the problem and to visit Fort St. James to investigate. Writing from the fort on 30 August 1903, he recommended that since Morice knew the Sikani and the grievances best, he should be given the right to order the distribution of relief supplies from the Hudson's Bay Company stores.[99] This was exactly the kind of extra power that McNab, and probably Murray too, did not want Morice to have.

Thus, while the Hudson's Bay Company was trying to check Morice's power, the Indian agent was attempting to bolster it. In his "Annual Report for the Year ending June 30th, 1903," Loring lavishly praised the Oblate missionary. While he did admit, rather reluctantly and defensively, that the Carrier had no schools, he emphasized that the natives were taught the syllabic script and had weekly and monthly newspapers printed for them at Fort St. James.[100] But no weekly paper had ever been produced, and there is no evidence that Morice was still publishing his monthly Carrier journal.

The Lorings were certainly Morice's loyal allies, but they were not powerful enough to save him from himself. In the autumn of 1903, Bishop Dontenwill decided to remove him from Fort St. James. It is unlikely that Morice's highhanded, autocratic manner of dealing with Indians was, in itself, considered grounds for dismissal, since other Oblates were equally dictatorial—and continue to be well into the twentieth century. Father Coccola, the Corsican who had arrived with Morice from France and who was to succeed him at Fort St. James, used the whip freely, being convinced that Indians "submit only to an iron hand."[101] Priests like Blanchet, Conan, and Lejeune may not have agreed with this attitude,[102] but there had been no official renunciation of public confessions and whippings. What did bring down Father Morice were the reports of his negligence from Bellot and Conan and complaints from the Hudson's Bay Company.[103] There appears to have been some communication between the bishop and the company's manager James Thomson, and while the nature of the complaints is not known, they probably concerned the use of threats by Morice to force Murray to carry his goods as well as his other attempts to interfere in company affairs.[104] Fortunately, the bishop chose to act cautiously, for transferring Morice was like deposing a king. Rather than sending him an order to leave his beloved mission, Dontenwill apparently planned to inform Morice of his decision when the latter came down to Vancouver to spend the winter of 1903–4 preparing the manuscript of his *History of the Northern Interior* for publication.[105] It would be a one-way trip. Morice did not know this, though other white residents of the Northern Interior guessed as much. When Morice left Fort St. James in early November, he carried with him a letter addressed to Mr. Thomson of the Hudson's Bay Company. The letter was written by Murray, and it was mainly concerned with company business. But Murray briefly mentioned Morice's departure, and noted in parentheses that he was leaving "perhaps forever."[106] Obviously the bishop had intimated to the Company that something would be done about Morice.

On 10 November, Morice's boat reached Quesnel, where Louis Dixon, the Hudson's Bay Company clerk, handed him a telegram. Dated 7 November 1903, it was from Bishop Dontenwill. It read as follows: "Tell Indians wait for priest to go Stuart's Lake." According to Dixon, the fact that a replacement priest was coming was a "great surprise" to Morice, who was "very much upset over the matter." He assured Dixon that it was a mistake and rushed off to the telegraph office to send a Latin cable to the bishop. This done, Morice returned to the company's building and hinted that he might cancel his plans to winter at the coast.[107] Either Morice had an extraordinary fear of the influence that another priest might have upon his flock and ultimately his power, or else he suspected that the priest who was on his way up was intended to replace him permanently.

When the stage arrived with the replacement, Morice was thrown into a real panic. It was Conan, whom Morice later accused of "having set everything upside down" while he was alone at Stuart Lake during Morice's exploration in August. Exactly what Conan had done was never clarified, though, in Morice's words, it concerned "the capital question of Christian education," which probably meant that Conan was too lax and explicitly or implicitly challenged Morice's rigorous rules for admission to baptism and communion.[108] Possibly Conan had heightened the discontent of the Carrier and acted as a focus for it, which would explain why Morice was particularly opposed to his return to the district. The Indian boatmen who waited patiently to take Conan up later reported to their fellows at Fort St. James that Morice told the young priest that the Stuart Lake Indians were "no good' and that the best thing for him to do would be to turn back. Conan refused, arguing that since he was under orders from the bishop, he had no choice but to proceed.[109]

Morice was faced with a dreadful dilemma. If he continued south, he risked losing his kingdom by default; if he turned back, he would be unable to finish his book on schedule. He needed to consult works that were not available at his remote mission.[110] As he weighed the consequences of either course, Father Morice must have been aware that a retreat to Fort St. James would be just the prelude to a fierce battle with Dontenwill. Yet this prospect probably did not intimidate him, since he had fought and won similar struggles before. Indeed, perhaps the fact that he had always triumphed over his superiors persuaded him that he need not jeopardize his book by returning to the fort immediately. Even if Dontenwill wanted to remove him, he would ultimately prevail. In any event, Morice continued his journey. Throughout these deliberations, Morice and Conan were studied intently by Louis Dixon. On 12 November, when Morice was preparing to board the southbound stage, Dixon penned a letter to Thomson in which he described in detail the little drama which he and the Indian voyageurs had witnessed. At the end of the letter, he explained that he was sending such information "as it is evident that something is working in the Bishop's mind which may very possibly relieve the northern country of Father Morice."[111] This remark suggests that Dixon, like Murray, was privy to the bishop's intent and that he too relished the prospect of getting rid of Morice.

Both men got their wish. While it is impossible to establish the exact nature of the charges levelled against him, the question of priestly negligence clearly decided Morice's fate.[112] After examining various documents and soliciting the opinion of men who knew Morice, the Oblate historian Father George Forbes reached the following conclusion:

> Father Morice's Oblate confrères ... seem to agree with his Bishop
> that he would have been a greater missionary had he given more time
> to the evangelization of the Indians and less to his studies, explora-
> tions, and writings.[113]

This judgment is characteristic of the charitable and magnanimous spirit
which the order always displayed in its relations with Morice.

Sadly, he was incapable of reciprocating. Otherwise, he would not have
left the Sikani without the sacraments for years or kept pressing Murray
for more favours and concessions. Morice was so infatuated with his own
success that he was not able to make the calculated compromises that
might have saved his kingdom. Just a little more attention to his priestly
duties and to the aspirations of the more acculturated Indians might have
satisfied his flock. This, together with a little respect and delegation of authority, would no doubt have prevented his young assistants from running
to the bishop with their damaging reports. But there is no evidence whatsoever to indicate that Morice was conscious of either the major elements
of his personality or of his strategic blunders. Foremost among the latter
was the fact that he ceased to pay enough attention to administrative detail
once he considered that his power base was secure. Instead, he turned to
conquests further afield. In doing so, he lost the "kingdom" which was
his childhood dream come true. At the age of forty-four, Father Morice
was forced once again to experience what was for him the dreadful prospect of living in the white man's world. He was, as was Prospero, "the es-
capist deeply reluctant to give up his magic, to leave his desert island and
to return to the society of people who would argue with him."[114] Only in a
colonial situation such as existed on the British Columbia frontier could
Morice satisfy his need for human relations of inequality and acknowledged subordination—for a paternalism long overthrown in his native
France.

EPILOGUE

"A fish cannot thrive out of water; how could Father Morice have flourished away from his beloved Indians?" Morice himself asked this rhetorical question in the autobiography he wrote in 1930 under the pseudonym "D. L. S." He answered it by claiming that since leaving Fort St. James he had been the unhappy victim of all manner of indignities and malicious conspiracies at the hands of his Oblate superiors.[1] What actually happened after 1903 was that Morice's inability to live in a European society caused him to behave erratically and to become convinced, unjustifiably, that he was being persecuted.[2] Unfortunately, the only historian to have written about Morice's career after he left British Columbia seems to have been influenced by the accusations made in his autobiography, for he has implied that the Oblates failed to give Morice "the necessary support and encouragement" in his academic pursuits. But Morice did not *have* to "finance his creative activities" by the "private sale of books," as Raymond Huel has suggested; he chose to do so in order to assert his independence from his superiors.[3]

It was this perennial anarchic individualism that prevented Morice from living peacefully in any Oblate community. He always clashed, often violently, with his fellow priests, and in 1908, after he was badly beaten in a fight, the Oblate authorities in Rome concluded that they would be forced to have him certified insane and committed to an asylum.[4] But constrained by the difficulty of proving madness in an acclaimed scholar and anxious to avoid a public scandal, they instead, and as a last resort, transferred Father Morice from British Columbia to Manitoba. He was described upon his arrival as having a sick heart and a ruined body.[5] The change did little to improve his demeanour, which closely resembled the rebelliousness he had exhibited at Williams Lake in the mid-1880's when he was refused permission to work among the Carrier. The most dramatic manifestation of this new malaise occurred at the Oblate Juniorate in St. Boniface. Morice had been given a room there in 1913, and by 1919 he regarded the college's director, Father Louis Péalapra, as an implacable and cunning enemy. According to Morice, Péalapra was jealous of his literary successes and was conspiring to rob him of the tranquillity which he needed in order to write: lights were positioned to annoy him, a student sent to play the piano nearby, and the cleaner was instructed to put a pungent disinfectant on his bed.[6] Finally, Morice could tolerate this "persecution" no longer, and he retaliated in kind. One evening, as the Juniorate's other residents were beginning their night's sleep, he repeatedly dropped his walking stick, his ruler, and his scissors on the floor at regular intervals. The protest disturbance was so successful that after half an hour of the carefully-timed percussions Morice's two locked doors—the extra one was built because he constantly complained about the chatter and laughter of his colleagues—were forced open, and he was physically restrained.[7] Although Father Péalapra had no choice but to have the room broken into, Morice tried to use the "brigandage" as further proof of the supposed conspiracy. Henceforth, Morice referred to the Juniorate's director as the "Chief of the Brigands," and he attributed the refusal of the Father Provincial to punish him to Péalapra's ability to hypnotize superiors.[8]

Convinced that he could expect neither peace nor justice from the Oblates, Morice fled the St. Boniface Juniorate early in 1920 and was a "fugitive" for more than two years. Sympathetic parish priests took him in, but as he fought with all of them, he eventually found himself without a sanctuary.[9] In May 1923, he returned. But a few months later, the priests he was living with in Marieval, Saskatchewan, put him into a car and "dumped" him, without notice or authorization, on their colleagues in Lebret. Morice protested that he had been kidnapped, and, technically, the word seems apt. That priests should have resorted to such an extreme measure is an index of the exasperation and despair Morice was capable of provoking among those charged with caring for him. He already had been treated in hospital a number of times, and while at Marieval he was described as suffering from neurasthenia, a vague and now archaic diagnosis based on a speculative neurophysiological theory of nervous and physical exhaustion. Variously ascribed to hard work, to modern life, or to masturbation, the diagnosis contributes little to an understanding of Morice's condition. In any event, the doctor, probably prompted by Morice but in conformity with the standard practice in such cases, recommended that his patient live alone or in a place of absolute tranquillity, and in 1925 he was given permission to move into rented rooms in a house on Austin Street in Winnipeg.[10] Father Morice needed, as he always had, a refuge from the society of his peers and the authority of his superiors—in other words, a substitute for his Indian mission. At 200 Austin Street, he found it. The owner was killed in a street accident soon after Morice moved in, and the Oblates bought the house from his widow, who agreed to stay on as his housekeeper. Morice contributed toward the cost of the house, and he soon came to regard it as his own.[11] There his books were written, stored, and dispatched to libraries and individual readers. It became his private publishing house. Of course, his superiors knew he was breaking his vow of poverty, which forbade private property, but their only reaction was to send him strongly worded but impotent rebukes. Father N. J. Dozois, the *Assistant Général* in Rome, told Morice that whereas he was just one of a number of Oblates who wrote books, he alone had used this as a "pretext to create for yourself a situation practically independent of superiors."[12]

In 1929, these superiors were informed that Morice was openly defying a Church ban on membership in the *Action Française*. A radically anti-democratic and anti-semetic French monarchist movement which historian Ernst Nolte says "should be called early fascism," the *Action Française* was lead by atheistic "Catholics by calculation," who tried to use the Church to achieve their political ends.[13] Given his authoritarian personality and his evident hostility towards Jews, Morice's membership in the movement is natural enough. It could even be said that he resembled the leaders of the *Action Française* in that, as a missionary, he too had used the Church for his own non-religious purposes. But among French Catholic priests, Morice was far from alone in his attachment to the movement. After its interdiction by the Church in 1926, there were numerous examples of "furtive disobedience" by priests,[14] but in Morice's case the refusal to comply was blatant and at times provocative. A parish priest who had gone to collect a book from him was presented with it wrapped in a back issue of the journal of *Action Française*. When challenged by the priest and later by Father J. Magnan, the Oblate Father Provincial for Manitoba, Morice denied the right of the Church to rule on a matter which was as "purely political" as the case of Galileo had been "purely scientific."[15] Once again, his refusal to subordinate himself to the order and to the Church which he had vowed to obey, and to which he owed so much, was thrown in the face of his perplexed superiors. Magnan wrote to Dozois in Rome for guidance, though he did not hesitate to state that his own preference was to let the affair "remain hidden." Morice was "so dangerous" that a scandal would probably follow any official intervention. During previous conflicts, he had threatened to break with the Oblates and to publish his reasons for doing so; a court case was also hinted at. Magnan and others in Manitoba doubted whether he was responsible for his actions, and they believed that in his present mental state he could not be convinced of his error.[16] Father Dozois accepted Magnan's recommendation: the delusion from which the *"pauvre grand homme"* suffered was complete, and thus he was innocent in God's eyes.[17] Morice's disobedience was not proof of mental irresponsibility, but the subversive individualism out of which it grew was so abnormally assertive and uncompromising that insanity seemed to be the only explanation for it. It was surely an attractive explanation, too, for it gave his superiors grounds for avoiding a problematical confrontation, one which could have ended with his expulsion from the Oblates.

Yet from the time he moved into the house in Winnipeg until his death on 21 April 1938, Father Morice was an Oblate in name only, and, if anything, he seems henceforth to have become less agitated and erratic in his behaviour. His regained independence, and his housekeeper's kind and deferential service would account for this amelioration. Apparently, Mrs. Martha Worsick was a gentle and patient woman, and her relationship with Morice resembled that which had existed between him and Georges Blanchet after the old man had abandoned his initial resistance to Morice's rule.[18] Thus at 200 Austin Street Father Morice came as near as he could reasonably expect to duplicating the freedom and the kind of personal relationships which he had enjoyed in his Indian mission. His job in Manitoba was to write biographies and histories for the Church, but since the native languages and cultures remained his real love, he continued to devote much of his great energy to his linguistic and ethnographic researches. He also continued to desire and expect recognition for his impressive achievements in so many fields, and when this was not forthcoming, what the cartographer G. S. Andrews has called his "bitterness" and "vainglory" were displayed in the autobiographical *Fifty Years in Western Canada*. In 1929, when Andrews was still a student, he visited Morice in Winnipeg to express his appreciation of the priest's map and his *History of the Northern Interior*. Morice's reception of Andrews is revealing: "He finally jumped up, grasped my hands, and looking at me with earnest radiance, he exclaimed: 'How happy you make me! . . . It is the first time, . . . yes! you are the first to come from there to seek me out here in appreciation of my work!' " An animated conversation followed, one which gave Morice "exciting pleasure." Upon taking leave of Morice, Andrews was told by Mrs. Worsick that "the tycoons of the Church were content, for the sake of peace, to let Father Morice live . . . in the privacy and detachment of his own house, to work unfettered at his chosen researches."[19]

The most important of these researches, and the one which he considered to be his *magnum opus,* was the Carrier dictionary and grammar. It was the need to collect and verify data for this work that twice took him back to the Carriers at the Stuart Lake mission. He was not disappointed with his "beloved children."[20] At the conclusion of his first visit, in 1919, they gave him a substantial sum of money, and between 1920 and his second and last visit in 1927, Louis Billy Prince responded to his frequent requests for linguistic information. They corresponded in the Carrier syllabic script.[21] During the 1927 visit, Louis Billy, who had now succeeded his brother Joseph Prince as the chief of the Fort St. James band, spent eight hours a day for three weeks helping Morice prepare his manuscript for publication. But he received neither an acknowledgment in the preface nor a fee.[22] Indeed, Morice actually appealed to him and the other Carrier to contribute toward the cost of printing his massive and esoteric study. They gave him the then substantial sum of $130, and he apparently appreciated their generosity. When he addressed them in the church for the last time, he broke down and wept.[23] It has been said of the Jesuits in Paraguay that they gave "their muddled-headed love to the Indians in their Machiavelian way,"[24] and the same could be said of Morice. A woman had come to the priest's house to cook for him during his three-week visit, and as a token of his thanks she received a book—a printer's reject with the pages bound in the wrong order.[25] This incident was recounted by Louis Billy Prince's daughter, who felt that Morice had used her father and other Indians without adequately acknowledging their invaluable services.[26] Her resentment is understandable, though she probably did not fully comprehend the extent of Morice's debt to the Carrier and Sikani people. They had provided him with a geographical and human arena for the gratification of his will to power. Being their missionary and exploring their mountains and lakes helped to satiate his enormous appetite for conquest; writing about their language and culture spread his influence as a scholar. Morice longed for recognition from the white world, but he never really belonged to it. Essentially he was an outsider who was happiest when in the wilderness with his "primitive" native companions. In this respect, he resembled not only Petitot and Chateaubriand's hero, Réné, but also some of Britain's most famous nineteenth-century missionaries and Africanists. Mary Kingsley never felt a part of the upper class English society into which she was born, and the power gained from ascending uncharted African rivers and bringing "under her domination the most ruthless savages" convinced her that the "society of London [was] dull and pointless."[27] David Livingstone too was interested above all in exploration and fame; he found it difficult to tolerate either the companionship of his fellow whites or the monotony of trying to convert and "civilize" Africans at mission stations.[28]

Although Morice was an explorer, he was also an ordinary missionary in a way that Livingstone was not. He had his own mission district, and once he become ensconced among the Carrier, he became an excellent example of what anthropologist R. W. Dunning has called the "marginal man": a white leader whose "non-democratic" behaviour, though it contravenes "normal Canadian ethical standards," nevertheless allows him to "operate most successfully" as a powerful figure among native people. In his influential 1959 article on leadership in small northern communities, Dunning warned that the "often capricious, authoritarian, and discriminatory" behaviour of these white contact persons was undermining efforts to achieve native "developmental change." Dunning attributed the ethically unCanadian conduct of the marginal men to the social marginality created by geographic isolation: the man on the margin is no longer subject to the subtle but effective "social sanctions" imposed by peers in the course of occupational and recreational activities.[29] This explanation neglects both personality and social role as possible causes of the marginal man's comportment. It is clear that Morice's emotional alienation from his own world strongly influenced his decision to be a missionary. It offered an escape from the social sanctions of his peers. The same appears to have been true of certain key missionaries elsewhere in the world. They were misanthropic misfits who sought independence and status on the colonial margins of their societies, and their goals could hardly have been attained without the kind of behaviour which Dunning observed and criticized.[30] A missionary's conviction that he was transmitting a "superior" religion and culture would have reinforced a personal predisposition to act arbitrarily.

Among British Columbia missionaries, the leading Protestant, William Duncan, seems to have been as much of a misfit as Morice—and equally bent on creating a new world, a word free of constraints on his will. Both men were constantly at odds with their superiors, and neither of them faithfully implemented the policies of their respective missionary organizations. They also shared an inability to accept missionary colleagues as co-workers. Of the two, Duncan made the greater impact on native society, for his commitment to sweeping economic and social change apparently coincided with native wishes. Unlike Morice, Duncan also had the advantage of working with a geographically more concentrated population, and he did not try to combine proselytizing with exploration and scholarship.[31] Duncan was a radical and autocratic organizer of "progressive" social change—a thoroughly modern man. Morice was a reactionary eager to cultivate among his converts ties of dependence like those of a feudal, paternalistic community. Hence his refusal to teach English and his fear of any acculturation beyond religious conversion. His anachronistic aspirations were substantially realized on the British Columbia frontier in the period after the Hudson's Bay Company had lost its monopoly and before the officials of the settlement frontier were numerous and firmly in place. For Morice, the settlement frontier was anathema. It was the society he could not control catching up with him. Even if he had not neglected the Carriers' spiritual life, he could not have long prevailed against their desire to learn English and in other ways to prepare themselves to cope with the new reality of miner and settler encroachment. Preoccupied with exploration and writing, and apparently confident that his native "children" were still loyal and that the fur traders and officials remained too dependent on him to be a threat, Morice failed to adjust to the new circumstances. Thus it was ultimately his own blind egotism and ambition which precipitated his downfall. Father Morice was an exceptionally gifted man, as his enduring linguistic, ethnographic, and historical writings eloquently testify. But as a wiser Oblate once said with reference to him, "brilliant people too often allow themselves to be consumed with pride and then they become more foolish than the ignorant."[32]

ABBREVIATIONS

AD	Archives Deschâtelets, Oblates of Mary Immaculate, Ottawa
AHIBC	Aural History Institute of British Columbia
APW	Archives provinciales des Oblats, Winnipeg, microfilm records
C	Colombie records
CMS	Church Missionary Society, North Pacific Mission, Correspondence
HBCA	Hudson's Bay Company Archives, London
O	Oregon records
PABC	Provincial Archives of British Columbia, Victoria
PAC	Public Archives of Canada, Ottawa
UBCL	University of British Columbia Library, Special Collections Division, Vancouver
US	Archives of the University of Saskatchewan, Saskatoon

NOTES

NOTES TO THE PREFACE

1. Wilson Duff, *The Indian History of British Columbia: Vol. 1. The Impact of the White Man,* Anthropology in British Columbia, Memoir no. 5 (Victoria: Provincial Museum, 1964), p. 91.
2. D. L. S., *Fifty Years in Western Canada, Being the Abridged Memoirs of Rev. A. G. Morice, O.M.I.* (Toronto: Ryerson, 1930). Despite his denials, it is clear that Morice wrote *Fifty Years* himself. There are two possible reasons for him to have hidden this fact. In the first place, the book is luxuriant in its praise of Morice, and he probably felt that such self praise would have little credibility. Secondly, the book alleges (pp. 237–45) that Morice was persecuted by his superiors. These superiors would not have given the requisite approval for its publication; hence the need for subterfuge. Morice had previously used the pseudonym "de la Seine" (D. L. S.), and the Oblate archives in Winnipeg contain a contract between Morice and Ryerson Press for the publication of *Fifty Years.* The contract refers to Morice as the "author." "Agreement Between Rev. A. G. Morice, O.M.I. and the Ryerson Press," APO.
3. Thomas Flanagan, "Problems of Psychobiography," *Queen's Quarterly* 89 (1982): 596,608. For an example of an uncritical evaluation of Morice, see T. P. Jost, "Rev. A. G. Morice, Discoverer and Surveyor, and the Problems of the Proper Geographical Names in North Central British Columbia," *Revue de l'Université d'Ottawa* 37 (1967): 463–76.
4. G. R. Elton, *The Practice of History* (London: Collins, 1961), p. 169.
5. G. L. Granatstein, "Interviewing for Fun and Profit: The Conservative Party, 1956–1967," *Sound Heritage* 3 (1974): 18.
6. Leo LaClare, "Report of the Oral History Committee of the Canadian Historical Association's Archives Section," *Sound Heritage* 3 (1974): 19.
7. Imbert Orchard of the Canadian Broadcasting Corporation recorded stories about Morice which contain glaring inaccuracies. These recordings have been incorporated into the tape collection of the Aural History Institute of British Columbia (AHIBC). See, for example, the oral evidence of Constance Cox, cassette 313, 5, AHIBC, PABC.

184   *Will To Power*

NOTES TO CHAPTER ONE

1. D. L. S., *Fifty Years*, pp. 1–3.
2. Morice to W. Murray, 3 March 1911, Presidential Papers, Series 1; US; D. L. S., *Fifty Years*, pp. 4–5.
3. D. L. S., *Fifty Years*, pp. 4–5. The influence of the classical heroes is indicated by Morice's comparisons of their exploits with his own adventures. Morice to Tatin, 29 December 1899, *Missions de la Congrégation des Missionnaires de Marie Immaculée* (hereafter cited as *Missions*) 38 (1900): 142.
4. D. L. S., *Fifty Years*, pp. 5–6.
5. A. G. Morice, *Souvenirs d'un missionnaire en Colombie Britannique* (Winnipeg: La Liberté, 1933), p. 10; A. G. Morice, *Disparus et survivants; études ethnographiques sur les Indiens de l'Amérique du Nord* (Winnipeg: The Author, 1928), pp. 99–100.
6. Richard Switzer, *Chateaubriand* (New York: Twayne Publishers, 1971), pp. i–iv; Michel Lelievre, *Chateaubriand Polémiste* ([Picardie]: Presses Universitaires de France, Université de Picardie, 1983), pp. 202–4.
7. Ibid., pp. 10–11; D. L. S., *Fifty Years*, pp. 6–7.
8. Jean Lefron, *Eugène de Mazenod*, trans. Francis D. Flanagan. 3 vols. (New York: Fordham University Press, 1961–70), vol. 1, pp. ix, x, xii; vol. 2, pp. 19, 30–31; Gabriel Dionne, "Histoire des Méthodes Missionnaires Utilisées par les Oblats de Marie Immaculée dans l'Evangélisation des Indiens du 'Versant Pacifique' au dix-neuvième siècle" (M.A. thesis, University of Ottawa, 1947), pp. 37–38.
9. P. F. X. Charlevoix, *History and General Description of New France*, trans. John Gilmary Shea. 6 vols. (Chicago: Loyola University Press, 1970), vol. 2, p. 68; Gilbert Chinard, *L'exotisme américain dans l'oeuvre de Chateaubriand* (Paris: Libraire Hachette et Cie., 1918), pp. 104–5.
10. H. Alan C. Cairns, *The Clash of Cultures: Early Race Relations in Central Africa* (New York: Praeger, 1965), p. 29.

11. Morice, *Souvenirs*, p. 10.
12. Ibid., pp. 11–12; D.L.S., *Fifty Years*, pp. 7–8.
13. Morice, *Souvenirs*, p. 11.
14. Blanchet to Durieu, 21 February 1888, Blanchet file, Colombie records (hereafter cited as C), AD.
15. Petitot to Père [?], 30 September 1864, and Petitot to Père [?], 7 December 1863, *Missions* 5 (1867): 373–74, 382–83.
16. For a short and colourless account of Petitot's life in Canada, see Donat Savoie, *Les Amérindiens du Nord-Ouest Canadien au 19e siècle selon Emile Petitot*. 2 vols. (Ottawa: Ministère des Affaires Indienne et du Nord Canadien, 1971), vol. 1, pp. 37–65; A. G. Morice, "On the Classification of the Dene Tribes," *Transactions of the Canadian Institute* 6 (1898–99): 76.
17. Emile Petitot, *Géographie de l'Athabaskaw-Mackenzie*, pp. 103–4, cited in A. G. Morice, *Histoire de l'Eglise catholique dans l'Ouest canadien*. 4 vols. (St. Boniface: Chez l'auteur; Montréal: Granger Frères, 1921–23), vol. 2, p. 166.
18. Gaston Carrière, O.M.I., personal communication with author, February 1974; Petitot to Père [?], 7 December 1863, *Missions* 5 (1867): 373–74; Savoie, *Les Amérindiens*, vol. 1, pp. 89–95.
19. Petitot to Père [?], 3 April 1863 [sic, 1864], *Missions* 5 (1867): 365–71; Gaston Carrière, personal communication with author, February 1974.
20. Chinard, *L'exotisme américain*, pp. vi, 125, 204–5, 219, 239; Savoie, *Les Amérindiens*, vol. 1, pp. 90–101; Petitot to Père [?], 7 December 1863, pp. 369–71.
21. Savoie, *Les Amérindiens*, vol. 1, pp. 55–57; Morice, *Histoire*, vol. 2, p. 371.
22. D. L. S., *Fifty Years*, pp. 8–9.
23. Ibid., pp. 9–11.
24. Martinet to [d'Herbomez], 26 November 1883, Martinet file, C, AD.
25. Father Martinet, an assistant to the Oblate Father General, made this clear during a visit to British Columbia in 1882. Martinet, "Acte Général

de Visite de la Mission de la Colombie Britannique, 1882,'' Registre des Actes des Visites, C, AD.

26. Jolivet to [d'Herbomez], 25 March 1872, Jolivet file, C, AD; Adrien Dansette, *Religious History of Modern France*, trans. John Dingle. 2 vols. (New York: Herder and Herder, 1961), vol. 1, pp. 315–16; D. L. S., *Fifty Years*, p. 12.

27. Morice, *Souvenirs*, pp. 12–14.

28. D. L. S., *Fifty Years*, p. 12.

29. Dionne, "Histoire des Méthodes," pp. 30–32, 39–41; Morice, *Histoire*, vol. 4, pp. 245, 283; Margaret Whitehead, *The Cariboo Mission: A History of the Oblates* (Victoria: Sono Nis, 1981), p. 53.

30. D. L. S., *Fifty Years*, pp. 14–15.

31. Ibid., p. 16; Morice to Missions, 24 June 1881, *Missions* 19 (1881): 387–88; Jacqueline Kennedy-Gresco [Gresko], "Missionary Acculturation Programs in British Columbia," *Etudes Oblates* 32 (1973): 147; Jacqueline Gresko, "Roman Catholic Missions to the Indians of British Columbia: A Reappraisal of the Lemert Thesis," *Journal of the Canadian Church Historical Society* 24 (1982): 56–57.

32. Durieu to d'Herbomez, 7 August 1860, and Durieu to Lejacq, 27 November 1883, "Lettres de Mgr. Durieu au R. P. Lejacq sur la direction des sauvages," Oregon records (hereafter cited as O), AD. The existence of disciplinary whipping among the Oregon tribes preceded the arrival of the Oblates, and it is likely that they adopted the Indian practice. The "whipping complex" of the U.S. plateau tribes is believed to have reached them via Indian slaves who had run away from Spanish mission stations in the southwest. Thomas Garth, "The Plateau Whipping Complex and its Relationship to Plateau-Southwest Contacts," *Ethnohistory* 12 (1965): 141–45, 150–54; Dionne, "Histoire des Méthodes," pp. 89–91.

33. Gresko, "Roman Catholic Missions," pp. 57–58.

34. James Axtell, *The European and the Indian: Essays in the Ethnohistory of Colonial North America* (New York:

Oxford University Press, 1981), p. 85; Arthur Darby Nock, *Conversion: The Old and New in Religion from Alexander the Great to Augustine of Hippo* (London: Oxford University Press, 1933), pp. 160–61.

35. Morice to de l'Hermite, 11 August 1880, *Missions* 18 (1880): 360–62. "Pour rejoindre nos canots, il nous fallut accepter les services de porteurs Shwahomish, à qui nos personnes ne pesaient pas plus qu'une plume, que le pittoresque de cette scène mettait en grande liesse. Nous glissâmes bientôt sur les flots, ce qui nous délassait des fatigues de la veille. Les Shwahomish sont d'habiles marins; ils se servent de l'aviron avec une dextérité remarquable, et on nous a assuré que l'année dernière ils dépassèrent en vitesse un *steamboat* venant de Victoria."

36. Ibid., pp. 362–63.

37. Carion to [d'Herbomez], 3 January 1876, and Carion to d'Herbomez, 1 June 1881, Carion file, C, AD. In the latter document, Carion claimed to be possessed by a demon and said that he wanted to die.

38. Carion to [d'Herbomez], 20 January 1876, and Carion to [d'Herbomez], 21 March 1881, Carion file; Baudre to [d'Herbomez], 21 September 1884, Baudre file, C, AD.

39. Morice to [d'Herbomez], 18 July 1881, Morice file, C, AD.

40. Ibid.

41. Carion to d'Herbomez], 22 July 1881, Carion file.

42. Lejeune to d'Herbomez, 25 July 1881, Lejeune file, C, AD.

43. Morice to *Missions*, 24 June 1881, *Missions* 19 (1881): 389–94.

44. Carion to [d'Herbomez], 24 July 1881, Carion file; Morice to [d'Herbomez], 22 July 1881, Morice file; Lejeune to [d'Herbomez], 23 June 1881, Lejeune file.

45. Morice to [d'Herbomez], 13 June 1881, Morice file; Carion to [d'Herbomez], 24 July 1881, Carion file; d'Herbomez to [Morice], 1 June 1881, d'Herbomez file, C, AD; Lejeune to d'Herbomez, 25 July 1881, Lejeune file.

46. Morice to [d'Herbomez], 18, 19 May 1882, Morice file; Lejeune to [d'Her-

bomez], 25 July 1881, Lejeune file.
47. Carion to [d'Herbomez], 21 March 1881, Carion file; Lejeune to [d'Herbomez], [n.d.], and 25 July 1881, Lejeune file.
48. Lejeune to [d'Herbomez], 25 July 1881, Lejeune file; Carion to [d'Herbomez], 15 May 1882, Carion file.
49. Carion to [d'Herbomez], 22 July 1881, Carion file. D'Herbomez wrote between the lines of Carion's letter.
50. Lejeune to [d'Herbomez], [n.d.], Lejeune file; Morice to [d'Herbomez], 25 July 1881, Morice file; Carion to [d'Herbomez], 21 March 1881, Carion file; Lejeune to [d'Herbomez], 25 July 1881, Lejeune file.
51. Lejeune to [d'Herbomez], 25 July 1881, Lejeune file; Morice to [d'Herbomez], 22, 25 July 1881, 18 May 1882, Morice file; Carion to [d'Herbomez], 15 May 1882, Carion file.
52. Morice to [d'Herbomez], 8 September 1881, Morice file.
53. Carion to [d'Herbomez], 12, 15, 18 May 1882, Carion file.
54. Morice to [?], 29 June 1919, and 19 October 1920, and Magnan to Favier, 29 July 1909, microfilm 59, APW, AD.
55. D. L. S., *Fifty Years*, p. 23; Morice, *Souvenirs*, p. 15; Lettre du R. P. E. Chirouse, 24 January 1881, *Missions*, 19 (1881): 381–86.
56. D. L. S., *Fifty Years*, p. 23; Martinet, "Acte Général de Visite... 1882," Registre des Actes des Visites.
57. Martinet, "Acte Général de Visite... 1882," Registre des Actes des Visites.
58. McGuckin to Martinet, 27 November 1878, *Missions* 19 (1881): 208–9; McGuckin, balance sheet, 1 July 1871 to 30 June 1872, and McGuckin to Durieu, 2 December 1870, McGuckin file, C, AD.
59. McGuckin to Martinet, 27 November 1878, *Missions* 19 (1881): 208–9; Whitehead, *Cariboo Mission*, pp. 75–6; McGuckin to d'Herbomez, 9 July 1867, 7 May 1876, 19 December 1881, McGuckin file.
60. D. L. S., *Fifty Years*, p. 23.
61. McGuckin to d'Herbomez, 15 August 1880, 19 December 1881, McGuckin file; Morice, *Souvenirs*, p. 15; Baudre to [d'Herbomez], 21 April 1884, Baudre file; D. L. S., *Fifty Years*, p. 24.
62. D. L. S., *Fifty Years*, pp. 24–25.
63. O. Mannoni, *Prospero and Caliban, The Psychology of Colonization*, trans. Pamela Powesland (New York: Praeger, 1964), pp. 100–108.
64. Philip Mason, "Foreword," in Mannoni, *Prospero and Caliban*, pp. 11–12; Neal Salisbury, "Prospero in New England: The Puritan Missionary as Colonist," *Papers of the Sixth Algonquian Conference, 1974*, ed. William Cowan, National Museum of Man, Mercury Series, Canadian Ethnology Service Paper 23 (Ottawa: National Museum of Man, 1975), pp. 254–55.

NOTES TO CHAPTER TWO

1. Morice, *Souvenirs*, p. 16.
2. Ibid., pp. 18–24; D. L. S., *Fifty Years*, pp. 25–27; A. G. Morice, *Au pays de l'ours noir. Chez les sauvages de la Colombie Britannique* (Paris-Lyons: Delhomme et Briquet, 1897), pp. 2, 23; Robert B. Lane, "Cultural Relations of the Chilcotin Indians of West Central British Columbia" (Ph.D. diss., University of Washington, 1953), pp. 37–38.
3. Guertin to [d'Herbomez], 4 June 1881, Guertin file, C, AD; Morice, *Au pays*, p. 27; Lane, "Cultural Relations," p. 272.
4. A. G. Morice, *History of the Northern Interior of British Columbia, Formerly New Caledonia (1660–1880)* (London: John Lane -The Bodley Head, 1906), pp. 76, 122–23, 307, 315–20; Edward Sleigh Hewlitt, "The Chilcotin Uprising of 1864," *BC Studies* 19 (1973): 54–65, 71–72.
5. Robin Fisher, "Indian-European Relations in British Columbia, 1774–

1890'' (Ph.D. diss., University of British Columbia, 1974), pp. 273–74; Morice, *Au pays,* pp. 4–6; Morice, *Souvenirs,* p. 23.
6. Morice, *History,* p. 335; Grandidier to Fouquet, 20 June 1866, Grandidier file, C, AD; McGuckin to d'Herbomez, 5 July 1873, McGuckin file.
7. McGuckin to d'Herbomez, 19 December 1881, McGuckin file; Guertin to [d'Herbomez], 4 June 1881, Guertin file.
8. Guertin to [d'Herbomez], 4 June 1881, Guertin file.
9. McGuckin to d'Herbomez, 1 July 1882, McGuckin file; Morice, *Au pays,* p. 6.
10. Morice, *Au pays,* p. 6; D. L. S., *Fifty Years,* pp. 27–28; Morice to R. P. Tatin, 5 September 1883, *Missions* 21 (1883): 355.
11. Morice, *Souvenirs,* pp. 29–30; D. L. S., *Fifty Years,* p. 29.
12. Morice to Tatin, 5 September 1883, *Missions* 21 (1883): 357–58; Lejacq to d'Herbomez, 29 November 1872, *Missions* 47 (1874): 221–22, 230–32.
13. Ibid., pp. 358–60.
14. Ibid., p. 357; Guertin to [d'Herbomez], 4 June 1881, Guertin file.
15. Morice to Tatin, 5 September 1883, *Missions* 21 (1883): 362–65.
16. Ibid., pp. 365–67.
17. Ibid., pp. 365–68.
18. Ibid., p. 368. For an African example, see James W. Fernandez, "Fang Representations Under Acculturation," in Philip D. Curtin, ed., *Africa and the West: Intellectual Responses to European Culture* (Madison: University of Wisconsin Press, 1972), pp. 6, 7, 18–19. The process of religious acculturation in the Pacific islands is examined in Kenelm Burridge, *New Heaven, New Earth: a Study of Millenarian Activities* (New York: Schocken Books, 1969).
19. J. M. R. Owens, *Prophets in the Wilderness: The Wesleyan Mission to New Zealand, 1819–1827* (Auckland: Auckland University Press: Oxford University Press, 1974), pp. 134–40.
20. Morice to Tatin, 5 September 1883, *Missions* 21 (1883): 368.
21. Ibid., pp. 368–70; Morice, *Souvenirs,* p. 43; Garth, "Plateau Whipping," p. 147.
22. Morice, *Au pays,* pp. 21–22; Morice to Tatin, 5 September 1883, *Missions* 21 (1883): 369.
23. Morice to Tatin, 5 September 1883, *Missions* 21 (1883): 370–73.
24. Ibid., pp. 361, 372–74.
25. Ibid., pp. 351–53.
26. Ibid., pp. 355–56, 359–65.
27. James G. MacGregor, *Father Lacombe* (Edmonton: Hurtig Publishers, 1975), p. 70.
28. D'Herbomez to Martinet, [March]. 1883, d'Herbomez file; Baudre to [d'Herbomez], 28 October 1883, Baudre file; letters from Petitot to his superiors, 1877–78, Savoie, *Les Amérindiens,* vol. 1, pp. 100–102.
29. Baudre to [d'Herbomez], 28 October 1883, Baudre file; Martinet to [d'Herbomez], 26 November 1883, Martinet file.
30. Morice, *Au pays,* pp. 31–33.
31. Ibid., pp. 33–35.
32. Ibid., pp. 35–37.
33. Ibid., p. 39; Chirouse to Ricard, 22 July 1849, cited in Dionne, "Histoire des Méthodes," p. 74; Owens, *Prophets in the Wilderness,* pp. 199–200.
34. Martinet to [d'Herbomez], 25 February 1884 and 14 February 1884, Martinet file.
35. A. G. Morice, "Rapport sur la mission de Tloesko," [6 April, 1884], Morice file, C, AD; Baudre to [d'Herbomez], 21 April 1884, Baudre file; Morice, *Au pays,* p. 52.
36. Morice, "Rapport"; McGuckin to d'Herbomez, 5 August 1881, McGuckin file.
37. Morice "Rapport."
38. Morice to [d'Herbomez], 12 June 1884, Morice file; Baudre to [d'Herbomez], 21 April and 8 May 1884, Baudre file.
39. Martinet to [d'Herbomez], 28 July 1884, Martinet file.
40. Morice, *Au pays,* pp. 42–46.
41. Ibid., pp. 47–50.
42. Ibid., p. 51; Morice, *Souvenirs,* p. 68.
43. Irving Goldman, "The Alkatcho Carrier of British Columbia," in

Ralph Linton ed., *Acculturation in Seven American Indian Tribes* (New York: D. Appleton-Century, 1940), p. 372.
44. Nock, *Conversion*, pp. 7, 37.
45. Goldman, "The Alkatcho Carrier," pp. 372–76.
46. Ibid., pp. 349–50; A. G. Morice, "The Western Dénés: Their Manners and Customs," *Proceedings of the Canadian Institute* Series 3, no. 7 (1889–90): 157; Alexander Hamilton Thompson, *Bede, His Life, Times and Writings* (Oxford: Clarendon Press, 1969), p. 204.
47. Hilary Eileen Rumley, "Reactions to Contact and Colonization: An Interpretation of Religious and Social Change among the Indians of British Columbia" (M.A. thesis, University of British Columbia, 1973) p. 82; Robin Ridington, "Changes of

Mind: Dunne-za Resistance to Empire," *BC Studies* 43 (1979): 77–78.
48. Goldman, "The Alkatcho Carrier," pp. 375–76; Rumley, "Reactions," p. 82.
49. Martinet to d'Herbomez, 15 May 1885, Martinet file.
50. Guertin to [d'Herbomez], 8 August 1885, Guertin file: "gives no sign of life: he is dead."
51. Baudre to [d'Herbomez], 21 September 1884, Baudre file. Baudre read a letter from Morice to Carion and copied parts of the letter for d'Herbomez.
52. Martinet to d'Herbomez, 29 September 1885, Martinet file, C, AD. Evidence concerning Pandosy's early career comes from Whitehead, *Cariboo Mission*, pp. 11, 19.
53. Martinet to d'Herbomez, 29 September 1885, Martinet file.

NOTES TO CHAPTER THREE

1. "Colombie Britannique, Rapport lu au Chapitre Général de 1904," Missions 43 (1905): 285.
2. Morice, *Au pays*, p. 59. "Sots orgueilleux qui se croent civilisés parce qu'ils bouvent sans vergogne et baragouinent quelques mots d'anglais."
3. Bruce G. Trigger, "The French Presence in Huronia: The Structure of Franco-Huron Relations in the First Half of the Seventeenth Century," *Canadian Historical Review* 49 (1968): 140.
4. J. M. Lindsay-Alexander, "Report," Fort St. James, June 1885, HBCA, B188/e/6.
5. The population figures were arrived at after comparing figures given in the following sources: Lindsay-Alexander, "Report"; D. L. S., *Fifty Years*, pp. 40–41; Lejacq to Durieu, [n.d.], *Missions* 18 (1880): 58–59; A. G. Morice, "The Western Dénés," p. 112.
6. D. L. S., *Fifty Years*, p. 40; Morice, *History*, p. 4; Lejacq to Durieu, [n.d.], *Missions* 18 (1880): 58–59.
7. Goldman, "The Alkatcho Carrier," p. 333; A. G. Morice, "Are the Carrier Sociology and Mythology Indi-

genous or Exotic?," *Proceedings and Transactions of the Royal Society of Canada for the Year 1892* Section 2, no. 10 (1893): 109–15; Julian H. Steward, "Determinism in Primitive Society?," *The Scientific Monthly*, 43 (1941): 495–97.
8. Morice, "The Western Dénés," p. 143; Diamond Jenness, *The Carrier Indians of the Bulkley River: Their Social and Religious Life*, Anthropological Papers, No. 25, Bureau of American Ethnology, Bulletin 133, Smithsonian Institute, pp. 457–82.
9. Diamond Jenness, "The Sekani Indians of British Columbia," *Transactions of the Royal Society of Canada* Section 2, no. 25 (1931): 31–32.
10. Morice, *History*, p. 62.
11. Morice, "Carrier Sociology," p. 115; MacFarlane, "Memorandum for Quesnelle," December 1877, HBCA, B188/b/10; MacFarlane to Sinclair, [1877], HBCA, B188/b/10; Morice, *History*, pp. 112–13.
12. Jenness, *The Carrier*, p. 546.
13. Morice, "The Western Dénés," p. 157.
14. Ibid., pp. 157–59, 162–63; D. Jen-

ness, "The Ancient Education of a Carrier Indian," *Bulletin of the Canadian Department of Mines* 62 (1947): 23–25.

15. Deward E. Walker Jr., "New Light on the Prophet Dance Controversy," *Ethnohistory* 16 (1969): 245–51. Ridington claims, following Spier, that the Dunne-za prophet dance was a pre-contact development. Robin Ridington, *Swan People: A Study of the Dunne-za Prophet Dance*, National Museum of Man, Mercury Series, Canadian Ethnology Service Paper 38 (Ottawa: National Museums of Canada, 1978), pp. 4–5, 27–29.

16. Jenness, *The Carrier*, p. 549.

17. Ibid.; Morice, "History,' pp. 129, 211, 225, 264.

18. Morice, "History," p. 234; Robin Fisher, *Contact and Conflict: Indian-European Relations in British Columbia, 1774–1890* (Vancouver: University of British Columbia Press, 1977), p. 122.

19. Morice, "History," pp. 238–39; Jenness, *The Carrier*, p. 556; Marius Barbeau, *Indian Days in the Canadian Rockies* (Toronto: Macmillan, 1923), pp. 30–32.

20. Peter Worsley, *The Trumpet Shall Sound* (London: MacGibbon and Kee, 1957), pp. 43–44; Rumley, "Reactions," pp. 13, 14, 82; Owens, *Prophets*, p. 138.

21. Morice, "Carrier Sociology," p. 115; editor's summary of Goldman, "The Alkatcho Carrier," p. 389.

22. Burridge, *New Heaven, New Earth,* p. 22.

23. John Bernard McGloin, sj, "John Nobili, sj, Founder of California's Santa Clara College: The New Caledonia Years," *British Columbia Historical Quarterly* 17 (1955): 218; William H. McNeill, *Plagues and People* (New York: Anchor Books, 1976), pp. 107, 176–85.

24. James R. Gibson, "Smallpox on the Northwest Coast, 1835–1838," *BC Studies* 56 (1982): 61–81.

25. Burridge, *New Heaven, New Earth,* pp. 96–109.

26. Jenness, *The Carrier*, p. 552.

27. Nock, *Conversion*, p. 9.

28. Anthony F. C. Wallace, "Revitalization Movements," *American Anthropologist* 58 (1956): 264–81.

29. Barbeau, *Indian Days,* pp. 24, 41; Jenness, *The Carrier,* pp. 551–55.

30. Martha McCarthy, "The Missions of the Oblates of Mary Immaculate to the Athapaskans 1846–1870: Theory, Structure and Method," (Ph.D. diss., University of Manitoba, 1981), pp. 311, 319–20; Norman James Williamson, "Abishabis the Cree," *Studies in Religion/Sciences Religieuses* 9 (1980): 229.

31. Max Weber, *The Theory of Social and Economic Organization*, trans. A. M. Henderson and Talcot Parsons, ed. Talcot Parsons (New York: Free Press, 1964), p. 131. Handsome Lake, the Seneca, made perhaps the most ambitious of the native prophets' bids for power. See Anthony F. C. Wallace, *The Death and Rebirth of the Seneca* (New York: Vintage Books, 1972), pp. 253–54, 286.

32. Morice, *History*, p. 239.

33. Norman Cohn, *The Pursuit of the Millenium: Revolutionary Millenarians and Mystical Anarchists of the Middle Ages* (New York: Oxford University Press, 1970), pp. 19–20, 52, 55–60, 282.

34. McGuckin to d'Herbomez, 9 July 1867, McGuckin file; Lejacq to d'Herbomez, 12 September 1869, *Missions* 8 (1870): 139–40; "Rapport du R. P. McGuckin a d'Herbomez," November 1870, *Missions* 11 (1873): 103; Lejacq to d'Herbomez, 29 November 1872, *Missions* 12 (1874): 226–27.

35. Lejacq to Durieu, [n.d.], *Missions* 18 (1880): 70–72; Joseph Allard, "Memoirs," Allard file, C, AD; Blanchet to d'Herbomez, 18 January 1876, Blanchet file; Lejacq to d'Herbomez, [n.d.], *Missions* 12 (1874): 348–50.

36. D. L. S., *Fifty Years,* p. 50; Morice, *Au pays,* pp. 85–86.

37. D. L. S., *Fifty Years,* pp. 32, 104, 203.

38. McGuckin to d'Herbomez, 9 July 1867, McGuckin file; Lejacq to d'Herbomez, 5 March 1880, Lejacq file, C, AD; Blanchet to d'Herbo-

190 *Will To Power*

mez, 18 January 1876, Blanchet file.
39. A. G. Morice, "Northwestern Dénés and Northeastern Asiatics," *Transactions of the Royal Canadian Institute* 10 (1914): 131; D. L. S., *Fifty Years*, pp. 46–47; Morice, *Au pays*, p. 157.
40. A. G. Morice, "The Déné Languages Considered in Themselves and Incidentally in Their Relations to Non-American Idioms," *Transactions of the Canadian Institute* 1 (1891): 178–81.
41. Morice, *Souvenirs*, pp. 354–55, 358.
42. D. L. S., *Fifty Years*, p. 47.
43. A. G. Morice, "Carrier Onomatology," *American Anthropologist* n.s., no. 35 (1933): 637; D. L. S., *Fifty Years*, pp. 45, 60.
44. A. G. Morice, "The Déné Syllabary and its Advantages," *A First Collection of Minor Essays, Mostly Anthropological* (Stuart's Lake Mission: [The Author], 1902), p. 67; Morice, "The Western Dénés," pp. 165–166.
45. Morice, "The Déné Syllabary," p. 66.
46. Morice, *Au pays*, p. 93; A. G. Morice, "The Unity of Speech Among the Northern and Southern Déné," *American Anthropologist* n.s., no. 9 (1907): 735; Morice, "The Western Dénés," p. 166.
47. D. Walker, a linguist and lay missionary, believes that Morice's alphabet was not sufficient to carry the phonetic load of Carrier phonology and was lacking in about 16 phonetic symbols." D. Walker, personal communication with author, 24 May 1974.
48. D. L. S., *Fifty Years*, p. 88.
49. Morice, "The Déné Syllabary," p. 67.
50. Morice, "The Western Dénés," p. 166; Morice, *Au pays*, p. 107; McNab to Hall, 31 August 1900, HBCA, B188/b/19.
51. D. L. S., *Fifty Years*, p. 92.
52. Ibid.
53. Durieu to Lejacq, 23 February 1884, "Lettres de Mgr. Durieu," O, AD.
54. Lejacq to Durieu, [n.d.], Missions 18 (1880): 60; D. L. S., *Fifty Years*, p. 96.

55. Morice to d'Herbomez, 23 September 1887, Morice file.
56. D. L. S., *Fifty Years*, pp. 77–81, 163, 170; Morice, *Au pays*, pp. 113–14.
57. Morice, *Au pays*, pp. 60, 86, 249; Morice, *Souvenirs*, p. 345.
58. Morice, *Au pays*, pp. 89–92.
59. Ibid., p. 91; D. L. S., *Fifty Years*, pp. 106–8.
60. Fraser's Lake Journal, 25 December 1889, and 18 December 1888, HBCA, B74/a/2.
61. Morice, *Au pays*, p. 113; Goldman, "The Alkatcho Carrier," pp. 349–50.
62. Morice to d'Herbomez, 23 September 1887.
63. Fraser's Lake Journal, 18 April 1893, HBCA, B74/a/3; 25 August 1888, 25–27 June 1889, HBCA, B74/a/2.
64. Morice, "The Western Dénés," pp. 147–53. Although some tribes gave potlatches for other reasons—to wipe out shame, for example—these "minor deviations from the basic pattern do not obscure the fact that the potlatch was a formal function... given for a serious purpose, that of validating the assumption of hereditary rights." Philip Drucker, *Cultures of the North Pacific Coast* (Scranton, PA: Chandler, 1965), p. 58; Jenness, *The Carrier*, p. 489.
65. Morice, *Au pays*, pp. 147–48; Loring to Hamilton Moffat, 12 October 1889, Record Group 10 (hereafter cited as RG 10), C113, vol. 1585, p. 6, PAC.
66. D. L. S., *Fifty Years*, p. 116; Morice, *Au pays*, pp. 146–47.
67. Durieu to Lejacq, 23 February 1884, 25 February 1884, "Lettres de Mgr. Durieu."
68. D. L. S., *Fifty Years*, p. 116.
69. Morice to d'Herbomez, 23 September 1887, Morice file.
70. Fraser's Lake Journal, 1 November 1888, HBCA, B74/a/2; 8 June 1894, HBCA, B74/a/3.
71. Morice, *Au pays*, p. 113; Morice to d'Herbomez, 23 September, 29 November 1887, Morice file.
72. Morice, "The Western Dénés," p. 118; Alice Beck Kehoe, *North Amer-*

ican Indians: A Comprehensive Account (Englewoods Cliffs: Prentice-Hall, 1981), p. 495.

73. Morice, "The Western Dénés," p. 143.
74. Quoted in R. W. Dunning, "Ethnic Relations and the Marginal Man," *Human Organization* 18 (1959): 120.
75. Morice, *Au pays,* pp. 106–7; Lejeune to his brother, 6 March 1886, Lejeune file.
76. Edwin M. Lemert, "The Life and Death of an Indian State,' *Human Organization* 13 (1954): 24–25.
77. E. M. Bunoz, "Catholic Action and Bishop Durieu's System," mimeograph, C, AD; Morice to d'Herbomez, 23 September 1887, Morice file.
78. D. L. S., *Fifty Years,* pp. 50, 116; Morice, *Au pays,* 126–27, 129–30, 135–36. In 1892, a number of Sekani actually starved to death while awaiting the arrival of Father Blanchet at Bear Lake. Bear Lake Outpost Journal, 11 April 1892, HBCA, B249/a/1.
79. Morice, *Au pays,* pp. 115–16, 130–31, 136; D. L. S., *Fifty Years,* p. 73.
80. D. L. S., *Fifty Years,* p. 51; Morice, *Au pays,* pp. 60–61, 138–39, 154–56; Lejacq to Durieu, [n.d.], *Missions* 18 (1880): 66.
81. Morice, *Au pays,* pp. 156–57.
82. Ibid., pp. 148–49, 156.
83. Ibid., pp. 138–39, 158–59; Morice to d'Herbomez, 23 September 1887, Morice file.
84. Morice, *Au pays,* pp. 159–60; D. L. S., *Fifty Years,* pp. 52–53; Morice to d'Herbomez, 23 September 1887, Morice file.
85. Morice, *Au pays,* pp. 160–61.
86. Morice to d'Herbomez, 23 September, 29 November 1887, Morice file.
87. Loring to Vowell, 29 March 1892, RG 10, C113, vol. 1585, p. 155; Jenness, *The Carrier,* p. 478.
88. Morice, *Histoire de l'Eglise,* vol. 4, p. 265; Morice, *Au pays,* pp. 138–39; D. L. S., *Fifty Years,* p. 51.
89. Peytavin to McGuckin, 21 February 1887, *Missions* 25 (1887): 247; Dozois to Lejeune, 11 February 1908, Dozois file, C, AD.

90. Lejacq to Durieu, [n.d.], *Missions* 18 (1880): 66; Morice, *Au pays,* pp. 170–71.
91. Morice to d'Herbomez, 23 September 1887, Morice file; Morice, *Au pays,* pp. 148–49.
92. Morice, *Au pays,* p. 186; Morice to d'Herbomez, 23 September 1887, Morice file.
93. Blanchet to [d'Herbomez], 4 December 1887, Blanchet file.
94. D'Herbomez to Morice, 5 January 1888, d'Herbomez file; Morice to d'Herbomez, 29 November 1887, Morice file; Morice, *Au pays,* p. 172.
95. Blanchet to [d'Herbomez], 30 September 1887, Blanchet file.
96. George Forbes, "Biographical Notes on Rev. Georges Blanchet (1818–1906)," George Forbes Papers, UBCL; D. L. S., *Fifty Years,* p. 33.
97. Blanchet to d'Herbomez, 9 January 1875, 15 March 1880, Blanchet file; Marchal to d'Herbomez, January 30, 1881, Marchal file, C, AD; Forbes, "Biographical Notes."
98. Bermond, "Reflexions sur la visite," Cahiers des Actes de Visite, O, AD; "Colombie Britannique, Rapport lu au Chapitre Général du 1904," *Missions* 43 (1905): 275.
99. Blanchet to d'Herbomez, 4 December 1887, Blanchet file.
100. Morice to d'Herbomez, 29 November 1887, Morice file.
101. D'Herbomez to Blanchet, 5 December 1888 [sic 1887], d'Herbomez file.
102. Morice to Durieu, 21 February 1888, Morice file; Blanchet to Durieu, 21 February 1888, Blanchet to d'Herbomez, 7 December 1887, Blanchet file.
103. Morice to Durieu, 21, 22 February 1888, Morice file.
104. Durieu to Lejacq, 25 February 1884, "Lettres de Mgr. Durieu."
105. Ibid.
106. Ibid.
107. Ibid.; Durieu to Lejacq, 24 November 1884, Durieu file, C, AD.
108. Dionne, "Histoire des Méthodes," p. 17; Bunoz, "Catholic Action," p. 11; "Lettres de Mgr. Durieu."
109. Martinet, "Acte Général de Visite, 1881."
110. Morice to Durieu, 21, 22 February

192

1888, "Lettres de Mgr. Durieu."
111. Blanchet to Durieu, 21 February 1888, ibid.
112. Ibid.; Morice to MacFarlane, 22 February 1894, microfilm 59, APW, AD.
113. Morice to de l'Hermite, 2 July 1888, *Missions* 27 (1889): 63–64; Morice, *Au pays*, p. 221.
114. Lejacq to [?], 16 November 1887, *Missions* 26 (1888): 82, 88; Bunoz, "Catholic Action," p. 28.
115. Morice to de l'Hermite, 1 July 1888, *Missions* 27 (1889): 58; Morice to Durieu, 21 February 1888; D. L. S., *Fifty Years*, p. 231.
116. Morice, *Au pays*, pp. 212–15.
117. Morice to de l'Hermite, 1 July 1888, pp. 60–62.
118. Ibid., pp. 62–63; Morice, *Au pays*, pp. 212–15.
119. Marchal to Supérieur Général, 24 February 1891, *Missions* 29 (1891): 155; Durieu to Auger, 28 June 1890, cited in Dionne, "Histoire des Méthodes," p. 131.
120. Marchal to Supérieur Général, 24 February 1891, *Missions* 29 (1891): 155–56.
121. "Colombie Britannique, Rapport lu au Chapitre General de 1904," p. 275.
122. Lemert, "Life and Death," pp. 25–26; Morice to de l'Hermite, 1 July 1888, pp. 65–66; Bunoz, "Catholic Action," pp. 14, 28.
123. Harlan I. Smith, "An American Oberammergau: The Passion Play by American Indians," *Putman's* 5 (1908): 297.
124. Bunoz, "Catholic Action," p. 29; Marchal to Supérieur Général, 24 February 1891, *Missions* 29 (1891): 154–55; Durieu to Auger, 28 June 1890, p. 131; Morice, *Au pays*, p. 232.
125. Smith, "An American Oberammergau," p. 296; Marchal to Supérieur Général, 24 February 1891, *Missions* 29 (1891): 155–58.
126. Morice, *Au pays*, pp. 211, 226–28.
127. Morice to de l'Hermite, 1 July 1888, pp. 67–68.
128. Morice to Directeur, 2 February 1893, *Petites Annales de la Congrégation des Missionnaires de Marie*

Immaculée (hereafter cited as *Petites Annales*), 3 (1893): 270–71; Blanchet to Durieu, 21 February 1888, Blanchet file, Fort Babine Journal, 7, 14 June, 22 July 1888, HBCA, B11/a/6; D. L. S., *Fifty Years*, p. 53.
129. J. D. Y. Peel, "Syncretism and Religious Change," *Comparative Studies in Society and History* 10 (1968): 125, 129.
130. MacFarlane to Smith, 25 July 1888, HBCA, B188/b/13; Morice, *Au pays*, pp. 162–64.
131. The way the Carrier turned to Christianity following the outbreak of disease conformed to an historical pattern. See Peel, "Syncretism," p. 134.
132. Morice, *Au pays*, pp. 165, 247.
133. Ibid., pp. 164–67; Loring to Hamilton Moffat, 28 February 1890, p. 5.
134. Morice, *Au pays*, p. 169; D. L. S., *Fifty Years*, p. 54.
135. D. L. S., *Fifty Years*, p. 54–55; Morice, *Au pays*, pp. 167–68; Morice to Directeur, 2 February 1893, p. 271.
136. Oral evidence of Mr. John Prince, Fort St. James, [n.d.], cassette 1043: 1:1, AHIBC.
137. Morice to Directeur, 2 February 1893, *Petites Annales*, p. 272; Morice, *Au pays*, p. 254.
138. Morice, *Au pays*, p. 204. "Un missionnaire à la voix éloquente et aux accents persuasifs. . . ."
139. Ibid., pp. 204, 248–49; Loring to Superintendent General of Indian Affairs, 25 July 1894, RG 10, C 113, vol. 1585, p. 98.
140. Morice, *Au pays*, pp. 204, 255.
141. Ibid., p. 256; Morice to Murray, 19 March [1895], A. G. Morice, Correspondence Outward, 1892–95 (hereafter cited as Morice Correspondence), PABC.
142. Morice, *Au pays*, p. 255; Morice to Directeur, 2 February 1893, *Petites Annales*, p. 273.
143. Morice, *Au pays*, pp. 171–72.
144. Ibid., pp. 174–80, 204.
145. Ibid., pp. 180–82.
146. Fraser's Lake Journal, 4 August 1889, HBCA, B74/a/2; Morice, *Au*

pays, pp. 185–86.
147. Morice, *Au pays,* pp. 186–87.
148. Ibid., pp. 188–89, 200–202.
149. Ibid., pp. 203–4.
150. Ibid., pp. 193–94; Loring to Vowell, 21 July 1893, RG 10, C 113, vol. 1585, p. 307.
151. Morice, *Souvenirs,* p. 369; Jean Usher, *William Duncan of Metlakatla: A Victorian Missionary in British Columbia* (Ottawa: National Museums of Canada, 1974), p. 15.
152. Morice, *Souvenirs,* p. 369; Mr. Justa Hansen, personal interview with author, Taché, B.C., 30 July 1974.
153. D. L. S., *Fifty Years,* p. 60.
154. Jenness, *The Carrier,* pp. 556–57.
155. D. L. S., *Fifty Years,* pp. 83–84; Dionne, "Histoire des Méthodes," p. 77.
156. "Rapport, Vicariat de la Colombie Britannique," *Missions* 11 (1873): 338–39.
157. Fraser's Lake Journal, 10 January 1890, HBCA, B74/a/2.
158. D. L. S., *Fifty Years,* p. 57.
159. Ibid., pp. 58–59.
160. R. W. Dunning, "Ethnic Relations," p. 18.
161. Owens, *Prophets,* p. 122.
162. Patron-broker-client theory is complex, and I have chosen to use the definitions of Robert Paine. For him, "what distinguishes the patron from his client is that only *values of the patron's choosing are circulated* in their relationship. There may be goods and services that are passed in the relationship in one direction only,

but these do not provide a basis for distinguishing the patron and client roles. Further, the client demonstrates, to his patron and others, his acceptance of the value which the patron has chosen for circulation between them; herein lies the 'loyalty' and 'dependence' for which the client is rewarded. The reward of the patron is in this acceptance by the client of the chosen value." Paine adds, "Patrons 'protect' their clients [and] the patron *chooses* for the client those values in relation to which the patron protects the client." A "broker," on the other hand, is involved with the "processing of information," and Paine restricts the term broker "to one who, while purveying values that are not his own, is also purposively making changes of emphasis and/or content." According to Paine, "an excellent example" of a broker "is the missionary who, while ensconced as a patron, cultivates a broker role so that he may manipulate also the values passing between other whites and the Indians." Robert Paine, "A Theory of Patronage and Brokerage," in Robert Paine, ed., *Patrons and Brokers in the Eastern Arctic,* Newfoundland Social and Economic Papers, No. 2 (St. John's: Institute of Social and Economic Research, Memorial University of Newfoundland, 1971), pp. 15, 19, 21.
163. Morice to Dozois, 19 May 1926, microfilm 59, APW, AD.

NOTES TO CHAPTER FOUR

1. Morice, *History,* pp. 227–30, 337.
2. Graham to Hamilton, 21 July 1873, HBCA, B226/b/47.
3. MacFarlane to McIntosh, 19 January 1889, HBCA, B188/b/14.
4. Bermond, Directoire des Missions, 1858, "Cahiers des Actes de Visite," O, AD.
5. Lejacq to d'Herbomez, 29 November 1872, *Missions* 12 (1874): 226.
6. Dunning, "Ethnic Relations," p. 117.
7. Morice, *History,* p. 198.
8. Ibid., pp. 197–98, 286.
9. Blanchet to d'Herbomez, 8 January 1881, Blanchet file.
10. Alexander J. M. Lindsay, "Report," Fort St. James, 1885, HBCA, B188/e/6.
11. Blanchet to [d'Herbomez], 4 December 1887, d'Herbomez to Blanchet, 5 December 1888 [?], d'Herbomez file.
12. MacFarlane to Smith, 6 October 1887, HBCA, B188/b/10.
13. "Rapport du R. P. McGuckin a Mgr.

194

d'Herbomez," pp. 73–80; MacFarlane to Clut, 29 November 1887, Roderick MacFarlane, Correspondence and Papers, 1834–1915 (hereafter cited as MacFarlane Papers), MG 29, D 9, vol. 1, pp. 1133–37, PAC.

14. MacFarlane to McKenzie, 10 December 1888, and MacFarlane to Sinclair, 10 December 1888, HBCA, B188/b/14.

15. MacFarlane, "Memorandum for Quesnelle," December 1887, HBCA, B188/b/18.

16. MacFarlane to Davie, 12 November 1888, and MacFarlane to McKenzie, 24, 26 November 1888, HBCA, B188/b/14; Murray to MacFarlane, 1 February 1891, MacFarlane Papers vol. 2, pp. 1353–60.

17. MacFarlane to Smith, 6 October, 24 December 1887, HBCA, B188/b/10; Blanchet to [d'Herbomez],, 4 December 1888 [?], d'Herbomez file.

18. MacFarlane to Smith, 24 December 1887 HBCA, B188/b/10; MacFarlane to Smith, 5 May 1888, HBCA, B188/b/12.

19. MacFarlane to Sinclair, 29 December 1888, HBCA, B188/14.

20. Morice to MacFarlane, 9 February 1892, MacFarlane Papers, D9, vol. 2, pp. 1553–55; Morice to MacFarlane, 10 November 1890, microfilm 59, APW, AD.

21. Morice to MacFarlane, 10 November 1890, microfilm 59, APW, AD; Murray to MacFarlane, 15 June 1890, MacFarlane Papers, D9, vol. 2, pp. 1221–24; numerous entries in the Fort St. James Journal, 1892–93, HBCA, B188/2/22; Nicholas Coccola, "The Memoirs of Rev. Nicholas Coccola, O.M.I., Veteran Missionary of British Columbia," p. 47, AD.

22. Lejacq to d'Herbomez, 9 September 1869, p. 138 Lejacq file; Fraser's Lake Journal, 3 September 1890, HBCA, B74/a/2.

23. M[urray] to MacFarlane, 1891, MacFarlane Papers, D9, vol. 2, pp. 1353–56; Fort St. James Journal, 24 April 1895, 15 June 1895, 21 July 1896, HBCA, B188/a/23; Fort St.

James Journal, 17 June 1893, HBCA, B188/a/22; McNab to Hall, 3 January 1900, HBCA, B188/b/19.

24. MacFarlane to McKenzie, 11 July 1888, HBCA, B188/b/13; A. C. M[urray] to MacFarlane, 1 February 1891 MacFarlane Papers, D9, vol. 2, pp. 1356–60; D. L. S., *Fifty Years,* p. 253.

25. Arthur J. Ray, *Indians in the Fur Trade* (Toronto: University of Toronto Press, 1974), p. 141.

26. Durieu to Martinet, 10 September 1884, *Missions* 21 (1885): 40–41.

27. Fort St. James Journal, 21 July 1896, HBCA, B188/a/23; Morice, *History,* p. 324.

28. Morice to MacFarlane, 10 November 1890 microfilm 59, APW, AD; A. C. M[urray] to MacFarlane, 1 February 1891, MacFarlane Papers, D9, vol. 2, pp. 1356–60; McNaught to Smith, 12 April 1890, HBCA, B171/d/14.

29. Morice to Traill, 26 January 1891, and 4 February 1893, Morice Correspondence, PABC.

30. Traill to MacFarlane, 14 October 1892, MacFarlane Papers, D9, vol. 2, pp. 1629–31.

31. Morice to Traill, 26 January 1893, Morice Correspondence.

32. *The Month* 1, no. 6, (1892): 123–33; Traill to Morice, 23 January 1893, HBCA, B188/b/18.

33. Morice to Murray, 15 December 1894, Morice Correspondence; Camsell to Anderson, 10 January 1898, HBCA, B188/b/17.

34. D. L. S., *Fifty Years,* p. 205.

35. Traill to Morice, 23 January 1893, HBCA, B188/b/18.

36. Ibid.; Morice to Traill, 23 January 1892 [sic, 1893], Morice Correspondence.

37. *The Daily Colonist,* Victoria, 8 May 1892; *The World,* Vancouver, 6 May 1892, cited in *The Month* 1, no. 6, (1892): 130.

38. *The Daily Colonist,* 8 May 1892.

39. Morice to Traill, 24 January 1893, Morice Correspondence. A "whipping complex" did exist among the tribes of the Oregon plateau, with which the Oblates worked when they first arrived in northwest America,

and this probably explains why the missionaries claimed that disciplinary whipping was a part of Indian culture. Garth, "The Plateau Whipping Complex," pp. 141–45.

40. Traill to Morice, 23 January 1893, HBCA, B188/b/18.
41. Morice to Traill, 26 January 1893, Morice Correspondence.
42. Morice to Traill, 24 January 1893, ibid.
43. Traill to Morice, 26 January 1893, HBCA, B188/b/18.
44. Morice to Traill, 26, 27 January 1893, Morice Correspondence.
45. Traill to Morice, 27 January 1893, HBCA, B188/b/18; Traill to Ogden, 27 January 1893, William E. Traill, Letter to Charles Ogden, PABC.
46. Morice to Traill, 27 January 1893, Morice Correspondence.
47. Ibid.,
48. Traill to Morice, 28 January, 1 February 1893, HBCA, B188/b/18; Morice to Traill, 4 February 1893, Morice Correspondence.
49. Morice to Traill, 19 February, 9 March 1893, Morice Correspondence.
50. McKenzie to MacFarlane, 18 February 1893, MacFarlane Papers, D9, vol. 2, pp. 1685–86; Traill to Smith, 4, 9 August [189]1, HBCA, B188/b/18.
51. Fort St. James Journal, 1 August 1893, HBCA, B188/a/22; Murray to Hall, 17 September 1893, HBCA, B226/c/12.
52. Fort St. James Journal, 5 July 1892, HBCA, B188/a/22.
53. Ibid., 5 July 1892, 17 June 1893.
54. Murray to Hall, 17 September 1893, HBCA, B226/c/12.
55. Murray to Morice, 2 August 1893, HBCA, B188/b/16; Morice to Murray, 19 March [1895], Morice Correspondence; McDonald to Murray, 4 March 1895, Babine Portage, Correspondence Outward, 1894–95, PABC.
56. Fort St. James Journal, 22 May, 11 June 1894, HBCA, B188/a/23.
57. Morice to Murray, [16 December 1894], Morice Correspondence; Murray to Hall, 17 September 1893, HBCA, B226/c/12.

58. Morice to Murray, 31 January 1895, Morice Correspondence; Murray to Hall, 14 March 1895, HBCA, B226/c/16.
59. French to Murray, 25 August 1895, Babine Portage, Correspondence Outward.
60. Murray to Hall, 14 March 1895 HBCA, B226/c/16; Hall to Murray, 4 April 1895, HBCA, B226/b/99.
61. Morice to Murray, [9 February 1895], and [16 December 1894], Morice Correspondence.
62. Morice to Murray, 15 December 1894, and [16 December 1894], ibid.
63. Morice to Murray, 15 December 1894, ibid.
64. Loring to Vowell, 9 September, 10 October 1894, RG 10, C 113, vol. 1585, pp. 448, 458; Traill to Loring, 21 March 1890, HBCA, B188/b/15.
65. D. L. S., *Fifty Years*, p. 101.
66. Loring to Gosnell, 5 September 1896, RG 10, C 113, vol. 1584, pp. 436–37; Margaret Whitehead, personal communication with author, 1 August 1985.
67. D. L. S., *Fifty Years*, p. 101; [Ridley] to Turner-Smith, 6 October 1900, Church Missionary Society, North Pacific Mission, Correspondence, 1857–1900 (hereafter cited as CMS), G 102/03, A-125, PAC.
68. Traill to Loring, 21 March 1890, HBCA, B188/b/15; Loring to Vowell, 9 September, and October 1894, RG 10, C 113, vol. 1583, pp. 448, 458.
69. Loring to Vowell, 29 September 1892, RG 10, C 113, vol. 1585, pp. 453–56; Fort St. James Journal, 1 January 1894, and 21 July 1896, HBCA, B188/a/23.
70. D. L. S., *Fifty Years*, p. 253; Coccola, "Memoirs," pp. 47–48.
71. Lejacq to d'Herbomez, 29 November 1872, *Missions* 12 (1874): 218–19.
72. Morice to MacFarlane, 10 November 1890, microfilm 59, APW, AD.
73. Fraser's Lake Journal, 3 September 1890, HBCA, B74/a/2; D. L. S., *Fifty Years*, pp. 254–55; Morice, *Au pays*, pp. 239–40.
74. D. L. S., *Fifty Years*, pp. 255–56.
75. Fort St. James Journal, 9 September 1895, HBCA, B188/a/23; Loring to

Vowell, 30 September 1895, RG 10, C 113, vol. 1585, p. 581.

76. Fitzstubbs to Maurice [*sic*], 7 August 1889, RG 10, C 113, vol. 1584, pp. 43–44.

77. Jacqueline Judith Kennedy, "Roman Catholic Missionary Effort and Indian Acculturation in the Fraser Valley, 1860–1900," (B.A. Essay, University of British Columbia, 1969), p. 70; Peytavin to McGuckin, 21 February 1887, *Missions* 25 (1887): 265–66.

78. Fitzstubbs to Attorney General, 23 April 1889, RG 10, C 113, vol. 1584, p. 34; McDonald to Murray, 4 March 1895, Babine Portage, Correspondence Outward.

79. Niel Gunson, *Messengers of Grace: Evangelical Missionaries in the South Seas, 1797–1860* (Melbourne: Oxford University Press, 1978), pp. 28–30; Usher, *William Duncan*, p. 3; Clarence R. Bolt, "The Conversion of the Port Simpson Tsimshian: Indian Control or Missionary Manipulation?" *BC Studies* 57 (1983): 44.

80. Morice, *Au pays*, pp. 190–95.

81. Ibid., pp. 195–99. Morice's friendship with Loring is attested to by the latter's stepdaughter, Mrs. Constance Cox, oral evidence, Cassette 313, 4, AHIBC.

82. D. L. S., *Fifty Years*, pp. 101–3; Loring to Vowell, 31 January, 31 March 1896, RG 10, C 113, vol. 1584, pp. 614, 641.

83. Loring to Vowell, 7 August 1896, RG 10, C 113, vol. 1585, pp. 725–26.

84. D. L. S., *Fifty Years*, pp. 103–4.

85. Loring to Smith, 6 April 1896, RG 10, C 113, vol. 1584, pp. 429–30.

86. D. L. S., *Fifty Years*, p. 104; Fitzstubbs to Holmes, 30 September 1888, RG 10, C 113, vol. 1583, p. 545.

87. Loring to Vowell, 31 March 1896, RG 10, C 113, vol. 1584, p. 641.

88. Charles H. French, "Autobiography of Charles H. French, 1867–1940," p. 58; Loring to Vowell, 7 August 1896, RG10, C 113, vol. 1585, pp. 725–26.

89. D. L. S., *Fifty Years*, pp. 103–4.

90. Morice to MacFarlane, 22 February 1894, microfilm 59, APW, AD.

91. Morice to Murray, 7 February 1895, and [November 1895], Morice Correspondence.

92. Morice to Murray, 3 April 1895, ibid.

93. Fort St. James Journal, 18 October 1892, HBCA, B188/a/22; Murray to Morice, 3, 4 April 1895, HBCA, B188/b/16; Morice to Murray, 3 April 1895, Morice Correspondence.

94. Morice to Murray, [5 April 1895], Morice Correspondence.

95. Murray to Morice, 4 April 1895, HBCA, B188/b/16.

96. Ibid.

97. Murray to Morice, 6 April 1896, HBCA, B188/b/16; Murray to Traill, 14 September 1893, Fort St. James, Correspondence Inward, 1891–93, PABC.

98. Morice to Murray, [6 April 1895], Morice Correspondence.

99. Hall to Murray, 4 April 1895, HBCA, B226/b/99.

100. Fraser's Lake Journal, 27 December 1887, HBCA, B74/a/2; Morice to Murray, [winter 1895], Morice Correspondence.

101. Morice, *Au pays*, pp. 105–6.

102. Georg Henriksen, "The Transactional Basis of Influence: White Men Among the Naskapi Indians," in Robert Payne, ed. *Patrons and Brokers*, pp. 26–31.

103. Fort St. James Journal, 24 April 1895, HBCA, B188/a/23; Murray to Morice, 3 April 1895, HBCA, B188/b/16; Morice to Murray, 3 April 1895, Morice Correspondence.

104. Loring to Deputy Commissioner of Lands and Works, 11 September 1899, RG 10, C 113, vol. 1584, pp. 186–87; Morice, *Au pays*, p. 240.

105. Morice to Murray, [n.d.], and 31 January 1895, and Morice to Traill, [February 1893], Morice Correspondence.

106. Hall to Murray, 15 February 1895, HBCA, B226/b/99; Fort St. James Journal, 25 December 1894, HBCA, B188/a/23.

NOTES TO CHAPTER FIVE

1. This intention is made abundantly clear throughout Morice's *Fifty Years in Western Canada*, which was obviously written to win recognition for his missionary and scholarly achievements. See in particular pp. 177–202.
2. There were other nineteenth-century missionary refugees with similar ambitions, David Livingstone being the most famous example. See Jim Jeal, *Livingstone* (London: Heinemann, 1973) pp. 42, 93–94, 108–9, 225. Morice, of course, modelled himself on Petitot, that most radical rejector of the comforts of civilization. Petitot had become renowned as a linguist, anthropologist, explorer, and cartographer, and Morice set out to excel him in all these fields.
3. D. L. S., *Fifty Years*, pp. 90–91; Morice, *Au pays*, p. 94; A. G. Morice, *Carrier Reading Book* (Stuart's Lake Mission: The Author, 1890); A. G. Morice, *Catéchisme en caractères syllabiques* (Stuart's Lake Mission: The Author, 1890).
4. Morice, *Au pays*, pp. 94–95.
5. Morice to MacFarlane, 9 February 1892, MacFarlane Papers, D9, vol. 2, pp. 1353–56.
6. Morice to Directeur, 2 February 1893, *Petites Annales* 3 (1893): 273–74.
7. H. S. Somerset, *The Land of the Muskeg*, pp. 226–28, cited in Morice, *History*, pp. 343–44.
8. J. M. Lejeune, "Comment la Sténographie a été introduite chez les sauvages," Lejeune file.
9. Durieu to Lejeune, March 1891, lettres divers, O, AD.
10. Lejeune to M., 1 April 1892, 3 March 1894, and Nicolaye to Lejeune, 28 August 1899, Lejeune file.
11. Lejacq to Lejeune, 1 December 1895, and Durieu to Lejeune, 28 October 1894, lettres divers, O, AD.
12. Lejacq to Lejeune, 25 January 1894, 19 January 1895, and Durieu to Lejeune, 11 January 1895, lettres divers, O, AD.
13. D. L. S., *Fifty Years*, p. 23.
14. Morice, "The Western Dénés," pp.

109–74; A. G. Morice, "Notes Archeological, Industrial and Sociological on the Western Denes With an Ethnographic Sketch of the Same," *Transactions of the Canadian Institute* 4 (1895): 1–222; A. G. Morice, "Three Carrier Myths, With Notes and Comments," *Transactions of the Royal Society of Canada for the year 1892* 2, no. 10 (1893): 109–26; Morice to MacFarlane, 25 January 1891, MacFarlane Papers, D9, vol. 2, pp. 1338–39.
15. William N. Fenton, Introduction to *The Iroquois Book of Rites*, ed. Horatio Emmons Hale (Toronto: University of Toronto Press, 1963), pp. vii, xi.
16. Morice, "The Western Dénés," p. 21; H. Hale, "Language as a Test of Mental Capacity," *Transactions of the Royal Society of Canada* 9 (1891): 77–78.
17. Morice to Hill-Tout, 7 January 1896, Charles Hill-Tout Papers, 1892–1941, UBCL; Morice, "Notes," p. 17. For the work of Boas, see Robert F. Berkhofer, *The White Man's Indian: Images of the American Indian from Columbus to the Present* (New York: Vintage Books, 1979), pp. 62–64.
18. Joyce C. Barkhouse, *George Dawson, the little giant* (Toronto: Clarke, Irwin, 1974).
19. Morice, "Carrier Sociology," p. 116. Loring found that the opposite was true: the Gitksan were "progressive," while the Carrier clung to their old ways. Loring to Vowell, 31 August 1899, RG 10, C 113, vol. 1589, pp. 188–89.
20. Morice, "Carrier Sociology," pp. 113–14, 118.
21. Ibid., p. 123.
22. Morice, *Souvenirs*, p. 369.
23. Morice, "The Western Dénés," p. 118.
24. D. L. S., *Fifty Years*, p. 67.
25. Morice, "The Western Dénés," pp. 144, 147–152.
26. Drucker, *Cultures of the North Pacific Coast*, pp. 58–60; H. G. Barnet, *The Nature and Function of the Pot-*

198   *Will To Power*

latch (Eugene, OR: Department of Anthropology, University of Oregon, 1968), pp. 100, 127.
27. Morice, "The Western Dénés," p. 165; Morice, "Carrier Sociology," pp. 114–15.
28. Morice, *Au pays,* pp. 59–60.
29. Morice, "The Western Dénés," p. 165.
30. Ibid., pp. 115, 147, 160; Morice, *Au pays,* pp. 78, 154.
31. Cornelius J. Jaenen, *Friend and Foe: Aspects of French-Amerindian Cultural Contact in the Sixteenth and Seventeenth Centuries* (Toronto: McClelland and Stewart, 1976), pp. 20–21. A good example of a work trying to establish racial affinities is J. Campbell, "The Dénés of America Identified with the Tungus of Asia," *Transactions of the Canadian Institute* 5 (1896–97): 167–213.
32. A. G. Morice, "L'Abbé Emile Petitot et les découvertes géographiques au Canada; étude géographico-historique," *Bulletin de la Société neuchâteloise de Géographie* 29 (1920): 9–10; Jaenan, *Friend and Foe,* pp. 20–21, 45–46.
33. Morice, "Notes," p. 162; Morice, "L'Abbé Emile Petitot," pp. 9–10.
34. Morice, "Notes," p. 21; Morice, "The Déné Languages," p. 170.
35. Morice, "The Western Dénés," p. 162.
36. Lane, "Cultural Relations of the Chilcotin," pp. 27–28. Morice's thesis concerning Carrier's adoption of coastal practices was later confirmed. See, for example, Goldman, "The Alkatcho Carrier," p. 333.
37. Morice to MacFarlane, 22 February 1894, microfilm 59, APW, AD; D. L. S., *Fifty Years,* p. 210.
38. Lejacq to Lejeune, 22 August 1894, lettres divers, O, AD; Morice, "The Western Dénés," p. 141.
39. Morice to MacFarlane, 10 November 1890, microfilm 59, APW, AD; Morice to Murray, 14 November 1895, Morice Correspondence.
40. D. L. S., *Fifty Years,* p. 210; Morice to Hill-Tout, 7 January 1896, Hill-Tout Papers.
41. Morice, *Au pays,* p. 23.
42. Jeal, *Livingstone,* pp. 42–43, 116;

Morice to MacFarlane, 22 February 1894, microfilm 59, APW, AD; Morice, *Au pays,* p. 266.
43. Morice, *Au pays,* pp. 204–5, 272–73. "And what mountains! Fortresses with crenelated ramparts, Gothic or Byzantine cathedrals with sturdy buttresses, colossal saws which rent the clouds, gigantic pyramids perhaps as old as the stars towards which they bear their white summits."
44. Ibid., pp. 207, 260–62, 267–68.
45. Ibid., pp. 259, 270, 275–76, 279, 291–92; D. L. S., *Fifty Years,* pp. 139, 140–41.
46. D. L. S., *Fifty Years,* pp. 140–41.
47. Ibid., p. 137; Morice, *Au pays,* pp. 204–5.
48. Morice, *Au pays,* pp. 286–88.
49. Ibid., pp. 258–60; D. L. S., *Fifty Years,* pp. 145–46.
50. Morice, *Au pays,* pp. 248, 260, 262.
51. Ibid., p. 264.
52. Ibid., pp. 265–67.
53. Ibid., pp. 266–67, 268–72.
54. Even such a ruthless and egotistical missionary explorer as David Livingstone was much more inclined to commit himself to God's care than was Morice. Jeal, *Livingstone,* pp. 117–18.
55. Morice, *Au pays,* pp. 274–77.
56. Ibid., pp. 279–82.
57. Ibid., pp. 283–86, Morice mistakenly referred to Ware as Wade; McLeod's Lake Journal, 18 August 1895, HBCA, B119/a/7.
58. Morice, *Au pays,* pp. 286–88.
59. Ibid., pp. 289–90.
60. Ibid., p. 86; D. L. S., *Fifty Years,* p. 138.
61. Morice, *Au pays,* pp. 290–92; A. G. Morice, "British Columbia Maps and Place Names," *A First Collection of Minor Essays* p. 46.
62. Morice, *Au pays,* pp. 291–92; D. L. S., *Fifty Years,* p. 158. Morice's "Dawson Lake" is now known as Whitesail Lake.
63. D. L. S., *Fifty Years,* p. 160.
64. A. G. Morice, "Carrier Onomatology," *American Anthropologist* 35 n.s. (1933) : 658.
65. A. G. Morice, "Du Lac Stuart à l'océan Pacifique," *Bulletin de la Société Neuchâteloise de Géogra-*

phie 15 (1904): 24.
66. Morice, *Au pays*, p. 261.
67. Ibid., pp. 295–96.
68. Ibid., pp. 297–301.
69. A. G. Morice, *Map of the Northern Interior of British Columbia* (Victoria: Chief Commissioner of Lands and Works, 1907); *Atlas and Gazetteer of Canada* (Ottawa: Canada, Department of Energy, Mines and Resources, 1969), p. 43.
70. Morice, *Au pays*, pp. 299–301.
71. Ibid., pp. 301–2.
72. D. L. S., *Fifty Years*, p. 132; Jeal, *Livingstone*, p. 225; Savoie, *Les Amérindiens*, vol. 1, pp. 55–57, 90–101.

73. Jeal, *Livingstone*, p. 224.
74. Ibid., pp. 100–101, 196, 367.
75. Morice to MacFarlane, 22 February 1894, microfilm 59, APW, AD.
76. After leaving Fort St. James in 1903, Morice was the victim of periodic mental breakdowns and was diagnosed as a neurasthenic. Morice to Père[?], 6 February 1924, microfilm 58, APW, AD.
77. Lejacq to Lejeune, 22 February 1896, lettres divers, O, AD.
78. Murray to Hall, 14 April 1896, HBCA, B188/b/17.
79. Morice, *Au pays*, p. 249.

NOTES TO CHAPTER SIX

1. Morice to Brulé, [November, 1898], Morice file.
2. D. L. S., *Fifty Years*, p. 204.
3. Fort St. James Journal, 6, 16, 28 June 1897, and 1 July 1897, HBCA, B188/a/23; Loring to Vowell, 31 March 1897, and 31 May 1897, RG 10, C 113, vol. 1585, pp. 789–90, 830.
4. Fort St. James Journal, 14 July 1896, 17, 19, 21 October 1896, HBCA, B188/a/23.
5. Ibid., 17, 19 October 1896, and 7 November 1896; McNab to Murray, 29 October 1896, HBCA, B171/b/5.
6. Fraser's Lake Journal, 30 June 1897, HBCA, B74/a/3.
7. McNab to Hall, 31 August 1900, HBCA, B188/b/19.
8. Fraser's Lake Journal, 7, 8, 13, 15, 22 September 1897, HBCA, B74/a/3.
9. Ibid., 3 January 1897, and 19 May 1897.
10. Loring to Vowell, 15 July 1897, RG 10, C 113, vol. 1585, p. 872.
11. Morice to Brulé, [n.d.], *Petites Annales* 9 (1899): 124–25; Fraser's Lake Journal, 24 June 1897, and 15, 22 September 1897, HBCA, B74/a/3.
12. Morice to Brulé, *Petites Annales*, p. 125.
13. Mr. John Prince, personal interview

with author, Fort St. James, 31 July 1974.
14. Fort St. James Journal, 27 October 1897, HBCA, B188/a/23.
15. Marchal to d'Herbomez, 30 January 1881, Marchal file.
16. Fort Babine Journal, 1 November 1902, HBCA, B11/a/7; Fort St. James Journal, 20–27, 30 November 1897, HBCA, B188/a/23.
17. Fraser's Lake Journal, 21–25 December 1897, HBCA, B74/a/3.
18. Ibid., 7, 8, 13, 14, 17, 18, 24, 27 November 1897, and 5 December 1897.
19. MacFarlane to McIntosh, 19 January 1889, HBCA, B188/b/14.
20. D. L. S., *Fifty Years*, p. 92; John Prince, personal interview, Fort St. James, 31 July 1974.
21. D. L. S., *Fifty Years*, p. 92.
22. Ibid.
23. Usher, *William Duncan*, pp. 51, 145; Dionne, "Histoire des Méthodes," pp. 135–39; Kennedy-Gresco [Gresko], "Missionary Acculturation Programs," pp. 148–58.
24. D. L. S., *Fifty Years*, p. 94; Plamandon to Forbes, 26 October 1950, Forbes Papers.
25. Morice to Brulé, *Petites Annales*, p. 125; Fort St. James Journal, 5 April 1898, HBCA, B188/a/23; oral evidence of Mrs. Lizette Hall, cassette 1041:1;1, AHIBC.

200   Will To Power

26. Morice to Brulé, *Petites Annales*, pp. 125, 273; Conan to Lejeune, August 22, [1903], lettres divers, O, AD.
27. Fisher, *Contact and Conflict*, p. 136; Usher, *William Duncan*, p. 95.
28. Morice to Brulé, *Petites Annales*, p. 273.
29. [Durieu], "Rapport du Vicariat de la Colombie Britannique," *Missions* 36 (1898): 245–46.
30. Martinet to d'Herbomez, 29 September 1885, Martinet file.
31. [Durieu], "Rapport," p. 225.
32. Morris Zaslow, *The Opening of the Canadian North, 1870–1914* (Toronto: McClelland and Stewart, 1971), p. 106; Morice to Brulé, *Petites Annales*, pp. 95–96, D. L. S., *Fifty Years*, p. 120.
33. Zaslow, *Opening*, p. 107; D. L. S., *Fifty Years*, p. 120.
34. Morice to Brulé, [November 1898], Morice file. "En voilà toujours un qui ne reviendra pas."
35. Ibid.; Morice to Brulé, *Petites Annales*, p. 94.
36. Loring to Deputy Attorney general, 12 November 1898, RG 10, C 113, vol. 1584, p. 261.
37. Loring to Tomlinson, 19 October 1899, and Loring to Vowell, 11 January 1900, RG 10, C 113, vol. 1584, pp. 140–41, 173.
38. Morice to Brulé, *Petites Annales*, pp. 97–98; Morice to Brulé, [November 1898], Morice file.
39. Morice to Brulé, *Petites Annales*, p. 98; Fraser's Lake Journal, 30 August 1898, HBCA, B74/a/3.
40. Beeston, "Inspection Report on Fort St. James," September 1900, HBCA, B188/e/11.
41. Alexi de Tocqueville, *La démocratie en Amérique*, cited in Paul Zweig, *The Heresy of Self-Love. A Study of Subversive Individualism* (New York: Basic Books, 1968), pp. 249–50.
42. Camsell to Anderson, 10 January 1898, HBCA, B188/b/17.
43. Morice to Brulé, *Petites Annales*, pp. 272–73.
44. Ibid.
45. Ibid.,
46. Lejeune to Supérier Général, 24 November 1894, *Missions* 33 (1895): 43–45.
47. John Prince, personal interview, Fort St. James, 31 July 1974.
48. Ibid.; Morice to Brulé, *Petites Annales*, pp. 98, 273.
49. Camsell to Ware, 28 August 1898, HBCA, B188/b/18.
50. Loring to Vowell, 31 December 1897, and 30 November 1898, RG 10, C 113, vol. 1585, p. 928, and vol. 1586, pp. 37–38. Some Indians were more fortunate. Charles Martin, a Gitksan, earned over $300 in the 1898 mining season. Loring to Harris, 28 January 1899, ibid, vol. 1584, p. 232.
51. Loring to Vowell, 17 September 1898, and 29 September 1898, RG 10, C 113, vol. 1586, pp. 15–17.
52. Fort St. James Journal, 9, 19 April, 4 May 1898, HBCA B188/a/23.
53. Ibid., 7 January 1898; Loring to Vowell, 28 February 1898, RG 10, C 113, vol. 1585, pp. 937–39; Loring to Vowell, 24 March 1899, ibid, vol. 1586, p. 74.
54. Morice to Vowell, 10 January 1899, Morice file; Fisher, *Contact and Conflict*, p. 139.
55. Loring to Vowell, 17, 29 September RG 10, C 113, vol. 1586, pp. 15–17; Loring to Vowell, 19, 23 October 1899, ibid., vol. 1584, pp. 169–79.
56. Loring to Vowell, 31 May 1897; Loring to Vowell, 19 October 1899, ibid, vol. 1585, p. 830.
57. Oral evidence of Constance Cox, cassette 313, 5, AHIBC; Loring to Vowell, 19 October 1899, and 23 October 1899, RG 10, C 113, vol. 1584, pp. 169–79.
58. Loring to Vowell, 24 March 1899, RG 10, C 113, vol. 1586, p. 74.
59. Ibid.
60. Morice to Vowell, 10 January 1899, Morice file.
61. Ibid.; Loring to Vowell, 24 March 1899, RG 10, C 113, vol. 1586, p. 74.
62. John Prince, personal interview, Fort St. James, 31 July 1974.
63. Morice to Vowell, 10 January 1899, Morice file.
64. A. G. Morice, "On the Classifications of the Déné Tribes," *Transactions of the Canadian Institute* 6 (1898–99): 76.
65. See Epilogue.

66. Morice to Vowell, 10 January 1899, Morice file.
67. Ibid.; D. L. S., *Fifty Years,* pp. 98–99; Fort St. James Journal, 29 October 1897, HBCA, B188/a/23.
68. Morice to Vowell, 10 January 1899, Morice file; D. L. S., *Fifty Years,* pp. 99–100.
69. D. L. S., *Fifty Years,* pp. 99–100; Morice to Vowell, 10 January 1899, Morice file.
70. Morice to Brulé, *Petites Annales,* p. 272; Morice to Vowell, 10 January 1899, Morice file.
71. Morice to Vowell, 10 January 1899, Morice file; D. L. S., *Fifty Years,* pp. 96–97; Magnan to Dozois, 6 June 1929, microfilm 59, APW, AD.
72. Morice to Vowell, 10 January 1899, Morice file.
73. Ibid.
74. Ibid.
75. Ibid.
76. Ibid.
77. D. L. S., *Fifty Years,* p. 97.
78. Ibid., pp. 95–100.
79. Beeston, "Inspection Report," HBCA, B188/e/11.
80. John Prince, personal interview, Fort St. James, 31 July 1974; Lizette Hall, cassette 1041:1;1, AHIBC.
81. Morice to Editor, *Missions* 38 (1900): 47–48; Fort George Journal, 31 May 1899, HBCA, B280/a/7.
82. Morice to Brulé, *Petites Annales,* p. 129.
83. John Prince, personal interview, Fort St. James, 31 July 1974.
84. Morice to Brulé, *Petites Annales,* p. 162. "Le sorcier par excellence, le grand médecin guérit ou tue par sa seule volonté ou du moins par l'effet de ses prières."
85. Oral evidence of John Prince, cassette 1043:1;2. AHIBC.
86. Mrs. Marie-Anne Joseph, personal interview with author, Portage, Stuart Lake, 30 July 1974; John Prince, personal interview with au-

thor, Fort St. James, 28 July 1974; Lizette Hall, personal interview with author, Fort St. James, 25 July 1974; Mr. Justa Hansen, personal interview with author, Taché, Stuart Lake, 30 July 1974.
87. Fort St. James Journal, 27 May, 4 June 1897, HBCA, B188/a/23.
88. Ibid., 7 January 1898.
89. Camsell to Anderson, 10 January 1898, HBCA, B188/b/17.
90. Vowell to Hall, 24 January 1901, HBCA, B226/c/29.
91. Fort St. James Journal, 16 February 1897, HBCA B188/a/23.
92. Camsell to Anderson, 10 January 1898. HBCA, B188/b/17.
93. Camsell to Hall, 9 January 1898, cited in Loring to Vowell, 5 April 1898, RG 10, C 113, vol. 1585, p. 963; Camsell to Hall, 4, 15 April 1898, HBCA B188/b/17.
94. Hall to Sinclair, 29 March 1899, HBCA, B229/b/117; Hall to Vowell, 15 February 1898, cited in Loring to Vowell, 5 April 1898, RG 10, C 113, vol. 1585, p. 963.
95. Coccola, "Memoirs," on the back of page 47; Lizette Hall, Fort St. James, 25 July 1974; Loring to Vowell, 2 July 1898, RG 10, C 113, vol. 1584, p. 271.
96. McNab to Morice, [November 1898], HBCA, B188/b/18.
97. McNab to Morice, 30 December 1898, and 3 January 1899, HBCA, B188/b/18; McNab to Morice, 11 May 1899, HBCA, B188/b/19.
98. McNab to Boyd, 13 May 1899, HBCA, B188/b/19.
99. Fort George Journal, 30 April 1899, HBCA, B280/a/7.
100. McNab to Hall, 20 October 1899, HBCA, B188/b/19.
101. Beeston, "Inspection Report," HBCA B188/e/11.
102. Ibid.; NcNab to Hall, 31 August 1900, HBCA B188/b/19.

NOTES TO CHAPTER SEVEN

1. Usher, *William Duncan,* pp. 66–69.
2. Kennedy-Gresco [Gresko], "Missionary Acculturation Programs," pp. 155–57.
3. Hall to Sinclair, 29 March 1899, HBCA, B226/b/17; Beeston, "Inspection Report." HBCA B188/e/11.

4. Morice to Brulé, *Petites Annales*, p. 269; Usher, *William Duncan*, p. 47; Martinet, Acte de Visite de la Maison de St. Louis (Kamloops), Cahiers de Actes de Visite, O, AD; Bunoz, "Catholic Action," pp. 25–26.
5. Justa Hansen, Taché, personal interview, 30 July 1974.
6. McGuckin to Martinet, 27 November 1878, *Missions* 19 (1881): 213.
7. Morice to Brulé, *Petites Annales*, p. 299–301.
8. Ibid., p. 270; Morice to Editor, *Missions*, pp. 42–43.
9. Durieu to Lejacq, 23 February 1884, "Lettres de Mgr. Durieu." Michael Foss, *The Founding of the Jesuits* (London: Hamilton, 1969), pp. 90–98.
10. Durieu to Lejacq, 23 February 1884, "Lettres de Mgr. Durieu,"; Fisher, *Contact and Conflict*, p. 125; Usher, *William Duncan*, p. 96.
11. Morice to Editor, *Missions*, pp. 61–62.
12. Morice to Brulé, *Petites Annales*, pp. 162–63.
13. Morice to Editor, *Missions*, p. 61.
14. Jenness, *The Carrier*, pp. 560–61.
15. Morice to Editor, *Missions*, pp. 40–41, 44, 62–63.
16. Ibid., pp. 63–64.
17. Ibid., pp. 64–65; Jenness, *The Carrier*, pp. 563–64.
18. Morice to Editor, *Missions*, pp. 65–66; Loring, "Statement as to occupancy of property in claim for purchase," [1898], RG 10, C 113, vol. 1585, p. 992; re: Mrs. Loring, Margaret Whitehead, personal communication, 1 August 1985.
19. D. L. S., *Fifty Years*, pp. 257–58; Loring, Travelling Expenses No. 1, [1898], RG 10, C 133, vol. 1584, p. 265.
20. Justa Sam, Fort St. James, personal interview, 28 July 1974; Morice to Editor, 19 June 1900, *Missions* 38 (1900): 375.
21. Morice to Brulé, [November 1898]; Morice to Brulé, *Petites Annales*, pp. 192–93. His efforts to get his map published and his references to it in his autobiography indicate that Morice expected the map to bring recognition. D. L. S., *Fifty Years*, pp.

138–45; Morice to [Provincial Secretary], [October 1905], Morice Correspondence; Young to Fraser, 12 March 1968. A copy of this letter was sent to the author from G. S. Andrews, former Chief Cartographer with the British Columbia government. W. R. Young was the Head, Geographic Division, B.C. government.
22. Morice to Editor, *Missions*, pp. 48–52.
23. Morice to Tatin, 6 November, 29 December 1899, *Missions* 38 (1900): 140–58; D. L. S., *Fifty Years*, p. 130–50.
24. Morice to Tatin, 6 November, 29 December 1899, *Missions*, pp. 156–60; D. L. S., *Fifty Years*, pp. 130, 152–53; Morice, *Souvenirs*, pp. 286–87; Morice, *Map of the Northern Interior*.
25. Morice to Editor, 19 June 1900, *Missions*, pp. 385–90; Morice, "Du lac Stuart à l'océan Pacifique," *Bulletin de la Societé Neuchâteloise de Géographie*, 15 (1904): 39–44.
26. Morice, "Du lac Stuart à l'océan Pacifique," pp. 47–51; Morice to Editor, 19 June 1900, *Missions*, p. 392; Morice to MacFarlane, 3 July 1906, MacFarlane Papers, D 9, vol. 2, pp. 2035–36.
27. Young to Fraser, 12 March 1968. See note 21 above.
28. G. S. Andrews, "Surveys and Mapping in British Columbia Resources Development," *Transactions of the Seventh British Columbia Natural Resources Conference* (1954): 12.
29. Morice to Tatin, 6 November, 29 December 1899, *Missions*, p. 136.
30. Campbell, "The Dénés of America," pp. 167–213.
31. A. G. Morice, "The Use and Abuse of Philology," *Transactions of the Canadian Institute* 6 (1898–99): 84–86, 96; A. G. Morice, "On the Classifications of the Dénés Tribes," *Transactions of the Canadian Institute* 6 (1898–99): 76, 81.
32. Morice, "The Use and Abuse of Philology," pp. 90–95.
33. Ibid., p. 95; Campbell, "The Dénés of America," pp. 211–13.
34. Morice to Tatin, 6 November, 29 De-

cember 1899, *Missions,* p. 134; Fort
George Journal, 13 September 1898,
HBCA, B280/a/6; D. L. S., *Fifty
Years,* p. 132.
35. Morice to Tatin, 6 November, 29 December 1899, *Missions,* pp. 133–34.
36. Ibid., pp. 133–35.
37. A. G. Morice, "Déné Surgery," *Transactions of the Canadian*

Institute 7 (1900–1901): 22, 24–27.
38. Ibid., pp. 15–27; Morice to Tatin, 6 November, 29 December 1899, *Missions,* pp. 136–41; Morice to Vicaire General, 24 September 1900, Morice file.
39. McNab to Hall, 12 November 1899, HBCA, B188/b/19.

NOTES TO CHAPTER EIGHT

1. Morice to Barrier, 24 September 1900, Morice file; Jenness, *The Carrier Indians,* p. 576.
2. Morice to Barrier, 24 September 1900, Morice file.
3. Ibid. "Le bon prédicateur que la maladie!"
4. N. Coccola, "Carrier or Déné Prayers," Our Lady of Good Hope, Stuart Lake, [n.d.], PABC.
5. Personal conclusion from observations during fieldwork.
6. Fisher, *Contact and Conflict,* p. 124; Gibson, "Smallpox," pp. 78–79, 81.
7. Morice to Barrier, 24 September 1900, Morice file.
8. Fort Babine Journal, 12, 14 June 1900, HBCA, B11/a/7.
9. Morice to Barrier, 24 September 1900, Morice file.
10. Ibid.; oral evidence of Martin Starrett, cassette 399;19;1, AHIBC.
11. Morice to Barrier, 24 September 1900, Morice file; Loring to Vowell, 30 June 1900, RG 10, C 113, vol. 1586, pp. 299–301.
12. Morice to Barrier, 24 September 1900. Morice file.
13. Loring to Vowell, 11 January 1900, RG 10, C 113, vol. 1584, p. 141; Loring to Vowell, 31 July 1902, RG 10, C 113, vol. 1586, pp. 739–40.
14. Loring to Vowell, 11 January 1900, RG 10, C 113, vol. 1584, pp. 131–40.
15. Ibid., pp. 140–41.
16. Ibid., p. 141; Loring to Vowell, 25 September 1900, RG 10, C 113, vol. 1584, pp. 95–96.
17. Loring to Valleau, 24 July 1900, Loring to Coothe, 21 May 1900, RG 10, C 113, vol. 1586, pp. 198, 340.

18. Morice to Barrier, 24 September 1900, Morice file.
19. Ibid.
20. McNab to Hall, [June 1900], and September 1900, HBCA, B188/b/19; McNab to Hall, 4 November 1900, HBCA, B188/b/20.
21. McNab to Thomson, [April 1901], HBCA, B188/b/20; Vowell to Hall, 24 January 1901, HBCA, B226/c/29. Vowell quoted Morice's letter to Hall.
22. McNab to Hall, 4 November 1900, and Murray to Ware, 29 March 1902, HBCA, B188/b/20; Vowell to Hall, 24 January 1901, HBCA, B226/c/29.
23. McLeod Lake Journal, 26 June 1901, HBCA, B119/a/10; Fraser's Lake Journal 23 October 1903, HBCA, B74/a/5; Fort George Journal, 10 November 1901, and 26 September 1902, HBCA, B280/a/7.
24. Oral evidence of Martin Starrett, cassette 399;19;2, and cassette 399: 18;2, AHIBC.
25. Fort Babine Journal, 28 January, 5 February 1900, HBCA, B11/a/7; Fort George Journal, 16 February 1902, HBCA, B280/a/7.
26. McNab to Thomson, [April 1901] HBCA, B188/b/20; Thomson to Vowell, 29 January 1901, HBCA, B226/b/122.
27. Vowell to Hall, 24 January 1901, HBCA, B226/c/29.
28. Morice to Barrier, 24 September 1900, Morice file.
29. Conan to Lejeune, 22 August [1903], lettres divers O, AD.
30. Morice to Barrier, 24 September 1900, Morice file.
31. Oral evidence of Lizette Hall, cas-

sette 1044:1;1, AHIBC.
32. Oral evidence of John Prince, cassette 1043:1;1, AHIBC.
33. Ibid.
34. John Prince, personal interview, Fort St. James, 31 July 1974.
35. Oral evidence of William Brennan, cassette 667, 2, AHIBC.
36. John Prince, personal interview, Fort St. James, 31 July 1974.
37. Ibid.
38. Fort Babine Journal, 13 November, 4, 18, 19 December 1900, HBCA, B11/a/7.
39. Fraser's Lake Journal, 23 June 1901, HBCA, B74/a/3.
40. Oral evidence of Mrs. Annie Rottacker [née Murray], cassette 1037: 1;1, AHIBC; McLeod Lake Journal, 20 June 1901, HBCA, B119/a/10; McNab to Wright, 12 June 1901, HBCA, B188/b/20.
41. Oral evidence of Mrs. Constance Cox, cassette 313, 4 and 5, AHIBC.
42. Loring to Vowell, 30 July 1901, RG 10, C 113, vol. 1586, p. 538.
43. Based on the assumption that three-quarters of the Hotsoten population attended, plus a hundred members of Carrier and Sikani bands. For population statistics, see Loring to Superintendent of Indian Affairs, 18 July 1900, ibid., p. 344.
44. Loring to Vowell, 31 December 1901, ibid., p. 503.
45. D. L. S., *Fifty Years,* pp. 118–19.
46. Fort George Journal, 17 July, 10, 13 August 1901, HBCA, B280/a/7.
47. Ibid., 14, 15, 16, 17, 18 August 1901; Loring to Superintendent General of Indian Affairs, 3 July 1902, RG 10, C 113, vol. 1587, pp. 1–26.
48. Loring to Superintendent General of Indian Affairs, 18 July 1900, and Loring to Vowell, 31 August 1901, ibid., vol. 1586, pp. 344–66, 561.
49. Loring to Vowell, 30 June 1902, ibid., vol. 1586, p. 715.
50. Loring to Superintendent General of Indian Affairs, 3 July 1902, and Loring to Vowell, 31 January 1903, ibid., vol. 1587, pp. 20, 68–69, Loring to Vowell, 31 December 1908, ibid., 1589, pp. 27–28.
51. Jenness, *The Carrier,* p. 513.
52. Ibid., pp. 557, 577.

53. Ibid., pp. 558–59.
54. Nock, *Conversion,* p. 156.
55. Jenness, *The Carrier,* pp. 561–62.
56. Fort George Journal, 30 October 1901, HBCA, B280/a/7.
57. D. L. S., *Fifty Years,* p. 132; Thomas to Forbes, 13 November 1950, and Forbes, "Notes on Fr. Plamondon's two letters," Forbes Papers.
58. Fort George Journal, 23 April 1902, HBCA, B280/a/7; Fraser's Lake Journal, 6 June 1902, HBCA, B74/a/4.
59. McLeod's Lake Journal, 4, 12 December 1901, 5 July, 11, 14 August 1902, HBCA, B119/a/10.
60. Ibid., 25 December 1901, 9 July 1902, 7 February 1903, HBCA, B119/a/10 & 11.
61. Murray to Thomson, 16 June 1902, HBCA, B188/d/20.
62. Ibid.; Fraser's Lake Journal, 18 June 1902, HBCA, B74/a/3.
63. Murray to Thomson, 8 April 1902, HBCA, B188/b/20.
64. Murray to Thomson, 18 April 1903, HBCA, B226/c/33.
65. Fraser's Lake Journal, 25 December 1902, HBCA, B74/a/3.
66. A. G. Morice, *The History of the Northern Interior of British Columbia, Formerly New Caledonia (1660–1880)* (Toronto: William Briggs, 1904; London: John Lane-The Bodley Head, 1906).
67. A. G. Morice, *The History of the Northern Interior . . . (1660–1880)* (Fairfax, Washington: Ye Galleon Press, 1971), p. xvii.
68. A. G. Morice, "Impartiality and Accuracy: Ramblings in the Field of Early British Columbia History," Morice file, p. 4.
69. Ibid., p. 10.
70. Lizette Hall, personal interview, Fort St. James, 25 July 1974.
71. Morice, *History* (1906), pp. 142–44. This story is well told in Charles Bishop, "Kwah: A Carrier Chief," in Carol M. Judd and Arthur J. Ray, eds., *Old Trails and New Directions: Papers of the Third North American Fur Trade Conference* (Toronto: University of Toronto Press, 1980), pp. 199–201.

72. Personal observation, 28 July 1974.
73. Morice, *History* (1906), pp. 144–46.
74. Morice, "Impartiality and Accuracy," pp. 4–5.
75. Ibid., p. 5.
76. Oscar Lewis, *The Effects of White Contact Upon Blackfoot Culture, with Special Reference to the Role of the Fur Trade* (New York: [Columbia University Press], 1942), pp. 3–6.
77. Murray to Thomson, 18 April 1903, HBCA, B188/b/20.
78. Ibid.
79. Fraser's Lake Journal, 25 February, 12 May 1903, HBCA, B74/a/5.
80. Fort George Journal, 29 May 1902, HBCA, B280/a/7.
81. Loring to Vowell, 29 December 1902, RG 10, C 113, vol. 1587, p. 55.
82. Plamondon to Forbes, 26 October 1950, Forbes Papers.
83. Fraser's Lake Journal, 18 May 1903, HBCA, B74/a/5; Conan to Lejeune, 22 August [1903], lettres divers, O, AD.
84. Conan to Lejeune, 22 August [1903] lettres divers, O, AD; Plamondon to Forbes, 26 October 1950, and G. Forbes, "Notes on Father Plamondon's two letters," Forbes Papers; Fort Babine Journal, 11 July 1903, HBCA, B11/a/7; A. G. Morice, "Exploration de la rivière Bulkley (Colombie Britannique)," *Bulletin* 21 (1911–12): 103.
85. Morice, "British Columbia Maps and Place Names," p. 49.
86. Conan to Lejeune, 22 August [1903], lettres divers, O, AD. "Mène les sauvages en esclaves du haut de sa grandeur."
87. George Webster Grant, *Moon of Wintertime: Missionaries and the Indians of Canada in Encounter since 1534* (Toronto: University of Toronto Press, 1984), p. 127.
88. Conan to Lejeune, 22 August [1903], lettres divers, O, AD.
89. Ibid.
90. Ibid.; Fort George Journal, 31 August 1903, HBCA, B280/a/8.
91. Forbes, "Notes on Fr. Plamondon's two letters," Forbes Papers.
92. Justa Hansen, personal interview, Taché, Stuart Lake, 30 July 1974.
93. Ibid.; John Prince, personal interview, Fort St. James, 31 July 1974.
94. Ibid.; Michel Sam, personal interview with author, Fort St. James, 28 July 1974.
95. Elizabeth Graham, *Medicine Man to Missionary: missionaries as agents of change among the Indians of Southern Ontario, 1784–1867* (Toronto: Peter Martin Associates, 1975), pp. 87–89; Bolt, "The Conversion of the Port Simpson Tsimshian," pp. 39–46.
96. Jolivet, "Acte de Visite, 1869"; Martinet, "Acte Générale de Visite, 1882."
97. Loring to Vowell, 9 May 1903, RG 10, C 113, vol. 1587, p. 105.
98. Usher, *William Duncan*, pp. 50–52.
99. Loring to Vowell, 9 May, 16 July, 30 August 1903, RG 10, C 113, vol. 1587, pp. 102, 128, 194.
100. Loring to Superintendent General of Indian Affairs, 18 July 1903, ibid., pp. 139–45.
101. Coccola, "Memoirs," pp. 88–89; Oral evidence of Lizette Hall, cassette 1044:1;2, AHIBC. "Well he used to rule the people with an iron hand. More so than the others."
102. Margaret Whitehead, personal communication with author, 1 August 1985.
103. Victor [Rohr] to Forbes, 5 March 1951, Forbes Papers.
104. Murray to Thomson, 4 November 1903, and Dixon to Thomson, 12 November 1903, HBCA, B226/c/34.
105. D. L. S., *Fifty Years*, p. 237.
106. Murray to Thomson, 4 November 1903, HBCA, B226/c/34.
107. Dixon to Thomson, 12 November 1903, ibid.
108. D. L. S., *Fifty Years*, p. 237.
109. John Prince, personal interview, Fort St. James, 31 July 1974.
110. Morice, "Impartiality and Accuracy," p. 4.
111. Dixon to Thomson, 12 November 1903, HBCA, B226/c/34.
112. Victor [Rohr] to Forbes, 5 March 1951, Forbes Papers.

113. Handwritten footnote signed G. F. [George Forbes] on a copy of E. C. Bellot, "St. Paul's Church," ibid.

114. Mason, Foreword to Mannoni, *Prospero and Caliban*, p. 12.

NOTES TO THE EPILOGUE

1. D. L. S., *Fifty Years*, pp. 198, 239–40, 244.
2. A. G. Morice, "Mon Testament," 31 May 1934, and Morice to Beys, 17 March 1938, microfilm 59, APO, AD.
3. Raymond Huel, "Adrien-Gabriel Morice, O.M.I. Brief Sojourn in Saskatchewan," *Revue de l'Université d'Ottawa* 41 (1971): 283.
4. Morice to Dozois, 19 May 1926, and Morice to [Magnan], 6 August 1908, microfilm 59, APW, AD; Dozois to Lejeune, 21 February 1908, lettres divers, O, AD.
5. Dozois to Lejeune, 6 July 1907, and 11 February 1908, lettres divers, O, AD. Magnan to Favier, 29 July 1908, microfilm 59, APW, AD.
6. Morice to [Beys], 10 November 1919, microfilm 59, APW, AD.
7. Ibid.; Morice to Beys, 7 November 1919, microfilm 59, APW, AD.
8. Morice to [Dozois], 19 January 1924, and Morice to [Beys], 4 February 1920, microfilm 59, APW, AD.
9. Dubois to Beys, 16 February 1923, Beys to Dozois, [1923], Dozois to Morice, 2 February 1922, and Dozois to Beys, 18 November 1922, microfilm 59, APW, AD.
10. Certificat du Docteur [V. Mitchell], 9 February 1923, copy enclosed in Morice to Beys, 21 July 1923, microfilm 59, APW, AD; Henri F. Ellenberger, *The Discovery of the Unconscious: The History and Evolution of Dynamic Psychiatry* (New York: Basic Books, 1970), pp. 242–44, 375.
11. Morice to Howay, 8 January 1931, Howay Papers, UBCL; Morice to Magnan, 17 March 1938, microfilm 59, APW, AD.
12. Dozois to Morice, 2 May 1928, and Magnan to Morice, 13 June 1934, microfilm 59, APW, AD. "Pretexte pour vous créer une situation pratiquement indépendante des supérieurs."
13. Ernst Nolte, *Three Faces of Fascism: Action Française, Italian Fascism, National Socialism* (New York: New American Library, 1969), pp. 46, 111.
14. Ibid., p. 110.
15. Magnan to Dozois, 6 June 1929, microfilm 59, APW, AD.
16. Ibid. "Reste cachée," "si dangereux"; Beys to Morice, 18 June 1923, and Morice to Cardinal President, Congrégation des Religieux, 11 February 1922, microfilm 59, APW, AD.
17. Dozois to Magnan, 25 June 1929, microfilm 59, APW, AD.
18. Morice, [Handwritten Will], 31 December 1926, Morice to [Mrs. Worsick], 3 July [1934], and Morice, "Mon Testament," 31 May 1934, microfilm 59, APW, AD.
19. G. S. Andrews, "Impressions of Father Morice," Morice file.
20. Morice to W. Murray, 9 April 1929, 1 Series, US; Morice to Howay, 22 October 1926, 25 September 1929, Howay Papers; D. L. S., *Fifty Years*, p. 158.
21. D. L. S., *Fifty Years*, pp. 258–61; Morice to Beys, 9 August 1919, microfilm 59, APW, AD; Lizette Hall, personal interview, Fort St. James, 25 July 1974.
22. Lizette Hall, personal interview, Fort St. James, 25 July 1974; A. G. Morice, *The Carrier Language (Déné Family). A Grammar and Dictionary* (2 vols.; St. Gabriel-Molding, near Vienna: Anthropos, Collections internationale des monographies linguistiques. Bibliothèque Anthropos, vol. 9–10, 1932).

22. Lizette Hall, personal interview, Fort St. James, 25 July 1974; A. G. Morice, *The Carrier Language (Déné Family). A Grammar and Dictionary* (2 vols.; St. Gabriel-Molding, near Vienna: *Anthropos, Collections internationale des monographies linguistiques. Bibliothèque Anthropos*, vol. 9–10, 1932).

23. Lizette Hall, personal interview, Fort St. James, 25 July 1974.

24. R. B. Cunninghame Graham, *A Vanished Arcadia: Being Some Account of the Jesuits in Paraguay, 1706–1767* (London: William Heineman, 1901), p. 281.

25. Lizette Hall, personal interview, Fort St. James, 25 July 1974.

26. Ibid.

27. Cecil Howard, *Mary Kingsley* (London: Hutchinson, 1957), pp. 12, 159–60.

28. Jeal, *Livingstone,* pp. 43, 66, 108.

29. Dunning, "Ethnic Relations," pp. 118–22.

30. Gunson, *Messengers of Grace,* p. 29.

31. Fisher, *Contact and Conflict,* pp. 125–36.

32. Dommeau to Lejeune, 21 April 1908, lettres divers, O, AD. "Les gens d'esprit se laissent trop souvent envalir par l'orgueil et alors ils deviennent plus bêtes que les ignorants."

BIBLIOGRAPHY

PRIMARY SOURCES

Manuscripts

Canada. Department of Indian Affairs. Record Group No. 10. PAC.
Church Missionary Society. North Pacific Mission. Correspondence, 1880–
    1900. PAC. Microfilm.
Coccola, Nicholas. "Carrier or Déné Prayers." PABC.
──── . "The Memoirs of Rev. Nicholas Coccola, O. M. I., Veteran Mission-
    ary of British Columbia." AD.'
Forbes, George. Papers, 1948–69. UBCL.
French, Charles H. "Autobiography of Charles H. French, 1867–1940." PABC.
Hill-Tout, Charles. Papers, 1892–1941. UBCL.
Howay, Frederick W. H. Correspondence and papers, 1764–1943. UBCL.
Hudson's Bay Company. Archives, London.
    B 11/a. Fort Babine Journal, 1887–1905.
    B 74/a. Fraser's Lake Journal, 1887–1907.
    B 119/a. McLeod Lake Journal, 1900–1903.
    B 171/b. Quesnel. Correspondence Books, 1890–97.
    B 188/a. Fort St. James Journal, 1892–98.
    B 188/b. Fort St. James. Correspondence Books, 1887–1902.
    B 188/e. Fort St. James Inspection Reports, 1885, 1900.
    B 226/b. Victoria. Correspondence Books.
    B 226/c. Victoria. Correspondence Inward, 1893–1903.
    B 249/a. Bear Lake Outpost Journal, 1891–93.
    B 180/a. Fort George Journal, 1887–1904.
Hudson's Bay Company. Babine Portage. Correspondence Outward, 1894–95.
    PABC.
──── . Fort St. James. Correspondence Inward, 1891–93. PABC.
MacFarlane, Roderick. Correspondence and Papers, 1834–1915. PAC.
Morice, Adrien Gabriel. "Agreement Between Rev. A. G. Morice, O.M.I. and
    the Ryerson Press." APO.

———. Correspondence Outward, 1892–95. PABC.
Oblates of Mary Immaculate. Oregon Records. AD.
———. Records, Archives provinciales o.m.i., Winnipeg. AD. Microfilm.
———. Records of St. Peter's Province, Colombie. AD.
Traill, William E. Correspondence Outward, 1889–92. PABC.
———. Letter to Charles Ogden, Stuart's Lake. 27 January 1893. PABC.
University of Saskatchewan. Presidential Papers, 1 series, General Correspondence. US.

Oral Testimony

Taped interviews [n.d.]. Aural History Institute of British Columbia. PABC.
    William Brennan - cassette 677,2.
    Constance Cox - cassette 313,4-5.
    William Ferrier - cassette 1042:1;2.
    Lizette Hall - cassette 1044:1;1.
    John Prince - cassette 1043:1;1-2.
    Annie Rottacker - cassette 1037:1;1.
    Martin Starrett - cassette 399:19;1.
Personal interviews. Tapes and notes in the possession of the writer.
    Lizette Hall, Fort St. James, 25 July 1974.
    Julia Hansen, Taché, Stuart Lake, 30 July 1974.
    Marie-Anne Joseph, Portage, Stuart Lake, 30 July 1974.
    Joseph Prince, Fort St. James, 28, 31 July 1974.
    Justa Sam, Fort St. James, 28 July 1974.
    Michel Sam, Fort St. James, 28 July 1974.

Printed Documents

Canada. Department of Indian Affairs. *Annual Reports, 1880–1904*. Ottawa: Queen's Printer.

Contemporary Newspapers and Periodicals

The Daily Colonist. Victoria, 1890–1905.
Missions de la Congrégation des Missionnaires Oblats de Marie-Immaculée. Paris: A. Hennuyer, 1862–1905.
The Month. New Westminster: Oblate Fathers, 1892–1906.
Petites Annales de la Congrégation des Missionnaires Oblats de Marie-Immaculée. Paris: Chez les Oblats, 1891–1905.

SECONDARY SOURCES

Books and Articles

Axtell, James. *The European and the Indian: Essays in the Ethnohistory of Colonial North America.* New York: Oxford University Press, 1981.

Barbeau, Marius. *Indian Days in the Canadian Rockies.* Toronto: Macmillan, 1923.

Barkhouse, Joyce C. *George Dawson, the Little Giant.* Toronto: Clarke, Irwin, 1974.

Barnett, H. G. *The Nature and Function of the Potlatch.* Eugene, OR: Department of Anthropology, University of Oregon, 1968.

Berkhofer, Robert F. *Salvation and the Savage: An Analysis of Protestant Missions and American Indian Response, 1787–1862.* Lexington: University of Kentucky Press, 1965.

Bolt, Clarence R. "The Conversion of the Port Simpson Tsimshian: Indian Control or Missionary Manipulation?" *BC Studies* 57 (1983): 38–56.

Burridge, Kenelm. *New Heaven, New Earth: A Study of Millenarian Activities.* New York: Schocken Books, 1969.

Cairns, H. Alan C. *The Clash of Cultures: Early Race Relations in Central Africa.* New York: Praeger, 1965.

Canada. Department of Energy, Mines and Resources. *Atlas and Gazetteer of Canada.* Ottawa: Queen's Printer, 1969.

Campbell, John. "The Dénés of America Identified with the Tungus of Asia." *Transactions of the Canadian Institute* 5 (1896–97):167-213.

Carrière, Gaston. "Adrien-Gabriel Morice, o.m.i. (1859–1938). Essai de bibliographie." *Revue de l'Université d'Ottawa* 42 (1972): 325-41.

Charlevoix, P. F. X. *History and General Description of New France.* Trans. John Gilmary Shea. 6 vols. Chicago: Loyola University Press, 1970.

Chinard, Gilbert. *L'exotisme américain dans l'oeuvre de Chateaubriand.* Paris: Librairie Hachette et Cie., 1918.

Cohn, Norman. *The Pursuit of the Millenium: Revolutionary Millenarians and Mystical Anarchists of the Middle Ages.* New York: Oxford University Press, 1970.

Cowan, William, ed. *Papers of the Sixth Algongquian Conference, 1974.* (National Museum of Man, Mercury Series, Canadian Ethnology Service Paper 23.) Ottawa: National Museums of Canada, 1975.

Curtin, Philip D., ed. *Africa and the West: Intellectual Responses to European Culture.* Madison: University of Wisconsin Press, 1972.

D.L.S. [A. G. Morice]. *Fifty Years in Western Canada, Being the Abridged Memoirs of Rev. A. G. Morice, O.M.I.* Toronto: Ryerson, 1930.

Dansette, Adrien. *Religious History of Modern France.* Trans. John Dingle. 2 vols. New York: Herder and Herder, 1961.

Drucker, Philip. *Cultures of the North Pacific Coast.* Scranton, PA: Chandler, 1965.

Duff, Wilson. *The Indian History of British Columbia: Vol. I. The Impact of the White Man*. (Anthropology in British Columbia Memoir no. 5.) Victoria: Provincial Museum, 1964.

Dunning, R. W. "Ethnic Relations and the Marginal Man." *Human Organization* 18 (1959): 117-22.

Ellenberger, Henri F. *The Discovery of the Unconscious: The History and Evolution of Dynamic Psychiatry*. New York: Basic Books, 1970.

Elton, G. R. *The Practice of History*. London: Collins, 1961.

Fisher, Robin. *Contact and Conflict: Indian-European Relations in British Columbia, 1774–1890*. Vancouver: University of British Columbia Press, 1977.

Flanagan, Thomas. "Problems of Psychobiography." *Queen's Quarterly* 89 (1982): 596-610.

Foss, Michael. *The Founding of the Jesuits*. London: Hamilton, 1969.

Garth, Thomas R. "The Plateau Whipping Complex and its Relationship to Plateau-Southwest Contacts." *Ethnohistory* 12 (1965): 141-70.

Gibson, James R. "Smallpox on the Northwest Coast, 1835–1838." *BC Studies* 56 (1982): 61-81.

Graham, Elizabeth. *Medicine Man to Missionary: missionaries as agents of change among the Indians of Southern Ontario, 1784–1867*. Toronto: Peter Martin, 1975.

Graham, R. B. Cunninghame. *A Vanished Arcadia: Being Some Account of the Jesuits in Paraguay. 1706–1767*. London: William Heinemann, 1901.

Granatstein, J. L. "Interviewing for Fun and Profit: The Conservative Party, 1956-1967." *Sound Heritage* 3 (1974): 17-18.

Grant, John Webster. "Missionaries and Messiahs in the Northwest." *Studies in Religion/Sciences Religieuses* 9 (1980): 125-36.

———. *Moon of Wintertime: Missionaries and the Indians of Canada in Encounter since 1534*. Toronto: University of Toronto Press, 1984.

Gresko, Jacqueline. "Roman Catholic Missions to the Indians of British Columbia: A Reappraisal of the Lemert Thesis," *Journal of the Canadian Church Historical Society* 24 (1982): 51-62.

Gunson, Niel. *Messengers of Grace: Evangelical Missionaries in the South Seas, 1797–1860*. Melbourne: Oxford University Press, 1978.

Hale, Horatio Emmons. "Language as a Test of Mental Capacity." *Transactions of the Royal Society of Canada* 9, Section II (1891): 77-112.

———. ed. *The Iroquois Book of Rites*. Toronto: University of Toronto Press, 1963.

Hewlitt, Edward Sleigh. "The Chilcotin Uprising of 1864." *BC Studies* 19 (1973): 50-72.

Howard, Cecil. *Mary Kingsley*. London: Hutchinson, 1957.

Huel, Raymond. "Adrien-Gabriel Morice, O.M.I., Brief Sojourn in Saskatchewan." *Revue de l'Université d'Ottawa* 41 (1971): 282-93.

Jaenen, Cornelius J. *Friend and Foe: Aspects of French-Amerindian Contact in the Sixteenth and Seventeenth Centuries*. Toronto: McClelland and Stewart, 1976.

Jeal, Jim. *Livingstone*. London: Heinemann, 1973.

Jenness, Diamond. "The Sekani Indians of British Columbia." *Transactions of the Royal Society of Canada* Series 3, no. 25, Section II (1931): 21-35.

——. *The Carrier Indians of the Bulkley River: Their Social and Religious Life*. Anthropological Papers, No. 25. Washington: Smithsonian Institution Bureau of American Ethnology, Bulletin 133, 1943.

——. "The Ancient Education of a Carrier Indian." *Bulletin of the Canadian Department of Mines* 62 (1947): 22-27.

Jost, T. P. "Rev. A. G. Morice, Discoverer and Surveyor, and the Problems of the Proper Geographical Names in North Central British Columbia." *Revue de l'Université d'Ottawa* 37 (1967): 463-76.

Judd, Carol M., and Arthur J. Ray, eds. *Old Trails and New Directions: Papers of the Third North American Fur Trade Conference*. Toronto: University of Toronto Press, 1980.

Kehoe, Alice Beck. *North American Indians: A Comprehensive Account*. Englewood Cliffs: Prentice Hall, 1981.

Kennedy-Gresco [Gresko], Jacqueline. "Missionary Acculturation Programs in British Columbia." *Etudes Oblates* 32 (1973): 145-58.

LaClare, Leo. "Report on the Oral History Committee of the Canadian Historical Association's Archives Section." *Sound Heritage* 3 (1974): 18-21.

Leflon, Jean. *Eugène de Mazenod*. Translated by Francis D. Flanagan. 3 vols. New York: Fordham University Press, 1961–70.

Lelievre, Michel. *Chateaubriand Polémiste*. [Picardie]: Presse Universitaires de France: Université de Picardie, 1983.

Lemert, Edwin M. "The Life and Death of an Indian State." *Human Organization* 13 (1954): 23-27.

Lewis, Oscar. *The Effects of White Contact Upon Blackfoot Culture, with Special Reference to the Role of the Fur Trade*. New York: [Columbia University Press], 1942.

Linton, Ralph, ed. *Acculturation in Seven American Indian Tribes*. New York: D. Appleton-Century, 1940.

Mannoni, O. *Prospero and Caliban: The Psychology of Colonization*. Translated by Pamela Powesland. New York: Praeger, 1964.

McGloin, sj, John Bernard. "John Nobili sj, Founder of California's Santa Clara College: The New Caledonia Years." *British Columbia Historical Quarterly* 17 (1955): 215-22.

McNeill, William H. *Plagues and People*. New York: Anchor Books, 1976.

Morice, A. G. "The Western Dénés: Their Manners and Customs." *Proceedings of the Canadian Institute* Series 3, no. 7 (1889–90): 109-74.

——. *Carrier Reading Book*. Stuart's Lake Mission, BC: [The Author], 1890.

——. *Catéchisme en caractères syllabiques*. Stuart's Lake Mission. BC: [The Author], 1890.

214   *Will To Power*

——. "The Déné Languages Considered in Themselves and Incidentally in Their Relations to Non-American Idioms." *Transactions of the Canadian Institute* 1 (1891): 170-213.

——. "Are Carrier Sociology and Mythology Indigenous or Exotic?" *Proceedings and Transactions of the Royal Society of Canada for the year 1892* Section 2, no. 10 (1893): 109-26.

——. "Three Carrier Myths, With Notes and Comments." *Transactions of the Royal Canadian Institute* 5 (1894–95): 1-36.

——. "Notes Archeological, Industrial and Sociological On the Western Dénés With an Ethnographical Sketch of the Same." *Transactions of the Royal Canadian Institute* 4 (1895): 1-222.

——. "On the Classification of the Dénés Tribes." *Transactions of the Canadian Institute* 6 (1898–99): 75-84.

——. "The Use and Abuse of Philology." *Transactions of the Canadian Institute* 6 (1898–99): 84-100.

——. "Déné Surgery." *Transactions of the Canadian Institute* 7 (1900–1901): 15-27.

——. *A First Collection of Minor Essays, Mostly Anthropological.* Stuart's Lake Mission, B.C. [The Author], 1902.

——. "The Nah•ane and their Language." *Transactions of the Royal Canadian Institute* 7 (1902–3): 517-34.

——. "Du Lac Stuart à l'océan Pacifique." *Bulletin de la Société Neuchâteloise de Géographie* 15 (1904): 32-80.

——. *The History of the Northern Interior of British Columbia, Formerly New Caledonia (1660–1880).* Toronto: William Briggs, 1904; London: John Lane – The Bodley Head, 1906; Fairfax, Washington: Ye Galleon Press, 1971 [reprint of the 1906 edition].

——. *Map of the Northern Interior of British Columbia.* Victoria: Chief Commissioner of Lands and Works, 1907.

——. The Unity of Speech Among the Northern and Southern Déné." *American Anthropologist* 9, n.s (1907): 720-37.

——. "Exploration de la rivière Bulkley (Colombie Britannique)." *Bulletin de la Societé Neuchâteloise de Géographie* 21 (1911–12): 101-26.

——. "Northwestern Dénés and Northeastern Asiatics." *Transactions of the Royal Canadian Institute* 10 (1914): 131-93.

——. "The Northern Interior of British Columbia and its Maps." *Transactions of the Royal Canadian Institute* 12 (1917): 25-39.

——. "L'Abbé Emile Petitot et les découverts géographiques au Canada; étude géographico-historique." *Bulletin de la Société Neuchâteloise de Géographie* 29 (1920): 5-58.

——. *Histoire de l'Eglise catholique dans l'Ouest canadien.* 4 vols. St. Boniface: Chez l'auteur; Montréal: Granger Frères, 1921–23.

——. *Disparus et survivants; études ethnographiques sur les Indiens de l'Amérique du Nord.* Winnipeg: The Author, 1928.

——. *The Carrier Language (Déné Family). A Grammar and Dictionary.* 2

vols. St. Gabriel-Molding, near Vienna: *Anthropos,* Collection internationale des monographies linguistiques. Bibliothèque Anthropos, vols. 9-10, 1932.

———. "The Carrier Onomatology." *American Anthropologist* 35, n.s (1933): 632-58.

———. *Souvenirs d'un missionaire en Colombie Britannique.* Winnipeg: La Liberté, 1933.

Morice, R. P. [A.G.]. *Au pays de l'ours noir. Chez les sauvages de la Colombie Britannique.* Paris-Lyon: Delhomme et Briguet, 1897.

Muise, D. A., ed. *Approaches to Native History in Canada: Papers of a Conference held at the National Museum of Man, October 1975.* Ottawa: National Museums of Canada, 1977.

Nock, Arthur Darby. *Conversion: The Old and New in Religion from Alexander the Great to Augustine of Hippo.* London: Oxford University Press, 1933.

Nolte, Ernst. *Three Faces of Fascism: Action Française, Italian Fascism, National Socialism.* New York: New American Library, 1969.

Owens, J. M. R. *Prophets in the Wilderness: The Wesleyan Mission to New Zealand, 1819–1827.* Auckland: Auckland University Press: Oxford University Press, 1974.

Paine, Robert, ed. *Patrons and Brokers in the Eastern Arctic.* Newfoundland Social and Economic Papers, no. 2. St. John's: Institute of Social and Economic Research, Memorial University of Newfoundland, 1971.

Peel, J. D. Y. "Syncretism and Religious Change." *Comparative Studies in Society and History* 10 (1968): 121–41.

Ray, Arthur J. *Indians in the Fur Trade: their role as trappers, hunters, and middlemen in the lands southwest of Hudson Bay.* Toronto: University of Toronto Press: 1974.

Ridington, Robin. "Changes of Mind: Dunne-za Resistance to Empire." *BC Studies* 43 (1979): 65–80.

———. *Swan People: A Study of the Dunne-za Prophet Dance.* National Museum of Man, Mercury Series, Canadian Ethnology Service Paper 38. Ottawa: National Museums of Canada, 1978.

Savoie, Donat. *Les Amérindiens du Nord-Ouest canadien au 19e siècle selon Emile Petitot.* 2 vols. Ottawa: Ministère des Affaires indienne et du Nord canadien, 1971.

Smith, Harlan I. "An American Obermmergau. The Passion Play by American Indians." *Putman's* 5 (1908): 294–303.

Steward, Julian H. "Determinism in Primitive Society." *The Scientific Monthly* 53 (1941): 491–501.

Switzer, Richard. *Chateaubriand.* New York: Twayne Publishers, 1971.

Thompson, Alexander Hamilton. *Bede, His Life, Times and Writings.* Oxford: Clarendon Press, 1969.

Trigger, Bruce G. "The French Presence in Huronia: The Structure of Franco-Huron Relations in the First Half of the Seventeenth Century." *Canadian Historical Review* 49 (1968): 104–41.

Usher, Jean. *William Duncan of Metlakatla: A Victorian Missionary in British Columbia*. National Museum of Man Publications in History, no. 5. Ottawa: National Museums of Canada, 1974.

Walker, Deward E., Jr. "New Light on the Prophet Dance Controversy." *Ethnohistory* 16 (1969): 245–55.

Wallace, Anthony F. C. *The Death and Rebirth of the Seneca*. New York: Vintage Books, 1972.

———. "Revitalization Movements." *American Anthropologist* 58 (1956): 264–81.

Weber, Max. *The Theory of Social and Economic Organization*. Trans. A. M. Henderson and Talcot Parsons. Edited with an Introduction by Talcot Parsons. New York: Free Press, 1964.

Whitehead, Margaret. *The Cariboo Mission: A History of the Oblates*. Victoria: Sono Nis, 1981.

Williamson, Norman James. "Abishabis the Cree." *Studies in Religion/Sciences Religieuses* 9 (1980): 217–45.

Worsley, Peter. *The Trumpet Shall Sound*. London: MacGibbon and Kee, 1957.

Zaslow, Morris. *The Opening of the Canadian North, 1870–1914*. Toronto: McClelland and Stewart, 1971.

Zweig, Paul. *The Heresy of Self-Love. A Study of Subversive Individualism*. New York: Basic Books, 1968.

Theses and Essays

Dionne, Gabriel. "Histoire des méthodes missionaires utilisées par les Oblats de Marie Immaculée dans l'évangelization des indiens du 'Versant Pacifique' au dix-neuvième siècle." M.A. thesis, University of Ottawa, 1947.

Fisher, Robin. "Indian-European Relations in British Columbia, 1774–1890." Ph.D. diss., University of British Columbia, 1974.

Kennedy, Jacqueline Judith. "Roman Catholic Missionary Effort and Indian Acculturation in the Fraser Valley, 1860–1900." B.A. essay, University of British Columbia, 1969.

Lane, Robert B. "Cultural Relations of the Chilcotin Indians of West Central British Columbia." Ph.D. diss., University of Washington, 1953.

McCarthy, Martha. "The Missions of the Oblates of Mary Immaculate to the Athapaskans 1846–1870: Theory, Structure and Method." Ph.D. diss. University of Manitoba, 1981.

Rumley, Hilary Eileen. "Reactions to Contact and Colonization: An Interpretation of Religious and Social Change among the Indians of British Columbia." M.A. thesis, University of British Columbia, 1973.

INDEX

Smiles, Samuel, 118
Society of the Missionaries of Provence. *See*
  Oblates
Soesradou'as, Indian guide, 144
Squamish Indians, 8, 9, 59, 63, 64
Stikine Valley, 106, 121, 162
Stations of the Cross, ceremony, 40, 48
Stene, John, Isaac Qasyak's son, 109, 145
Stone Chilcotin Indians, 17, 18, 25, 27-28
Stoney Creek, 46, 76, 120, 148-49, 164, 167,
  169
Stuart, John, 166
Stuart Lake, 29, 35-38, 44, 46-47, 53, 87, 105,
  108, 115, 120, 125, 149, 173
  Indians at, 42, 75, 116, 123, 150, 153, 158,
    165, 168, 173
  missions at, 28, 33, 36, 57, 76, 117, 119,
    151, 169
  and Morice, 26, 32-35, 114, 143, 148, 156,
    168
Sutherland, Jack, trader, 117-18

Taché, 42, 53, 150
Taya, Indian chief, 76-79, 84-87, 92-93,
  155, 163, 171
Thautil, Thomas, 109-10, 145
Thomson, James, Hudson's Bay Company
  manager, 155, 172
"Three Carrier Myths, with Notes and
  Comments," 98

Touzi, Indian chief, 21, 25, 28
Traill, W. E., 78-86, 133, 137, 147
Tsimshian Indians, 55, 99, 170
Turner, John H., premier of British Columbia,
  144
Typee, Alex, Indian chief, 89, 129

Valleau, F. W., 124, 125
Varice, Henri, trapper, 171
Victoria, B.C., 75, 85, 86, 90
Vowell, Indian affairs superintendent, 125-27,
  129-30, 134, 152-55, 167, 171

Waddington wagon road, 19
Wagner, Father, 158
Ware, William, Hudson's Bay Company clerk,
  108
"Western Denes: Their Manners and Customs,"
  97
Whipping, 80-83, 123, 134, 155, 157, 172
Williams Lake, B.C., 20-22, 25-26, 28-29, 57,
  62, 112, 116, 118-19
  Morice at, 14, 15, 18, 27, 28, 32, 33, 102, 156
Winnipeg, Manitoba, Morice at, 176-81
Worsick, Mrs. Martha, housekeeper, 178

Yale, B.C., 11